I WILL SEND MY MESSENGER

An Introduction to The Church of Jesus Christ of Latter-day Saints

C. PAUL SMITH

Archway Publishing books may be ordered through booksellers or by contacting:

Archway Publishing
1663 Liberty Drive
Bloomington, IN 47403
www.archwaypublishing.com
1 (888) 242-5904

ISBN: 978-1-4808-6947-9 (sc)
ISBN: 978-1-4808-6948-6 (hc)
ISBN: 978-1-4808-6946-2 (e)

Library of Congress Control Number: 2019904569

Print information available on the last page.

Archway Publishing rev. date: 06/27/2019

CONTENTS

EXPANDED CONTENTS

THE FUFILLMENT

PREFACE

No other Christian denomination makes the bold claims made by The Church of Jesus Christ of Latter-day Saints—that resurrected apostles of Jesus visited Joseph Smith and Oliver Cowdery and conferred their apostolic authority upon them; that a resurrected, ancient American prophet named Moroni visited Joseph Smith and delivered a volume of ancient scripture to him; that God the Father and His Son Jesus Christ, appeared to Joseph Smith; and that through the prophet Joseph Smith, God set up His Kingdom on earth.

Biblical prophets foretold that God would send divine messengers to the earth in the last days to prepare a people to receive the Lord Jesus Christ when He comes again in power and glory. In this book I will set forth many of these prophecies and recount the story of their fulfillment.

If someone really wants to learn the beliefs of The Church of Jesus Christ of Latter-day Saints ("Mormonism"), he must recognize that he cannot expect to get an understanding of that church's point of view by reading the words of a disgruntled ex-Mormon or by listening to the sermon of a competing minister. If someone really wants to know about The Church of Jesus Christ of Latter-day Saints he will go to a reliable source, where he can count on getting an accurate report of

Mormon doctrine. He will seek out the missionaries of The Church of Jesus Christ of Latter-day Saints and be taught by them.

I do not intend for this book to be a substitute for learning the gospel directly from the authorized servants of Jesus Christ—the Elders and missionaries of the Church. But I hope and believe that this book may be a helpful supplement to their efforts in many instances.

It is my purpose in this book to present a *Mormon's version of Mormonism.* You cannot comprehend Mormonism without learning the Mormon point of view. Though the enemies of Mormonism may deny it, the Mormon point of view is in total harmony with the Bible; the doctrines of The Church of Jesus Christ of Latter-day Saints are consistent with each other and are consistent with a logical interpretation of the Bible. The pages of this book will bear this out.

Man's intellect can verify that Mormon doctrine is harmonious with itself and with the Bible. But the greater question still remains—Is it divine? The answer to this question cannot be proved by reasoning alone any more than mere reasoning can prove that the Bible is the word of God. The ultimate test for all divine truth is whether the Spirit of God witnesses to the soul that it is true.

With this in mind, I undertake the task of setting forth in clear terms a divine message of unsurpassed importance for every living soul. The Lord has promised to confirm the divinity of this message to all sincere truth-seekers who will listen to this message and ask God with faith if it is His word.

As an Elder in The Church of Jesus Christ of Latter-day Saints, I have been called of God to assist in teaching the gospel of Jesus Christ to all who will hear me. With all my heart I want to do this. This book is my personal testimony of messages from God in our day that are of eternal importance for all the world.

This book is not an official statement of The Church of Jesus Christ of Latter-day Saints; but it is the individual testimony of one of its members.

2019 PREFACE

In the 30 years since the first edition of this book was published, Mormons have gained increased acceptance in the world, especially among those committed to high moral values, strong families and the sanctity of life. In 2012, Mormon Mitt Romney became the Republican Nominee for President of the United States. Mormons have come a long way from the days in the 1890s when Senator Reed Smoot was denied a seat in the United States Senate because he was a Mormon. The world knows the name "Mormon," but most do not know who Mormon was. The message of Mormonism—the restored gospel of Jesus Christ—continues to be unknown and misunderstood by most.

A significant portion of today's Christian community considers Mormonism to be a "cult" and a fake Christian church that actually promotes Satan's work. One recent example of this prejudice against Mormonism occurred in October of 2012, when Mitt Romney visited the venerable Reverend Billy Graham and obtained from Rev. Graham his endorsement as a candidate for President. Following this visit, Reverend Graham's evangelical organization took Mormons off of their cult list. But this action brought considerable criticism to Rev. Graham—accusing him of abandoning important principles for political expediency. A month later, Mitt Romney lost to Barack Obama in the Presidential Election, and within a few days after that Mormons were back on Rev. Graham's cult list. This incident demonstrates the enormous prejudice that still exists towards Mormons from some religionists. And as this book will demonstrate, such prejudice is primarily based upon ignorance of the teachings of Jesus Christ.

The name "Mormon" comes from the ancient American prophet named Mormon, who lived in the Fourth Century A. D. He was a prophet to whom Christ appeared. He was the principal compiler-writer of ancient gold plates which were translated into *The Book of Mormon*. Mormon was a prophet who saw our day in vision, and who invited all to come unto Christ—to be pure, to be patient and longsuffering, to exercise faith in Christ, to receive the love of God in their countenances, to experience the power of God in their lives, and ultimately to return to live with God in the hereafter. Mormon's record recounts a visit of the resurrected Jesus to some of his disciples in America after Jesus' ascension in Palestine. Jesus taught his gospel to these ancient Americans; He taught them that through faith on His name and obedience to God's commandments, including baptism, that the grace of Christ will redeem us from sin and death. Mormon was a valiant witness of Jesus Christ, as was the prophet Joseph Smith who, by the gift and power of God, translated the plates of Mormon into *The Book of Mormon*.

Thirty-five hundred years ago Moses prophesied that God would raise up a prophet like unto him, and that the people would be responsible to recognize and hearken unto the words of that prophet (Deuteronomy 18:18-19). After Jesus' resurrection, Peter alluded to this prophecy and told the "men of Israel" that Jesus was the one who was "raised up," and that if the people would not hearken to the words of Christ delivered through God's prophets, then they would suffer dire consequences (Acts 3:19-23); and see chapter 13). In 1823, a heavenly messenger appeared to Joseph Smith and quoted him this prophecy and said that the day would soon come when they who would not hear the voice of God's prophets would "be cut off from among the people" (Joseph Smith, History 1:40). The divine challenge for all mankind throughout history, and for us today, is to hear and hearken to the word of God which will be delivered through God's servants, the prophets. To succeed at this is the key to peace, happiness and eternal life. To fail at this will ultimately bring regret and estrangement from God because one cannot be in communion with Him and at the same time ignore or deny the messages that God's prophets deliver to the world.

Divine messages from God are being delivered today to all mankind through the Elders and missionaries of The Church of Jesus Christ of Latter-day Saints. The message they declare is the pure gospel of our Lord and Redeemer, Jesus Christ.

I bear testimony of the words of Jesus delivered to the ancient Americans, to the words of Jesus recorded in the New Testament, and to the words of Jesus delivered through living prophets today. All of this is in fulfillment of biblical prophecies, to prepare the world for the Lord's Second Coming. To believe this is to believe the words of Christ, delivered through God's prophets. Conversely, to reject or deny the words of God's messengers is to reject Jesus Christ. I hesitate to use such strong words. I do not wish to offend, but neither do I wish to detract from the import of this message by a fear of offending. My words are borne of my deepest desire to make sure that my friends and family know of the depth and breadth of my witness—it is without doubt or qualification; it is based upon the powerful witness that God has given me.

God has the power to reveal the truthfulness of His messages to those who ask with a sincere heart and real intent. Of this I am also a witness. Personal revelation is real and is available to all who seek the Lord with all their heart, mind and strength.

The message of Mormonism is a message from Jesus Christ. There is nothing in it that is not virtuous and holy. The Spirit of God bears witness of this to sincere truth seekers. The Spirit has borne witness to me that this is so. May the power of God attend you as you read this book and as you prayerfully consider the messages of The Church of Jesus Christ of Latter-day Saints.

ABBREVIATIONS

B of M   *The Book of Mormon—Another Testament of Jesus Christ*

D&C   *The Doctrine and Covenants*

P of GP   *The Pearl of Great Price*

HC   *History of the Church of Jesus-Christ of Latter-day Saints*

"BEHOLD, I will send my messenger, and he shall prepare the way before me: and the Lord, whom ye seek, shall suddenly come to his temple, even the messenger of the covenant, whom ye delight in: behold, he shall come, saith the LORD of hosts." Malachi 3:1

THE SETTING

PART I

Conflicting Doctrines of Salvation
in the Christian Community

CHAPTER 1

Which Gospel Is the Gospel of Jesus Christ?

The greatest event to ever occur in the history of the world is the atoning sacrifice of the great Messiah, Jesus Christ. He paid the penalty for the sins of mankind when he suffered in body and in spirit in the garden of Gethsemane and on the cross at Calvary.

The gospel that Jesus taught and that his apostles continued to preach outlined the things that all mankind must do in order for Jesus' sacrifice to have full effect in their lives.

The apostle Paul wrote that "as in Adam all die, even so in Christ shall all be made alive" (1 Corinthians 15:22). He clearly taught that all mankind would one day be resurrected whether or not they believe in Jesus. But Jesus also taught that "repentance and remission of sins should be preached in his name among all nations" (Luke 24:47), and that "except a man be born of the water and of the Spirit, he cannot enter into the kingdom of God" (John 3:5). "He that believeth and is baptized shall be saved; but he that believeth not shall be damned" (Mark 16:16).

Since the days of the ancient apostles many divergent interpretations have sprung up in Christianity concerning fundamental principles of the gospel of Jesus Christ. Since the days of Martin Luther, thousands of Christians have separated from the Roman Catholic Church because they felt the whole truth was not taught in that church. These denominations are generally characterized as Protestants because they "protested" against the Roman Catholic Church. Initially, the motivation for the creation of these denominations was the desire to return to the truth—the desire to reform that church back to the pure, original organization and doctrines established by Jesus and the apostles. When the Roman Catholic Church refused to reform, Christians abandoned that church as they attempted to hold fast to the truth as taught in the Bible.

The advent of the printing press was unquestionably one of the greatest forces behind the Protestant Reformation. As the Bible became available to the common man for the first time for private reading and study, the people were confronted with the fact that the Roman Catholic Church had departed from many of the fundamental principles of the gospel of Jesus Christ.

But today, the hunger and thirsting for truth that sparked and fueled the Reformation has given way to a growing complacency with error and a widely held belief that no religion has or can have all the truth. Thus, the search for truth has been quenched in the lives of many Christians.

I come from a different mold. When I consider the contradictory doctrines of salvation taught in different Christian denominations, I refuse to attempt mental gymnastics to reconcile them. It's not right that different Christian denominations should teach conflicting and contradictory doctrines of salvation. Many Christians are adhering to falsehoods; I don't believe there is any other way to look at it.

Amid this scene of multiple Christian denominations in the United States, there appeared in 1830 another Christian religion, The Church of Jesus Christ of Latter-day Saints, which is now commonly referred to as Mormonism. Its prophet-leader, Joseph Smith, said that the Lord Jesus Christ called him to be a prophet and restored to the earth the true gospel of Jesus Christ, in preparation for the Lord's Second Coming. This is not another protestant religion; it is not a reformation—it is the restored, pure gospel of Jesus Christ.

From 1830 until today there have been hundreds of thousands of divinely authorized servants of the Lord who have gone throughout the world proclaiming the message of this restoration of the truth. Millions have embraced this message with joy. But there have been many who have gone to great lengths to distort this message in efforts to destroy it and to prevent its dissemination. It is in some measure because of the falsity and the pervasiveness of these efforts that I have undertaken to set forth my testimony of the divinity of Mormonism in this book.

This work is not intended to be an answer to every question that may be raised about The Church of Jesus Christ of Latter-day Saints—but it is an effort to present the basic beliefs that are its foundation. I submit that no one can fairly evaluate the message of Mormonism—the message of the restored gospel of Jesus Christ—without coming to understand the Mormon point of view. And you won't get the Mormon point of view from those who are opposed to Mormonism. This book is addressed to those who are not afraid to learn the Mormon point of view.

A. Lies about the Gospel of Jesus Christ Are Being Sold to Christianity.

Printed Propaganda—When I opened a law practice in Montgomery County, Maryland in 1978, I rented office space from a Christian attorney. In the course of our association, we had occasion to share our beliefs with each other. He was a "born again" Christian, and I had also been "born again." As we became friends, I believe he recognized that I was just as much of a Christian as he was, though he knew that some self-proclaimed "Mormon experts" said otherwise.

My associate shared with me some anti-Mormon literature and tapes that he had been exposed to in his circle of Christian friends. In our discussion of these materials I told him that they presented a distorted picture of Mormonism; they contained a mixture of some truth, some erroneous interpretations of Mormon beliefs, some out-and-out falsehoods, some mistakes in distinguishing official doctrine from private opinion, and many derogatory adjectives and rhetorical devices. He urged me to speak out and correct any false teachings that I observed. He said this information was disseminated to Christians around the nation through channels that are considered trustworthy.

I judged that my associate was puzzled about Mormonism—that he wasn't sure what to make of it. On the one hand, he had heard many unfavorable things about it from people who had previously nourished him spiritually; this made Mormonism suspect in his mind. But on the other hand, from our relationship and our discussions, he came to understand and respect some things about Mormonism. I am sure that for my associate, the jury is still out on Mormonism; until he knows more about it he is reserving judgment.

My relationship with him and with a number of Christians has made me realize that thousands of Christians are being influenced by anti-Mormon ministries that teach a mixture of truths, half-truths, lies and distortions—all of which make Mormonism out to be a repulsive, counterfeit Christianity.

The disinformation campaigns against Mormonism are numerous. Current books published for mainstream Christian audiences label Mormonism as a false Christianity. Television and radio evangelists openly proclaim it to be anti-Christian. If public opinion were determinative, then Mormonism might indeed be a counterfeit Christianity.

Broadcast Slander—A few years ago I listened to a national radio broadcast of a well-respected evangelist from Florida whose program on this day addressed the growing influence of satanic cults in the world. Initially, I was impressed with the program and that the evangelist was sincerely devoted to the cause of Christ.

But then the evangelist and his guest went on to talk about religions that claim to be Christian, but which they said were really doing the work of Satan. The guest said that Mormonism was just such a religion. The problem with Mormonism, the guest said, was that it teaches that an individual "earns" salvation by his "works," thereby denying the efficacy of Christ's saving grace.

This program did not dwell on Mormonism for long, but instead it quickly moved on, mentioning another prominent Christian religion that they said was also satanic. But while Mormonism was not the focus of this program, nevertheless the slander had been launched— its impact would be felt by the countless listeners throughout the nation who were tuned in to that broadcast. The evangelist and his guest had misstated the Mormon belief about salvation in a way geared to prejudice someone else against Mormonism; they had used falsehood to condemn Mormonism.

When I returned home I wrote a letter to the evangelist explaining the correct Mormon doctrine about salvation and about the roles of grace, faith and works in obtaining it. (See chapters 16 and 17 below for a discussion of these doctrinal points.) I explained that he and his guest had misrepresented the Mormon belief about how to obtain salvation and that they had erroneously concluded that Mormonism was anti-Christian and satanic. I asked to be given some time on his program to correct the false information that he had broadcast.

Several weeks later, I received a response from one of the evangelist's associates, denying that they had misrepresented anything and not responding to my request for broadcast time to correct the misrepresentation. With his letter, he enclosed three small tracts of anti-Mormon propaganda that combined to give a provocative, superficial condemnation of Mormonism. If ever there was an example of speciousness, this was it; on the surface these tracts presented one thing that sounded convincing, but the truth was something different.

I was impressed that the associate sent me the materials with the honest intent of helping me to come to know the truth about Mormonism. But I also realized that he had not discerned the falsehoods and deceptions in the materials he was promoting.

The evangelist and his associate may sincerely believe Mormonism is in error. But based upon what they said and on what they wrote, and based upon the error-saturated propaganda for which they were vouching, I knew that they did not know what Mormon doctrine really was; they believed the propaganda of the anti-Mormon critics, but they had a superficial and flawed understanding of Mormonism.

I wrote back to the evangelist and his associate; I pointed out that they were disseminating falsehoods about Mormonism, and I offered to send additional information to help correct the false impressions they had. But I'm not convinced they really want to know the truth about Mormonism; the fact that they were so willing to condemn Mormonism by using materials saturated with errors and reeking with prejudice indicated to me that a thorough evaluation of Mormonism from reliable information was secondary to their anxiousness to condemn Mormonism. Without gathering complete and accurate facts, they had prejudged Mormonism to be satanic, and they were urging their followers to likewise condemn Mormonism on the same faulty basis. In his haste to condemn, the evangelist had been duped by the anti-Mormon propaganda that is popular in many Christian circles today.

This combination of intellectual laziness and of misplaced confidence in Mormon critics is responsible for the spread of a flood of provocative, anti-Mormon propaganda among thousands and thousands of devoted Christians throughout the United States. Thousands of honorable Christians are being duped unwittingly to misjudge Mormonism when they blindly accept the false conclusions and misrepresentations of the anti-Mormon ministers.

The amazing irony of this chain of deception is that there is considerable enthusiasm to condemn Mormonism, but little energy to make sure that condemnation is justified by facts and reason. The reasonable approach would be to withhold judgment until a thorough and mature evaluation can be made. But there are some anti-Mormon ministries who thrive on marketing their provocative deceptions to sincere, but gullible Christians through the channels of broadcast evangelists who are looking for sensational materials to fill their broadcast slots and convention programs.

In spite of this widespread prejudice, and based on the premise that reason can help establish truth, and that the Spirit of God can and will bear witness of truth to the souls of men, this book has been prepared to set forth the basic principles of The Church of Jesus Christ of Latter-day Saints. If Mormonism must be condemned, let the critics stick to the truth about it. This book is intended to supply some of the essential basics of Mormonism that are neglected and ignored by the anti-Mormon campaigners.

Criticisms of Mormonism—Some criticisms of Mormonism are aimed at tangential issues, while some attack Mormonism at the very core— such as the accusation that Mormonism is not Christian. It is these more fundamental criticisms that deserve the first and foremost attention; and it is these that will be treated in this book.

Mormons are criticized for our belief in another book of scripture called *The Book of Mormon*—a book we revere to be of equal stature with the Bible. Some Christians are critical of such a belief; they say that the Bible condemns the belief that any book other than the Bible could be scripture. Thus, they say, the Mormons don't really believe in the Bible. Some Christians say that Mormonism is a "cult"; they say that Mormons are not Christian and that the Mormons' professed belief in Christ is a false belief in a counterfeit gospel. "Mormons may be good people," they say, "but they have been duped by their leaders, and their faith is in supposed prophets rather than in Christ." Some Christians, such as the nationally prominent radio evangelist, falsely state that Mormonism teaches that a person "earns" his salvation by his "works" and that Mormonism thus denies the saving grace of Christ. Some even say that Mormonism is the great "antichrist" spoken of in the book of Revelation. Still others declare that the Mormon belief in God is blasphemous and that the Mormon leaders are false prophets teaching of a false Christ—both of which evils are prophesied to occur in the last days.

Although these criticisms are widely broadcast throughout Christianity, anyone who will seriously and sincerely investigate Mormonism will find that none of these criticisms has merit.

Two additional facets of Mormonism that are not always criticized (but which are almost always a cause of consternation and frustration to other ministers should be noted here because they are often found at the roots of Mormon criticisms.

First, The Church of Jesus Christ of Latter-day Saints proclaims itself to be "the only true" church of Jesus Christ; we claim that no other religion teaches the pure gospel of Jesus in its fullness, and that no other religion has God's actual authority. Many other denominations do not take such an exclusive stance about themselves any more—this is not popular today. Today, in the name of "tolerance" and "open-mindedness," it is not acceptable to teach of the preeminence of one religion or denomination over all the others. Thus, today, those who claim to belong to "the only true religion" are ridiculed by many as being presumptuous and proud.

But while this "all-accepting" attitude may be popular today, it is nevertheless fatally flawed—it rejects the belief in universal truth—and in its stead it seeks to enthrone the notion that each religious organization can be a law unto itself. But this attitude of excessive doctrinal tolerance repudiates the belief that God governs the world with laws equally applicable to all; it denies the existence of a divine truth that is valuable for all mankind. Embracing both truth and falsehood, this attitude pollutes the truth and ultimately denies the existence of absolute truths. All of this blocks the search for truth—for who will search for what he does not believe exists? Thus, this attitude that lacks the integrity and courage to denounce falsehood fosters a spiritually debilitating attitude that keeps its adherents chained in the bonds of ignorance and doubt.

Second, The Church of Jesus Christ of Latter-day Saints actively proselytes other Christians. This practice makes Mormons not only unpopular with competing ministers, but it altogether alienates many ministers, who are continually threatened to have their congregations diminished every time one of their members agrees to be taught by Mormon missionaries. And, of course, not only does this practice tend to diminish their congregations, but it hits them right where it really hurts—in the pocket book. Ministers whose very livelihoods depend on large congregations of generous donors cannot passively look on when their incomes are threatened and slashed by the convincing preaching of the Mormon missionaries. Thus, an evangelical market is created to stop the flow of people and pocket books away from paid ministries; the stage is set and the door opened for anti-Mormon ministers to stem the tide and stop the buck.

And the irony of this wallet war is that neither the Mormon missionaries nor the Mormon ministers are paid clergy—they labor without compensation. Mormon missionaries finance their own missions; and Mormon bishops are lay ministers who support themselves in the market place just like everyone else in their congregations.

Spurned by these and a host of other ignominious motives, Mormon critics have been marketing exploitative and slanderous reports on Mormonism for over 190 years. Every generation seems to spawn new challengers who develop an obsession with attempting to discredit the Mormon Church.

An Anti-Mormon Letter Campaign—Another example of an anti-Mormon campaign occurred a few years ago where my family was living, in Frederick, Maryland (about 45 miles from Washington, D. C.). Christian ministers from several different denominations in this area circulated a joint letter warning their members to be wary of Mormon missionaries in the area and counseling their members not to invite them into their homes. The Mormons, they said, were not really Christians, and they said that exposure to Mormon doctrine could jeopardize a person's salvation. But this campaign backfired. When the press got wind of it, a couple of excellent pro-Mormon articles appeared, and the letter-writing ministers ended up under fire themselves. Then the Mormon congregations had several curious people attending their services the next Sunday. As is sometimes the case, this letter campaign sparked more interest in Mormonism than it stifled.

Our critics acknowledge that we claim to be Christian, but they contend that our doctrine is un-Christian. One popular TV evangelist criticized our doctrine as being unsound in a recent book he published. I happily take issue with such criticism. But as this (my) book will bear out, the doctrine of The Church of Jesus Christ of Latter-day Saints is in total harmony with the teachings of Jesus Christ as found in the Bible.

The real basis of our critics' quarrel with us is that they interpret the scriptures differently than we do. Of course, the Mormon critics who live off of the proceeds of their anti-Mormon businesses will never acknowledge this—it would undermine their very livelihoods. Neither will they acknowledge the logic and consistency of Mormon doctrines. That, too, would be suicide to their businesses. Instead, they usually attack Mormonism with the shotgun approach—launching a barrage of accusations, and concluding that these accusations prove Mormonism is false. This approach always has some success with shallow thinkers and superficial Christians. But disciplined thinkers and dedicated followers of the word of God recognize that accusations without supporting facts prove nothing.

B.   Condemnation of Mormonism by Accusation—Without Supporting Evidence and Without a Full and Fair Hearing.

To refute Mormonism you must refute the best argument in favor of Mormonism. This the critics cannot do—they carefully avoid it! In their accusations they do not dare probe beneath the superficial; they do not dare to engage in an in-depth evaluation of actual Mormon doctrine. Instead they limit their efforts to merely repeating specious accusations. An in-depth discussion of any one of the multiple accusations that they make is always fatal to them. But fortunately for them, the radio, television and evangelistic convention medias are ideal for their shotgun method. In a 30-minute or one-hour program, they have just enough time to present their opening argument against Mormonism in a convincing manner—and then the time is up and the matter is concluded, and the audience is never given an opening statement in favor of Mormonism, and certainly no evidence and explanations that would favor it.

American citizens who have served as jurors can appreciate that the first opening statement at a trial usually sounds convincing; but they know that the opposition's opening statement usually sounds equally convincing; and they know that it is not until all the evidence is in that they can feel comfortable in making a decision. But why, in the case of Mormonism, is there a feeling that such a process of fundamental fairness is not necessary?

Yet that is precisely what is happening in the case of Mormonism. Thousands of evangelical supporters meekly endorse the conclusions that their shepherds announce to them when Mormonism is condemned; the evangelist is sustained as both prosecutor and judge of Mormonism, and his arbitrary conclusions are blindly accepted without question and without requiring fair justification. The evangelist and his sheep are more than willing to dispense with logic, reason and fairness in the case of Mormonism.

But what about an opening statement in support of the Mormon point of view? The mainline Christian evangelical community has no time for it and will have no part of it.

And what about a trial? What about a careful and rational consideration of what Mormonism really does teach and what the Bible says in support of it? What about a presentation of the Mormon point of view? Again, the mainline evangelical community has no time for it and will have no part of it. Their words and actions give the following message:

> A rational and reasoned basis for condemning is just not required in the case of Mormonism. The accusations against it are so terrible and sound so convincing that processes of fair evaluation can be dispensed with. And since Mormonism is the work of the devil, the investigation of it is likely to entice and ensnare the investigator and bind him with the chains of hell. Thus, normal processes of reason and fairness must be dispensed with in the case of Mormonism.

That such patent prejudice and irrationality and fear should exist in 2019 is incredible. And yet it does.

Make Judgment Based on Truth, Reason and the Confirming Witness of the Holy Ghost—This book is written for the courageous few, whose love of truth is not doused by scare tactics. It is written for those who will not tolerate lies and prejudice as acceptable bases for making a condemnation. If Mormonism must be condemned, truth lovers must condemn it based on facts and reason, not based on falsehood, supposition and speculation. Before one condemns Mormonism, he must refute, not ignore, the best arguments that support it. Anyone who condemns Mormonism while ignoring such facts and reasons is like a person who says that a building does not exist because all he can see is a smokescreen that blocks its view. Such condemnation stands as a monument to prejudice and intellectual sloth in a community that professes a commitment to truth.

Throughout the pages of this book information will be discussed that will provide answers to many fundamental questions that have been asked about Mormonism. But this is not written in response to any one particular question; and there are some questions that it does not specifically address. Rather than a defense, this book is a proclamation, an announcement and an introduction to a divine work of God unfolding in our day in fulfillment of numerous biblical prophecies. I leave to others or to another occasion to respond to specific accusations that might require correction, clarification or a defense. I do not undertake that here because an understanding of the foundation of Mormonism should be obtained first, before moving on to doctrinal matters that are built upon it. A proper understanding of tangential points of doctrine cannot be obtained without first learning the fundamental principles that underpin it.

Sincere truth seekers who learn the doctrines of The Church of Jesus Christ of Latter-day Saints acknowledge that its doctrines are logical. The real question is: Is Mormon doctrine true?

No man's private interpretation of the gospel of Jesus Christ has any value in and of itself. Only God's interpretation has intrinsic value. But a person can come to understand God's interpretation of scripture by receiving the same Spirit that inspired scripture. This we should do. Peter said:

> [N]o prophecy of the scripture is of any private
> interpretation. For the prophecy came not in old time
> by the will of man: but holy men of God spake as they
> were moved by the Holy Ghost. (2 Peter 1:20-21)

And as Paul said:

> [M]y speech and my preaching was … in demonstration
> of the Spirit and of power: That your faith should not
> stand in the wisdom of men, but in the power of God.
> (1 Corinthians 2:4-5)

What is the gospel of Jesus Christ? Is it sufficient to merely echo belief in a "Christ"? Or is it necessary to also believe the truth about Christ and about his commandments?

In this book I will set forth what I think of Christ and what I believe his gospel is. See if it isn't in harmony with the Bible. See if the Spirit of God does not witness it to be the truth.

C.   Conflicting Doctrines of Salvation.

Even a casual observer of the Christian religious scene must acknowledge that different denominations teach conflicting doctrines of salvation—thus, each has a different gospel of Jesus Christ. It is not popular today to point this out, but it is nevertheless true. And which gospel is the true gospel of Jesus Christ?

I, for one, would like to know the truth; I would like to sort out divine truth from the opinions of men. And it seems to me there is no more important matter in which to do this than the matter of the destiny of mankind and our relationship to God. The purpose of our earth experience must be discovered if we are to be successful and happy at living. There are thousands of witnesses in the world today who claim that the gospel of Jesus Christ gives the true answers to these fundamental questions about life. I agree. But there are so many contradictory doctrines taught in the multiple Christian denominations that reasonable men must admit that many purported "gospels" of Jesus Christ are false. Consider the following questions about salvation, for which there are almost as many answers as there are different Christian denominations:

1. What is the true nature of God?
2. What is man's relation to God?
3. Who is Jesus Christ?
4. What did Christ do for mankind?
5. What does it mean to be saved?
6. What must mankind do to be saved?
7. Is faith (or belief) in Jesus sufficient to save someone, without repentance, baptism and reception of the Holy Ghost?
8. What does it mean to have faith in Christ?
9. Must one be born of the water and of the spirit in order to be saved?
10. What does it mean to be born of the water?
11. What does it mean to be born of the spirit?
12. If someone is born of the water and of the spirit, can he thereafter fall from his salvation through transgressing the commandments of God?
13. Since salvation comes only by the grace of God, and since we will be judged by our works, what are the respective roles of grace and works in obtaining salvation?
14. Can one obtain salvation without repenting of his sins?
15. What does it mean to repent?
16. Is baptism a prerequisite to salvation?
17. What is the purpose and effect of baptism?
18. What is the purpose of life?
19. What is the eternal destiny of man?

Some people would answer many of these questions by saying, "It doesn't really matter." And some people ridicule those who profess to have answers to some of these questions. "These are beautiful mysteries," they will say. "We are not meant to understand them," they continue, "and anyone who thinks he does is only fooling himself."

Perhaps the best illustration of this attitude of *blessed ignorance* is found in a television sermon by one of the most famous evangelists of the twentieth century. In talking about the Trinity—how the three members of the Godhead are one and yet are three at the same time, the Reverend said that this was a mystery that we cannot understand. He said that they are three manifestations of the same thing, just like steam, water and ice are three different manifestations of water. And then he went on to ridicule the notion that someone might understand the Trinity better than he. He compared such a notion to a young school child who naively raised his hand in response to the teacher's question, "Who can explain how electricity works?" When the child noticed that no one else had raised his hand, he eventually dropped his hand also. But the teacher, noting that he *had* raised his hand, pressed him to respond. Finally, the student said, "I forgot." To which the teacher replied, "That's too bad, because you would be the only one in the world who did know." The audience laughed approvingly at the story and at its implicit message—that we cannot understand the mystery of the Trinity, and that those who think they do are only fooling themselves.

But contrary to the predominant Christian attitude—that the Trinity is a mystery, the Bible teaches us much more about God's nature than many ministers will admit. (See chapters 8 and 16, below.) The attitude that we cannot understand the nature of God contradicts the words of the Savior that "this is life eternal that they [we] might know thee the only true God, and Jesus Christ, whom thou hast sent" (John 17:3).

Neither does the Lord desire us to be content to believe false doctrines about salvation and baptism. And consider the matter of baptism further.

Is baptism essential for salvation or isn't it? Is it optional or isn't it? Must one be born of the water and the spirit to be saved? If so, what does this mean? Can anyone perform a baptism? Or, must it be done by an authorized servant of God? Can someone baptize himself? Is baptism by immersion essential, or is sprinkling sufficient? Should infants be baptized immediately after birth to insure their salvation? Or, is baptism necessary only for those who are responsible for their actions? What is the purpose of baptism? Does baptism automatically assure one of salvation? Or, must one also live a good life after baptism in order to be saved in the kingdom of God?

When you stop to think about the diversity of beliefs in Christianity about baptism and salvation—when you stop to think of the many contradictory teachings taught in the different Christian denominations, all of which are supposedly based in the same Bible—when you stop to think about such contradictions, you cannot help but realize that many Christian churches today must be teaching falsehoods about the gospel of Jesus Christ. All Christian denominations say they base their doctrines on the teachings of the Bible. But they each interpret the Bible differently. There can be no dispute that many false interpretations of the gospel of Jesus Christ are being passed off as truth—sold, if you will—to Christian audiences around the world.

What is your response to the diverse and contradictory doctrines taught by the many different Christian denominations today? Are these doctrinal differences important? Those who deny the significance of these doctrinal differences deny the importance of the very doctrines they profess. Thus, while it is a good thing to seek to unify the Christian world by focusing on common denominators in our beliefs, the quest for unity without a quest for the truth is just not a satisfactory goal. The purpose of the Church of Christ in the first place was to bring the saints to a "unity of the faith" (Ephesians 4:13). The Lord has promised that "the truth shall make [us] free" (John 8:32), but neither the Lord nor his prophets ever taught that we should come to a unity at the expense of truth. Any unity that includes ignoring or discounting Jesus' true doctrines is a flawed and problematic unity.

D. We Need Direct Revelation from God to Identify the True Gospel of Jesus Christ.

Every one of these 19 questions about salvation and God and the purpose of life are of prime importance for us. I am not satisfied with the point of view that downplays the importance of those questions it cannot answer. All of these questions are important. God has revealed and will reveal precise information in answer to them. God does not have different and conflicting answers to these questions depending on what a person's religion is. God has one, true answer for everyone on all of these important questions pertaining to the salvation of mankind. My faith in Christ makes me believe that God is willing today to make known His answers to these questions to all those who earnestly seek them of Him.

Answers to many of these questions have been communicated to mankind today by messengers from God. God has given us revelations today that are just as marvelous and important at those He gave to Moses. And the modern-day prophets to whom these revelations have come are of equal stature with Abraham, Isaiah and Moses.

The story I have to tell of angels and of God himself delivering these messages to a living prophet is magnificent and awesome. But it is a story that is vehemently denounced by some people who contend that God will not give the world any new scriptural revelation after the Bible; they claim that the Bible teaches this. But it does not. There is no reasonable interpretation of scripture that supports this defensive argument. In fact, the Bible teaches just the opposite. Numerous prophecies foretell of divine messages that will be given to the world in the latter days.

In the next four chapters I will set forth more than a dozen of these prophecies that establish that God will send messengers and messages to the world in the last days. Study these and see if they do not indeed prove this. Chapters 2-5 discuss these prophecies. Then, chapter 6 specifically refutes the notion that the Bible teaches that it is the last and final word of scripture for the world.

THE SETTING

PART II

Biblical Prophecies that God Will
Send Messengers to the Earth
Prior to the Second Coming

We are living in the last days, just prior to the Lord's Second Coming. The signs of the times foretold by Jesus (Matthew 24: 3-7, 11, 21-24, 29) are taking place all around us: We live in a time of wars, rumors of wars, famines and earthquakes; iniquity abounds; there are false Christs and false prophets among us; there have appeared great signs in the heavens; there have been signs and wonders wrought by holy men of God; and there have been signs and wonders wrought by false prophets.

Although the Christian world acknowledges that Christ will come again—and soon—most of the Christian world is not looking for messengers to be sent from God before the Second Coming. But biblical prophecies clearly predict that God will send messengers to the earth to prepare a people to receive Jesus when he comes again.

Many biblical prophets foretold of latter-day messengers and messages from God. The Savior prophesied that a divine messenger would precede his Second Coming. John the Revelator prophesied of an angel who would come to the earth in the last days. The apostles Peter and Paul wrote of a great restoration and of a new dispensation of authority from heaven that would be given in the last days. Likewise, many of the Old Testament prophets foretold of the coming of divine messengers and messages before the great and dreadful day of the Lord—Malachi, Isaiah, Ezekiel, Moses, Jeremiah, Daniel and Joel all prophesied of these things.

Prophecies of divine messengers coming in the last days is so well established in Holy Writ that no honest student of the Bible can deny it. Yet many Bible believers are not aware of these prophecies.

Consider the prophecies of all of these holy prophets and of the Savior himself. If you do, you must inescapably conclude that God will give new revelation to the world in the latter days to prepare the world for the Lord's coming in power and glory. Disciples of Christ will look with eager anticipation for the fulfillment of these prophecies. In the next four chapters, let's review over a dozen prophecies about messengers and messages from God in the last days.

Prophecies of Messengers and Messages from God to Come in the Last Days

Chapter 2
    Matthew 17:11
    Malachi 4:5-6
    Malachi 3:1
    Acts 3:21
    Ephesians 1:10
    Joel 2:28-29
    Revelation 14:6

Chapter 3
    Ezekiel 37:16-22
    Isaiah 29:1-18
    Jeremiah 23:1-4
    Deuteronomy 30:1-3
    Matthew 24:14, 28 & 31

Chapter 4
    Daniel 2:44
    Daniel 12:4 & 9
    Daniel 7:13-14
    Ephesians 4:11-14
    Ephesians 2:19-21

Chapter 5
    Summary of Prophecies

A Discussion of Scriptures that Are Sometimes Misconstrued and Used to Oppose Additional Revelation from God

Chapter 6
    Revelation 22:18-19
    2 Timothy 3:15
    Galatians 1:8

CHAPTER 2

"Elias Truly Shall First Come, and Restore All Things"

A.   The Transfiguration of Jesus.

One of the most spectacular events recorded in the Bible is the transfiguration of Jesus that was witnessed by Peter, James and John on a high mountain (Matthew 17). On that occasion, Matthew records that Jesus' "face did shine as the sun, and his raiment was white as the light" (verse 2). Seeing Jesus glorified in this manner must have been a strengthening experience for the three apostles. This undoubtedly helped the apostles to better understand the words they would hear Jesus speak a short time later, when he prayed: "And now, O Father, glorify thou me with thine own self, and with the glory which I had with thee before the world was" (John 17:5).

Except for the time of his transfiguration, Jesus put off his pre-mortal glory during his mortal sojourn on earth. At his Second Coming, however, the scriptures teach that he will come and reign in power and glory.

At the time of Jesus' transfiguration there were other spectacular things that also occurred. Matthew records that Moses and Elijah[1] appeared on this occasion. Such a manifestation was an additional miracle. For someone to return to the earth hundreds of years after he had lived on the earth is phenomenal. The scriptures teach that Elijah was taken to heaven in a chariot of fire without tasting death (2 Kings 2:11). And the prophet Malachi foretold that Elijah would return to the earth again before the coming of the great and dreadful day of the Lord (Malachi 4:5). The Jews had been looking for Elijah's return for hundreds of years. The apostles thought that this appearance may have fulfilled that prophecy.

Matthew records another miracle that occurred at the time of Jesus' transfiguration. The apostles heard the voice of God the Father bearing record of Jesus' divinity. Matthew writes: "[B]ehold, a bright cloud overshadowed them: and behold, a voice out of the cloud which said, This is my beloved Son, in whom I am well pleased: hear ye him" (Matthew 17:5).

Following these miraculous manifestations, as the apostles descended from the mountain with the Savior, they marveled at what they had seen and heard. They contemplated whether this appearance of Elijah was a fulfillment of Malachi's prophecy. And, if it was, they wanted to know why it was that Malachi had prophesied that Elijah would come *before* the Lord—for this appearance was *after*, rather than before their Lord's coming. With this in mind, the apostles asked Jesus: "Why then say the scribes that Elias must *first* come?" [Emphasis added.]

Jesus' answer to this question introduced a prophecy about his future, glorious return to the earth that was later repeated and amplified by his apostles—it was the prophecy of a restoration of all things by an "Elias" before His Second Coming: "And Jesus answered and said unto them, Elias truly shall first come, and restore all things" (Matthew 17:11).

To get the full import of this prophecy, we must examine it closely

---

[1] The text in Matthew uses the name "Elias" rather than "Elijah." But "Elias" is the name used in the New Testament to mean "Elijah." (See, e.g., Luke 4:25. Also, Smith's *Bible Dictionary* says that "Elias" is the Greek and Latin form of Elijah.)

and also examine some other prophecies that foretell of a restoration by divine messengers in the last days.

B.   Malachi Prophesied that God Would Send Elijah the Prophet Before the Second Coming.

When the apostles asked Jesus, "Why then say the scribes that Elias must first come?" they were undoubtedly referring to the prophecies in the third and fourth chapters of "Malachi. In chapter four, Malachi prophesied:

> Behold, I will send you Elijah the prophet before the coming of the great and dreadful day of the LORD:
> And he shall turn the heart of the fathers to the children, and the heart of the children to their fathers, lest I come and smite the earth with a curse. (Malachi 4:5-6)

Elijah will come before the "great and dreadful day of the LORD"—that is, before the judgment day, when the righteous saints will rise to meet the Lord, while the wicked will be burned by the brightness of the coming of the Lord (Malachi 4:1-2). When Elijah does come, it will be to perform a specific mission—to turn the hearts of the children to their fathers, and vice versa.

Because this prophecy pertains to the Lord's Second Coming, we know it was not fulfilled by Elijah's appearance to Jesus and his three apostles on the mount of transfiguration. And, of course, Jesus confirmed this interpretation when he answered his apostles' question with the statement: "Elias truly shall first come" (Matthew 17:11).

The coming of Elijah spoken of in Malachi 4:5-6 did not occur in New Testament times. It will occur in the last days, before the Second Coming.

C. Malachi Prophesied that God Would Send a "Messenger" to Prepare a People to Receive the Lord at His Second Coming.

In Malachi, chapter 3, the prophet foretold of a "messenger" that the Lord would "send" in advance, to prepare the way before His coming. The apostles were also undoubtedly aware of this prophecy just as much as the one in chapter four when they asked Jesus why the scribes said that "Elias must first come." Both prophecies speak of someone coming to prepare the way before the Lord. The text of the prophecy in chapter three is as follows:

> BEHOLD, I will send my messenger, and he shall prepare the way before me: And the Lord, whom ye seek, shall suddenly come to his temple, even the messenger of the covenant,[2] whom ye delight in: behold, he shall come, saith the LORD of hosts.
>
> But who may abide the day of his coming? and who shall stand when he appeareth? for he is like a refiner's fire, and like fullers' soap. (Malachi 3:1-2)

Is the "messenger" spoken of in chapter three one and the same as Elijah, who is identified by name in chapter four? And, was this "messenger" to come before the Lord's first coming or before his second coming? Let's look at this prophecy a little more closely. And then let's examine some other prophecies that shed further light on its meaning.

---

[2] The "messenger" and the "messenger of the covenant" identify two separate persons in this prophecy. The first "messenger" spoken of is to come "before"— to "prepare the way before" the "messenger of the covenant." The Lord himself is the "messenger of the covenant" who is to "suddenly come to his temple."

1. Malachi's Prophecy—The Second Coming.

There are biblical prophecies about both of Jesus' comings: His first coming was when he was born as a babe in Bethlehem; and His second coming will be when he comes in power and glory and with judgment and destruction of the wicked. It is sometimes difficult to grasp whether a prophecy pertains to the first or the second coming. And some prophecies have application to both comings. Malachi 3:1 is a prophecy that has been interpreted by Jesus to apply to both comings, but its main thrust clearly pertains to the Second Coming.

One aspect of the prophecy that applies to Jesus' second coming, but not to his first coming, is the prediction that He would "suddenly come to his temple." The "sudden" coming of the Lord to his temple would not seem to refer to Jesus' visits to the temple at Jerusalem during his mortal life. Jesus visited that temple several times, but he did not appear there "suddenly"; he came there gradually—that is, he walked there, and he could be seen gradually approaching the temple from a distance until he finally arrived there. At the time of Jesus' ascension to heaven, two angels declared to the eleven apostles that when Jesus comes again he will appear in like manner to his ascension; just as Jesus ascended straight up to heaven, so when He comes again He will descend straight out of heaven and suddenly appear (Acts 1:11). This is the type of sudden appearance about which I believe Malachi was speaking.

Another aspect of this prophecy that is applicable to the second coming, but not to the first, is the cleansing destruction of the wicked by fire that is to precede the Lord's coming. Malachi asked rhetorically: "Who shall stand when he appeareth? For he is like a refiner's fire. . . For, Behold, the day cometh that shall burn as an oven; and all the proud, yea, and all that do wickedly shall be as stubble" (Malachi 3:2 & 4:1). By these words Malachi unmistakably implies that the wicked would be burned at or before Jesus' coming. Of course, such destruction did not attend Jesus' first coming. Malachi refers to this second coming as the "great and dreadful day of the Lord" (Malachi

4:5). Malachi prophesied that the wicked will be burned at that day, while the righteous will be preserved to meet him (Malachi 4:1-2).

Malachi's prophecy that a messenger would prepare the way before the Lord's second coming is confirmed by Isaiah, who prophesied:

> The voice of him that crieth in the wilderness, Prepare ye the way of the LORD, make straight in the desert a highway for our God.
>
> Every valley shall be exalted, and every mountain and hill shall be made low: and the crooked shall be made straight, and the rough places plain:
>
> And the glory of the LORD shall be revealed, and all flesh shall see it together: for the mouth of the LORD has spoken it. (Isaiah 40:3-5)

It is the Lord's second coming that "all flesh shall see . . . together," and which will be accompanied by the exalting of valleys and the leveling of mountains. And Isaiah prophesied that a forerunner "that crieth in the wilderness" would come before the Lord to prepare the way.[3]

All of this makes it clear that the principal thrust of Malachi's prophecy in chapter 3, verse 1, pertains to the Lord's Second Coming. God's messenger will prepare the way before this event.

2. Double Fulfillment of Malachi's Prophecy.

At the time of his transfiguration, Jesus commented on this prophecy of Malachi, confirming that it had reference to both his coming at that time as well as to a subsequent coming. Let's consider Jesus' words more fully here. After Jesus told the apostles, "Elias truly shall first come, and restore all things." He then made the following

---

[3] John said that he came in fulfillment of this prophecy of Isaiah (John 1:23). But like Malachi's prophecy, the major thrust of this prophecy pertains to the Lord's later coming in power and glory. John the Baptist came in partial fulfillment of this prophecy. But its complete fulfillment will be in the coming of "Elias," preparing the way before the Lord's Second Coming.

comments: "But I say unto you, That Elias is come already, and they knew him not, but have done unto him whatsoever they listed. Likewise shall also the son of man suffer of them. Then the disciples understood that he spake unto them of John the Baptist" (Matthew 17:12-13).

After confirming that Malachi's prophecy would later be fulfilled by the coming of an "Elias" prior to His Second Coming, Jesus then explained that in another sense Malachi's prophecies had been fulfilled by the coming of John the Baptist. John was certainly a "messenger" who prepared the way before the Lord. Jesus said that in this sense, John had come in fulfillment of Malachi 3:1; in this sense, Jesus said John was an "Elias."[4]

3. The Meaning of "Elias"

Note how Jesus used the name "Elias." Did Jesus use the name "Elias" to be synonymous with "Elijah the prophet"? No. By his referring to John the Baptist as an "Elias," Jesus made it clear that he was not restricting the name "Elias" to refer only to Elijah the prophet. And Jesus was not saying that John the Baptist had come in fulfillment of Malachi 4:5. Jesus was saying that John the Baptist had come in a fulfillment of Malachi 3:1—the prophecy of a "messenger" to come before the Lord. Jesus taught that this "messenger" was an "Elias." Perhaps the apostles had previously understood that the "messenger" and "Elijah the prophet" were one and the same person. But Jesus made it clear that the "messenger" spoken of by Malachi did not refer only to Elijah the prophet. Certainly, Elijah would be a "messenger"— but not the only "messenger." Both on this occasion and earlier in his ministry, Jesus taught that John the Baptist had come as an "Elias" in a fulfillment of prophecy. On the previous occasion Jesus said: "For this is he, of whom it is written, Behold, I send my messenger before

---

[4] According to the Gospel of John, John the Baptist denied being Elias; when asked "Art thou Elias?" John the Baptist answered, "I am not" (John1:21). Nevertheless, Jesus said that in one sense John was "Elias," but he was not the "Elias" who would later come and restore all things.

thy face, which shall prepare the way before thee. . . . And if ye will receive it, this [John the Baptist] is Elias, which was for to come" (Matthew 11:10, 14). Later, as we discussed, in descending from the Mount of Transfiguration, Jesus reaffirmed that John the Baptist was an "Elias" and that he had come in fulfillment of Malachi's prophecy.[5]

By this explanation, the disciples came to understand a new meaning of the word "Elias." John had come as an "Elias" in preparing the way before the Lord. Before the birth of John the Baptist, the angel Gabriel announced to Zacharias, John's father, that his son would "go before [the Savior] in the spirit and power of Elias" (Luke 1:17). Both the angel Gabriel and Jesus used the name "Elias" as a title, indentifying a divine messenger, a forerunner, with a preparatory mission; and both said that John came as an "Elias." "Elias," then can denote a title and mission, as well as being a proper name. Thus, there are at least three possible meanings of "Elias": (1) Elijah the prophet; (2) John the Baptist; and (3) any messenger of God who comes in "the spirit and power of Elias" (Luke 1:17).

As we previously discussed, the main thrust of Malachi 3:1 pertains to Jesus' Second Coming. And, of course, Jesus confirmed that "Elias," the "messenger," would yet come to prepare the way before Jesus comes again. And who will this "Elias" be? It could be one or several divine messengers with preparatory missions. We know that Elijah the prophet will come to perform such a preparatory mission before the Second Coming (Malachi 4:5-6). But Jesus described the mission of this "Elias" differently from the mission that Malachi described for Elijah—Elias was to "restore all things," while Elijah was to "turn the heart of the fathers to the children and the heart of the children to their fathers." By Jesus' identifying John the Baptist to be an "Elias," this points to the possibility that the future "Elias" would be a different person with a preparatory mission similar to John's. And consider this: To whom will Elijah the prophet come? We could certainly expect him to come to a living prophet. Since the beginning of mankind, it has been the Lord's pattern to send divine

---

[5] *Id.*

messengers to his living prophets. Isn't it most probable that the Lord would raise up from birth a latter-day "Elias" just as the Lord raised up John the Baptist before the Lord's first coming. And while this later "messenger" is designated as an "Elias," he could very well be known by some other name, just as John was.

The name of the future "Elias" is not given in the Bible, but it is nevertheless clear that an "Elias" or "messenger" was prophesied to come before the Lord's Second Coming.

D. Jesus Prophesied that an "Elias" Would "Restore All Things" before His Second Coming.

Before leaving Jesus' prophecy about the coming of "Elias" in the last days, contemplate what Jesus said about the mission of this latter-day "Elias." Jesus said that "Elias truly shall first come, and *restore all things*" (Matthew 17:11). [Emphasis added.] By these last three words Jesus taught that Elias' mission would be exceedingly broad and comprehensive in scope.

The word "restore" means "to give back," "to put back," or "to put back into a former state" (Webster's Dictionary). The word "restore" implies that something was "lost" or "taken away" or "tarnished." For example, people "restore" antique cars and furniture—putting them back into their original condition. And we speak of a person's good health being "restored" after it has been absent for a period of time. So, when Jesus spoke of restoring things, he implied that something would be lost or tarnished—otherwise nothing would need to be restored.

And Jesus did not say "some" things would be restored, but rather he said "all" things. Jesus did not give a list of specific things to be restored, but there can be no question that the restorer was to have a broad and comprehensive mission to perform prior to the Lord's triumphal return to the earth.

The apostle Peter echoed the words of the Savior when he characterized the preparatory time before the Second coming as "the times of restitution of all things" (Acts 3:20-21). There can be no question but that these statements of Jesus and Peter refer to the same thing. There can likewise be no question but that Peter understood that a future "Elias" would play a major role in this restoration;[6] Peter had learned about this from Jesus as they descended from the Mount of Transfiguration. Let us now consider Peter's prophecy in further detail, because it, too, sheds additional light on the mission of the messenger spoken of by Malachi.

E.   Peter Prophesied of a "Restitution of All Things" Occurring before the Second Coming.

The Apostle Peter prophesied that Christ's Second Coming would not occur until a "restitution of all things" had taken place. He said: "And he shall send Jesus Christ which before was preached unto you: Whom the heaven must receive until the times of restitution of all things, which God hath spoken by the mouth of all his holy prophets since the world began" (Acts 3:20-21).

"Restitution" means "the act of restoring" or "the state of being restored"[7] (Webster's Dictionary). Peter does not elaborate on what is to be restored, except to say that "all things" spoken of by "all his holy prophets" must be restored before the Second Coming. This comment invites us to search the scriptures to learn what the prophets may have recorded as "things" to be restored in the last days.

The resurrection of the righteous dead is one important aspect of the restoration of all things that will immediately precede the Second

---

[6] It might be expected that God would involve a number of "Eliases" and "messengers" when He brings about the restoration of all things. The "Elias" who is to "restore all things" would necessarily have to deliver his message of restoration to someone; and that person would in turn be a "messenger" once he testifies to others of the restoration. It is also reasonable to believe that more than one heavenly messenger will be involved in the restoration. Moses and Elijah appeared on the Mount of Transfiguration. We know that Elijah was to return to the earth; perhaps Moses would likewise return again. And, when Jesus identified John the Baptist as an "Elias," one possible meaning would be that John the Baptist would later return to do a work. The "Elias" who will restore all things could very well be a composite of several individuals.

[7] Peter also referred to this time as "the times of refreshing" (Acts 3:19).

Coming. God's prophets have spoken of this. Daniel wrote that when Jesus comes he will come with the clouds of heaven (Daniel 7:13); and Jude adds that "ten thousands of his saints" will come with Him (Jude 1:14; see also 1 Thess. 4:16-17). The resurrection and return of these saints will certainly be a part of a great restoration. (Of course, not all will be resurrected before the Second Coming. See, e.g., Rev. 20:5.)

Jesus' apostles understood that the restoring of the kingdom of Israel was a part of this restoration of all things. (See Acts 1:6-7.) This aspect of the restoration could occur years before the actual Second Coming. Such a restoration includes the gathering of Israel or the restoring of the twelve tribes to their promised lands—an event that will occur over a period of time. (See chapter 3, below.) We know from the prophecies that much of this will occur before the Second Coming. The gathering of Israel is a dominant theme in the writings of Moses, Isaiah, Jeremiah and Ezekiel. The Old Testament prophets Nehemiah Amos, Micah, Zephaniah, Joel and Zechariah all mention the gathering or restoration of Israel. In the New Testament, Jesus, Peter, Paul, John and Matthew also speak of this great event. Each prophet gives additional insights to the great day of the "restitution of all things."

God's "messengers" will play a great role in the latter-day restoration, in gathering Israel "one by one" (Isaiah 27:12). To these "messengers" Isaiah wrote in the name of the Lord: "Go, ye swift messengers, to a nation scattered" (Isaiah 18:2). And to scattered Israel, Isaiah wrote: "All ye inhabitants of the world, . . . see ye, when he lifteth up an ensign on the mountains; and when he bloweth a trumpet, hear ye" (Isaiah 18:3). Clearly, God will send his messengers with his messages in the last days to gather scattered Israel.

Isaiah's many prophecies about the gathering of Israel in the last days are particularly enlightening. Isaiah wrote that in this day the Lord would "*restore* thy judges as at the first" (Isaiah 1:26) [emphasis added]. Isaiah described this time as a day of wickedness and apostasy among the "priests" and "prophets" (Isaiah 24:5; 28:7-8; & 29:10). Isaiah points out the futility of trying to correct this apostasy by teaching true doctrines to the wayward priests and prophets; he declared that precept must be upon precept, line upon line (Isaiah 28:9-13). So, Isaiah declares, in the midst of this hypocrisy, where lip service thrives, but hearts are far from God (Isaiah 29:13), the Lord would "do a marvelous work" among the people (Isaiah 29:14) through the instrumentality of one who is not learned (Isaiah 29:12). Isaiah writes that this marvelous work will cause the wisdom of the world's wise men to perish (Isaiah 29:14). Jeremiah wrote about the restoration of God's true shepherds back over the fold (Jeremiah 23:1-4). In Isaiah 3:2-4, the prophet describes how the Lord would put "children" and "babes" to rule over the sophisticated people of the world—a restoration of godly leaders over the people. In chapter 44, verses 25-26, Isaiah prophesied that in these days the Lord would make manifest the foolishness of the wise men of the world, and that he would "perform[] the counsel of his *messengers*" [emphasis added].

Isaiah repeatedly uses the word "ensign" to describe the work of the Lord in the latter days. In Isaiah 5:26 he writes that the Lord "will lift up an ensign to the nations," to which people from all nations would come. In chapter 11, verses 10 and 12, he writes that the "Gentiles" and "the outcasts of Israel" would seek and gather to the "ensign." (See also Isaiah 30:17.) He also refers to this marvelous work of God as "a banner upon a high mountain" (Isaiah 13:2), "a light to the Gentiles" (Isaiah 42:6; see also 49:6, 51:4 & 60:3), and "a standard to the people" (Isaiah 49:22; see also 62:10). In chapter 66, Isaiah says that the "sign" will consist of the gathering of his people by those whom he would "send" "unto the nations" to declare God's glory (Isaiah 66:19). So, the "sign" or "ensign" will include the Lord's sending messengers of salvation, who "will bring [their] brethren . . . out of all nations . . . to my holy mountain Jerusalem" (Isaiah 66:20; see also 18:2-3). It is of these messengers as well as of Jesus that Isaiah said: "How beautiful upon the mountains are the feet of him that bringeth good tidings, . . . that publisheth salvation" (Isaiah 52:7).

All of these marvelous happenings foretold by Isaiah are a part of the "times of restitution of all things" spoken of by Peter.

F.   Paul Prophesied that There Would Be a Special "Dispensation" from God to Man in the Last Days.

In his letter to the Ephesians, the Apostle Paul described "the times of restitution of all things" (Acts 3:21) as "the dispensation of the fulness of times" (Ephesians 1:10). Paul wrote that in Christ "we have obtained an inheritance" (Ephesians 1:11), so that we will be with Him in the day when He gathers together all things. About this day of gathering, Paul wrote: "That in the dispensation of the fulness of times he might gather together in one all things in Christ, both which are in heaven, and which are on the earth...." (Ephesians 1:10).

The reason I call attention to this prophecy is because of the insight Paul gives us about this great day through his use of the word "dispensation." Paul used the word in the sense that means "an ordering of events under divine authority" (Webster's Dictionary). "Divine authority" is a key element of Paul's use of the word "dispensation" from God "by revelation" to bring the gospel to them (Ephesians 3:2-3). Paul also told the Colossians that "the dispensation of God" to him gave him the authority to minister the gospel to them (Colossians 1:25). Paul clearly understood the word "dispensation" to include the meaning: *authority obtained from God through revelation*. And this is the sense in which he used it.

So, what additional light does this shed on the latter days? By denoting this period, "the dispensation of the fulness of times," Paul expresses his understanding that there will be a special dispensing of divine authority by revelation in this latter-day period. This is something for which the disciples of Christ will watch.

And if divine authority is to be dispensed in the last days, to whom will it be dispensed? The revelation and dispensation of God's authority is not complete until it is received by someone—until it is received by a prophet of God—for by definition such a recipient would have to be a prophet; such a recipient would be God's messenger. Malachi said God would send a messenger before the Lord's Second Coming. Clearly, this messenger will come with a special dispensation from God.

Paul characterizes the time when this dispensation will occur to be "the fulness of times." Peter described this time as "the times of restitution of all things." It is because of the great authority that is to be dispensed and because "all things" are to be restored in this day that it is most appropriately designated as "the fulness of times."

G. Joel Prophesied that There Would Be a Number of True Prophets in the Last Days.

In writing about the last days, the prophet Joel wrote:

> And it shall come to pass afterward, that I will pour out my spirit upon all flesh; and your sons and your daughters shall prophesy, and your old men shall dream dreams, and your young men shall see visions:
> And also upon the servants and upon the handmaids in those days will I pour out my spirit. (Joel 2:28-29)

While the prophet Joel does not refer to one specific messenger, as did Malachi, he nevertheless mentions that "sons" and "daughters" would prophesy in the last days. Thus, by definition, they would be "prophets"—plural. Joel said that God would pour out his spirit upon them, revealing things to them in dreams and in visions. Of course, for the first 4,000 years of the earth's existence God always communicated to man through prophets; and Joel foresaw that God would likewise communicate with mankind through prophecy and visions in the last days.[8]

---

[8] Peter said that the spiritual manifestations on the Day of Pentecost were what Joel had spoken of in his prophecy (Acts 2:16-19). But complete fulfillment of the prophecy did not occur then. The main thrust of Joel's prophecy pertains to a later time, just "before the great and dreadful day of the LORD," when the sun will be darkened and the moon turned to blood, when the Lord will "show wonders in the heavens and in the earth," and in a day of "fire, and pillars of smoke" (Joel 2:30-32). For a further discussion of this prophecy of Joel, see B. H. Roberts, "Introduction," *History of The Church of Jesus Christ of Latter-day Saints*

In light of Joel's prophecy, it is clear that Jesus' warning to beware of false Christs and false prophets in the last days, was not meant to imply that there would be no "true" prophets in the latter days. There is no scripture that says there will be no prophets in the last days. On the contrary, the scriptures teach that God will do a great and marvelous work in the latter days—and when God does anything, "he revealeth his secret unto his servants the prophets" (Amos 3:7). Joel foretold that God would give divine manifestations to men and women in the latter days. Thus, Joel's prophecy implies that God would give messages to the world in the last days. The messages from "Elias" and Elijah will undoubtedly be part of the fulfillment of this prophecy. And he to whom "Elias" and Elijah deliver these messages will be a prophet of God.

H. John the Revelator Prophesied that in the Last Days an Angel would Be Sent from Heaven to Preach the Everlasting Gospel to the World.

One of the events foretold by the Apostle John in his Book of Revelation refers to an angelic messenger having a message to be preached to every nation, kindred, tongue and people. John wrote: "And I saw another angel fly in the midst of heaven, having the everlasting gospel to preach unto them that dwell on the earth, and to every nation and kindred, and tongue, and people" (Revelation 14:6). The Apostle John wrote about numerous angels and heavenly messengers in his book. However, this one is particularly interesting because this angel was to bring "the everlasting gospel" to be preached to the inhabitants of the earth. Now, why would God send an angel to the earth with the gospel when we already have the gospel taught in the Bible? Well, either the angel would be bringing a repetitious message or else he would be bringing something new. But in either event, this angel *will* come. And he will come with a message—the

[hereafter HC], by Joseph Smith (Salt Lake City: Deseret Book Co., 1948) pp. xxxi-xxxiv.

everlasting gospel. And he will "preach" the message to people who need to hear it; he will call upon the people to worship God and prepare for the day of judgment (Revelation 14:7).

The disciples of Jesus will look for the angel's coming and will believe the angel's message when he comes and delivers it.

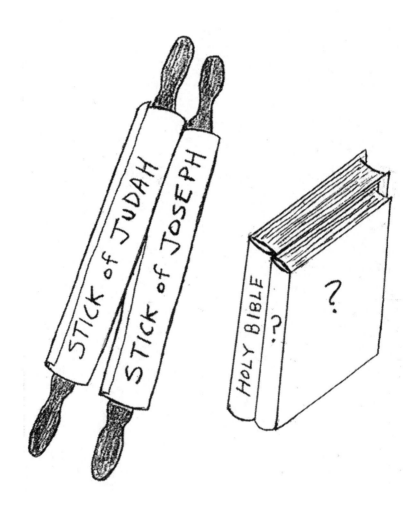

CHAPTER 3

The Gathering of Israel

One of the most frequently repeated prophecies in the Bible is that of the gathering of scattered Israel in the last days. A review of some of these prophecies shows that messengers and messages from God were foretold to play a key role in accomplishing this gathering.

A. Ezekiel and Isaiah Prophesied that a Book of Scripture Would Come Forth to Be Used with the Bible to Help Bring about the Gathering of Israel.

One of the most intriguing prophesies about the last days in all of the Bible is found in Ezekiel chapter 37. Ezekiel begins the chapter by speaking symbolically about the gathering of Israel, an event predicted to occur in the latter days. Ezekiel relates a vision he had of a valley of dry bones which took flesh upon themselves and were resurrected. Ezekiel then explained that just as God caused these dry bones to be brought to life again, so he would bring Israel out of their graves and into their lands again. Immediately following this allegory Ezekiel tells of two "sticks" or writings:

Moreover, thou son of man, take thee one stick, and write upon it, For Judah, and for the children of Israel his companions: then take another stick, and write upon it, For Joseph, the stick of Ephraim, and for all the house of Israel his companions;

And join them one to another into one stick; and they shall become one in thine hand.

And when the children of thy people shall speak unto thee, saying, Wilt thou not shew us what thou meanest by these?

Say unto them, Thus saith the Lord GOD; behold, I will take the stick of Joseph, which is in the hand of Ephraim, and the tribes of Israel his fellows, and will put them with him, even with the stick of Judah, and make them one in mine hand.

And the sticks whereon thou writest shall be in thine hand before their eyes.

And say unto them, Thus saith the Lord GOD; Behold I will take the children of Israel from among the heathen, whither they be gone, and will gather them on every side, and bring them into their own lands:

And I will make them one nation in the land upon the mountains of Israel; and one king shall be king to them all: and they shall be no more two nations, neither shall they be divided into two kingdoms any more at all. (Ezekiel 37:16-22)

The fascinating aspect of this prophecy has to do with the two "sticks" that are held together in one hand. In this passage the word "stick" is a figure of speech called a *metonymy*—that is a word used for another word or meaning that it suggests. For example, the word "bench" is used to mean the ball players on the bench, rather than to mean the piece of furniture on which those players sit. In the instance of Ezekiel's prophecy, the "stick" apparently has reference to the writings on parchment or some other material that are rolled up onto a stick. (See, e.g., Jeremiah 36:2, where such a writing is described as "a roll of a book.") So, when Ezekiel figuratively wrote that the "sticks" were to be written upon, this referred to the whole "scroll" or "stick," rather than to just the "stick" itself.[9] And when these writings would be held, it is undoubtedly the "stick" handles that were meant to be held, in order not to mar or damage the precious writings on the parchment or other material.

Our bible is acknowledged to come from the house of Judah; it could easily be "the stick of Judah" spoken of. But what about a record of the house of Joseph? Is there such a book in existence? If such another book were to exist, and were to be held in one hand with the Bible today—this would be a literal fulfillment of Ezekiel's prophecy. Of course, such a "stick of Joseph" would have to have some relationship to the gathering of Israel, and it would have to come from the same source—from the God of Israel. Isaiah prophesied of a book that would come forth in the latter days. He wrote:

> And thou shalt be brought down, and shalt speak out of the ground, and they speech shall be low out of the dust . . . .

---

[9] Recent archeological findings have shown that it was common in Ezekiel's time (approximately 587 B.C.) to write on waxen surfaces contained in wooden, frame boxes. The wax surface in the boxes or boards were erasable and reusable. It has been suggested that this was the recording medium referred to by Ezekiel in chapter 37. Scholars have explained that the word "stick" is the translation of the Hebrew word 'ets, which means "wood" or "of wood." Scholars explain that 'ets could mean "box," "board," "log," "stick," "beam" or a number of other particular forms of wood, depending on the context of the passage. (See Keith Merservy, "Ezekiel's Sticks," *Ensign*, March, 1987, pp. 4-13. See also, Hugh Nibley, *An Approach to the Book of Mormon* [Salt Lake City: Deseret Book Co., 1976] pp. 257-272.) Whether or not Ezekiel was referring to such a wax board, Ezekiel still used 'ets as a figure of speech; the writing would have been on some other material than the 'ets. Whether 'ets was used to mean "scroll stick" or "wax writing board," in either case the 'ets could be held together in one hand. (Merservy says that it was common to join more than one of these frame boards together with hinges. *Id.*)

And the vision of all is become unto you as the words of a book that is sealed, which men deliver to one that is learned, saying, Read this, I pray thee: and he saith, I cannot; for it is sealed:

And the book is delivered to him that is not learned, saying, Read this, I pray thee: and he saith, I am not learned.

Wherefore the Lord said, Forasmuch as this people draw near me with their mouth and with their lips do honour me, but have removed their heart far from me, and their fear toward me is taught by the precept of men:

Therefore, Behold, I will proceed to do a marvellous work among this people, even a marvellous work and a wonder: for the wisdom of their wise men shall perish, and the understanding of their prudent men shall be hid. . . .

And in that day shall the deaf hear the words of the book, and the eyes of the blind shall see out of obscurity, and out of darkness. (Isaiah 29:4, 11-14 & 18)

Isaiah said that this book and this marvelous work would happen at a time when a spirit of deep sleep was upon the people and when the eyes of the prophets and rulers were covered (Isaiah 29:10), and at a time of hypocrisy of people professing to believe in God—who render lip service—but whose hearts were far from God.

Is the book spoken of by Isaiah one and the same as the "stick of Joseph"? I believe it is. In chapter 29, Isaiah describes a people who came from "Ariel, the city where David dwelt" (verse 1—i.e., Jerusalem), against whom the Lord will lay siege (verse 3), and after which the people "shalt be brought down, and shall speak out of the ground" (verse 4). Since this describes a people coming from Jerusalem, they are undoubtedly an Israelite nation. (As will be discussed in chapters 10 and 11, below, the Book of Mormon fits the description of both of these writings.) Isaiah says that the words of this dead Israelite nation would someday be unsealed and speak to us "from the dust" or from the grave (Isaiah 29:11 & 4; see also Daniel 12:4 & 9, discussed below). Isaiah refers to this book in connection with a marvelous work of God. This book has a message which will cause the blind to see out of obscurity and darkness. And the message of that book will, or course, come from a messenger. When this book does appear, God's messenger will certainly be able to tell the world that it is the book spoken of by Isaiah. And he will also be able to tell us whether it is the "stick of Joseph" spoken of by Ezekiel.

B. Jeremiah Prophesied that God Would Set Up New Shepherds to Preach the Gospel and Gather Israel in the Last Days.

The prophet Jeremiah taught that God would use messengers to gather scattered Israel.[10] He said that in the latter days the Lord would give Israel "pastors according to mine heart" who would teach them "knowledge and understanding" (Jeremiah 3:15). Another time Jeremiah referred to these men as "shepherds" (Jeremiah 23:4). Jeremiah also wrote that God would send "many fishers" and "many hunters" to fish and hunt scattered Israel "from every mountain, and from every hill, and out of the holes of the rocks" (Jeremiah 16:16). These prophecies of Jeremiah make it clear that God will send

---

[10] The magnificence of some aspects of the gathering of Israel will be so great that they will eclipse the mighty miracles that God wrought through Moses in leading Israel out of Egypt—and those miracles were indeed great—the ten plagues, the passover miracle, and the dividing of the Red Sea. The prophet Jeremiah foretold that when the Lord does gather Israel, that it shall no more be said, The LORD liveth, that brought up the children of Israel out of the land of Egypt; But, the LORD liveth, that brought up the children of Israel from the land of the north, and from all the lands whither he had driven them; and I will bring them again into their land that I gave unto their fathers. (Jeremiah 16:14-15; see also Jeremiah 23:7-8) One of the magnificent happenings that will be a part of this gathering is the "highway" that the Lord would prepare for his people to use in returning (Isaiah 11:16; 35:8; 51:10 & 62:10).

his authorized servants to gather Israel, and that they will gather scattered Israel by teaching them a message from God.

The pastors spoken of by Jeremiah will have a message to deliver. Jeremiah said these pastors would "feed you [Israel] with knowledge and understanding" (Jeremiah 3:15). This means these "pastors" will teach Israel. Jeremiah said they would be "pastors according to mine [the LORD's] heart," which signifies that their teachings would be in harmony with God's will (Jeremiah 3:15).

That God would send men with messages to assist in gathering Israel is also foretold in the twenty-third chapter of Jeremiah, where the LORD says, through Jeremiah:

> Woe be unto the pastors that destroy and scatter the sheep of my pasture! saith the LORD.
>
> Therefore thus saith the LORD God of Israel against the pastors that feed my people; ye have scattered my flock, and driven them away, and have not visited them: behold, I will visit upon you the evil of your doings, saith the LORD.
>
> And I will gather the remnant of my flock out of all countries whither I have driven them, and will bring them again to their folds; and they shall be fruitful and increase.
>
> And I will set up shepherds over them which shall feed them. (Jeremiah 23:1-4)

The analogy used by Jeremiah is unmistakable; the "shepherds" God will "set up" to "feed" Israel will be his messengers sent to teach scattered Israel the true word of God. After "evil" pastors (and false prophets) had "driven them away" from Him, God will send good shepherds throughout the world to gather his flock back together (Jeremiah 23:14, 15, 21, 25-26 & 32).

C. Moses, Isaiah, Paul and Jesus Christ Himself Prophesied that in the Last Days God Would Use Divine Messengers to Gather Israel.

The gathering of scattered Israel is a theme that we have discussed a number of times in connection with prophecies about messengers God will send in the latter days. Many, many scriptures pertain to this latter-day event. Because of its importance, let us now explore the gathering of Israel in further depth, focusing on several prophecies about it. Doing this will help us to better understand how all of the previous prophecies are related.

Most Christians have heard of the gathering of Israel, but few grasp the full significance of it as it applies to modern day Christianity. The gathering of Israel is an integral part of the gathering of all the disciples of Jesus Christ. In the last days both blood descendants of Israel and non-blood descendants will be gathered and will participate in the gathering of God's "elect." This gathering will be accomplished through God's servants teaching a message from God to Israelites and Gentiles. All of the messengers prophesied to come in the latter days will play important roles in this gathering. Thus, the more fully we understand the gathering, the more readily we will be able to recognize God's messengers when they come and do their gathering work.

Consider the following questions and how the prophets of the Bible have answered them:

1. Who is scattered Israel?
2. Where will Israel be gathered?
3. What caused the scattering of Israel?
4. What will cause the gathering of Israel?
5. Who will comprise "gathered" Israel?

1. The Jews Are Only One of Twelve Tribes of Scattered Israel.

Many people equate the Jews with the Israelites. But this is not completely accurate. A Jew is a member of the tribe of Judah, one of the twelve tribes of Israel. The student of the scriptures realizes that there are eleven other scattered tribes of Israel that are not "Jews," but who are Israelites who will also be gathered together in the last days. (The term "Jew" can also refer to a citizen of the southern kingdom of Israel, called "Judah," being named after the largest tribe in the southern kingdom.)

We can for the most part identify who the Jews are and where they are. But who are these other tribes of Israel? And where are they? The identity and location of these other Israelites has not been known, and thus these other Israelites have sometimes been referred to as the "lost tribes."

In order to comprehend the full scope of the gathering of Israel, one must recognize that the biblical prophecies of the gathering of Israel are not limited to the tribe of Judah, but rather apply to all twelve of the tribes of Israel who have been scattered throughout the earth. One who believes that only the Jews will be gathered will miss seeing the major part of the gathering of Israel, even though it is unfolding right before his eyes.

2. All of the Tribes of Israel Will Not Be Gathered to Palestine.

Many of the Old Testament prophets wrote about the scattering and gathering of Israel. That some of the gathering of Israel is now taking place in the middle east is acknowledged by almost all Christians. The founding of the nation "Israel" in 1948 is one of the events that is certainly part of the fulfillment of these biblical prophecies.

However, not all of Israel will be gathered to the middle east, to the area of the new nation, "Israel." While this is the land where much of the tribe of Judah will be gathered, other tribes will be gathered to other lands that the Lord has covenanted to give them as long as they will love and serve Him with all their hearts and souls.

After Joshua led Israel across the Jordan River and into the promised land, the land was divided up and granted to the different tribes of Israel (Joshua, chapters 15-19). But these are not the only lands that the Lord has covenanted to give to Israel. Two tribes that have been given another land are the tribes of Ephraim and Manasseh (the two sons of Joseph).

Just prior to his death, Jacob blessed each of his twelve sons and prophesied about their posterity. To Joseph, Jacob said: "Joseph is a fruitful bough, even a fruitful bough by a well; whose branches run over the wall. . . . The blessings of thy father have prevailed above the blessings of my progenitors unto the utmost bound of the everlasting hills; they shall be on the head of Joseph" (Genesis 49:22 & 26). Joseph was promised to be blessed in a land of "everlasting hills."[11] The words of this blessing are not specific enough to make the identification of this land an easy and obvious task. However, the reference to "the utmost bound of the everlasting hills" does not fit the area in the mid-east where Joseph's descendants and the other tribes of Israel were given an inheritance. The reference to Joseph's posterity being a "fruitful bough" (being very numerous) "by a well; whose branches run over the wall" sounds like it could refer to a branch of Joseph's descendants who lived by a body of water, but who went from there to somewhere else to live where they would receive choice blessings. Joseph is the only son of Israel whose blessing referred to a mountainous place, a land characterized by everlasting hills."[12]

---

[11] Moses gave a slightly different blessing to the tribe of Joseph, as recorded in Deuteronomy 33:15. It is, however, strikingly consistent with Jacob's blessing of Joseph. Moses prophesied that Joseph's blessings would include: "the chief things of the *ancient mountains,* and for the precious things of *the lasting hills.*" [Emphasis added.] Moses used the word "precious" five times in describing the choice blessings that would come to the tribe of Joseph in its land. No land in the world better fits the description of "precious" than America.

[12] *The Book of Mormon* recounts the emigration of some of the descendants of Joseph to the Americas around 600 B.C. The prophets of this branch of the House of Israel taught that this land was to be a choice and blessed land for

The land of North and South America is perhaps the one land that fits Jacob's description of "everlasting hills." The geography of these two continents features a continuous ("everlasting") range of mountains stretching from the southern tip of South America to the northernmost part of North America (the Andes and Rocky Mountains).

Another important biblical reference to the existence of two great gathering places for Israel in the last days is written in Isaiah, chapter 2:

> And it shall come to pass in the last days, that the mountain of the LORD's house shall be established in the top of the mountains, and shall be exalted above the hills; and all nations shall flow unto it.
>
> And many people shall go and say, Come ye, and let us go up to the mountain of the LORD, to the house of the God of Jacob; and he will teach us of his ways, and we will walk in his paths: for out of Zion shall go forth the law, and the word of the LORD from Jerusalem. (Isaiah 2:2-3)

These verses specifically refer to people gathering to the tops of the mountains to learn about the LORD. Verse 2 refers to this mountainous land as "Zion" and distinguishes it as being separate and different from Jerusalem.

---

the posterity of Joseph and for others as long as they would serve the true and living God, who is Jesus Christ. *(Book of Mormon* [hereafter B of M] 1 Nephi 22:6-7; and Ether 2:7-12.) The prophets of this group of Israelites also taught that "the remnant of the house of Joseph shall be built upon this land" (B of M, Ether 13:8), and that the New Jerusalem would come down out of heaven to this land in the latter days. (B of M, Ether 13:3).

3. Causes of the Scattering and Gathering of Israel.

Moses wrote much about the scattering and gathering of Israel. In addition to predicting these occurrences, he also described their causes. In Deuteronomy chapter 28, Moses told Israel that "if thou shalt hearken diligently unto the voice of the LORD thy God and to do all his commandments," then Israel would be blessed above all other nations of the earth (Deuteronomy 28:1-14). But Moses also wrote of a corresponding cursing that awaited Israel if they would turn away from God and not obey his voice and his commandments (Deuteronomy 28:15). Moses predicted that Israel would be smitten by its enemies and vexed with pestilence, consumption and fever and would be an abused people (Deuteronomy 28:16-44). Another one of these predicted curses for Israel was a scattering:

> And the LORD shall scatter thee among all people, from the one end of the earth even unto the other; and there thou shalt serve other gods, which neither thou nor thy fathers have known, even wood and stone.
> And among these nations shalt thou find no ease, neither shall the sole of thy foot have rest. (Deuteronomy 28:64-65)

Moses emphasized and reemphasized that the cause of these curses and of this scattering would be that Israel would turn away from and reject God: "Moreover all these curses shall come upon thee . . . because thou hearkenedst not unto the voice of the LORD thy God, to keep his commandments and his statutes. . . . Because thou servedst not the LORD thy God with joyfulness, and with gladness of heart" (Deuteronomy 28:45 & 47). Moses prophesied that it would be known among the nations that the Lord had brought this cursing upon Israel: "Because they have forsaken the covenant of the LORD God of their fathers, . . . For they went and served other gods, and worshipped them, gods whom they knew not" (Deuteronomy 29:25-26). Moses further taught the people that even as Israel's turning away from God would bring the cursing and scattering, even so would God bless and gather Israel if they would return to the true and living God and obey him.

> And it shall come to pass when all these things are come upon thee, the blessing and the curse, which I have set before thee, and thou shalt call them to mind among all the nations, whither the LORD thy God hath driven thee,
>
> And shalt return unto the LORD thy God, and shalt obey his voice . . .
>
> That then the LORD thy God will turn thy captivity, and have compassion upon thee, and will return and gather thee from all the nations, whither the LORD thy God hath scattered thee. . . .
>
> If thou shalt hearken unto the voice of the LORD thy God, to keep his commandments and his statutes which are written in this book of the law, and if thou turn unto the LORD thy God with all thine heart, and with all thy soul. (Deuteronomy 30:1-3, 10)

Moses prophetically addressed this message to future generations, for their benefit. Since the scattering would not occur until future generations, Moses' admonition to return to the Lord with all their heart and soul was necessarily given to people of a later time who would have Moses' words to read and consider.

And Moses repeated this message to future Israel several times in the Book of Deuteronomy. In chapter four, Moses warned Israel to "take heed," or else they would forget to obey the covenant they had made with God. Moses said they would forget; they would begin to serve other gods; they would do evil in the sight of God; and, therefore the LORD would scatter Israel "among the nations" (Deuteronomy 4:23-25 & 27). But Moses also repeated the great promise to future generations: "But if from thence thou shalt seek the LORD thy God, thou shalt find him, if thou seek him with all thy heart and with all thy soul" (Deuteronomy 4:29). Israel was scattered because it rejected and disobeyed the true and living God. It will be gathered when it again accepts and obeys the true and living God.

4. The Gathering of Israel Will Be Accomplished through the Preaching of the Gospel of Jesus Christ.

In a previous section we discussed the prophecies that God would send his messengers to assist in the gathering of Israel. These messengers will help gather Israel by preaching the word of God.

And what will be the message of these pastors and shepherds that God will set up to teach Israel when God gathers them home? The message will be that Israel must seek to know the true and living God with all their heart and soul, and that they must keep His commandments. Moses taught repeatedly that when Israel would be gathered again, that they would not only be gathered together physically, but that they would be gathered together spiritually as they turned again to worship the only true and living God with all their heart and soul (Deuteronomy 4:29 & 30:1-3 & 10).

a. *Jesus Christ is JEHOVAH—the God of Israel.* Israel will be gathered again when they return to the true and living God. And who is the true and living God of Israel? Isaiah taught that the "God of Israel" was the Savior of Israel; he wrote: "Verily thou art a God that hidest thyself, O God of Israel, the Saviour" (Isaiah 45:15). On another occasion, speaking in the name of the LORD, Isaiah wrote: "I, *even* I, *am* the LORD; and beside me *there is* no savior" (Isaiah 43:11). Isaiah taught this in other passages, too. (E.g., Isaiah 47:4; 45:22; 44:24 & 43:10-11 & 25.) The apostle John identifies Jesus as the God of Israel, when he wrote that Jesus had fulfilled a prophecy spoken of by Isaiah (John 12:39-41; & Isaiah 6:1 & 10). And most importantly, Jesus himself testified that He is the God of the Old Testament. He taught this on one occasion, at the temple in Jerusalem, to a gathering of Jews that were contending with him. Jesus said:

> Your father Abraham rejoiced to see my day: and
> he saw it, and was glad.
>
> Then said the Jews unto him, Thou art not yet
> fifty years old, and hast thou seen Abraham?
>
> Jesus said unto them, Verily, verily, I say unto you,
> Before Abraham was, I am" (John 8:56-58).

Upon Jesus' identifying himself as "I am," the Jews immediately "took . . . up stones to cast at him" (John 8:59). The Jews understood that Jesus was declaring himself to be Jehovah, the great "I am," the God of Israel—and since the Jews did not believe Jesus to be Jehovah, they picked up stones to stone Jesus to death for blaspheming the name of God. But Jesus' time had not come, and so he miraculously "went out of the temple, going through the midst of them" without suffering any harm (John 8:59).

Among the Jews who were contending with Jesus on that occasion were certainly a number of Pharisees, who prided themselves in their knowledge of the scriptures. They were undoubtedly well familiar with the words by which God identified himself to Moses:

> Moses said unto God, Behold, when I come unto
> the children of Israel, and shall say unto them The
> God of your fathers hath sent me unto you; and they
> shall say to me, What is his name? what shall I say
> unto them?
>
> And God said unto Moses, I AM THAT I AM:
> and he said, Thus shalt thou say unto the children of
> Israel, I AM hath sent me unto you. (Exodus 3:13-14)

(See also, Exodus 6:2-3.) So, when Jesus said "Before Abraham was, I am," (John 8:58) he was not only saying that he existed before Abraham, but he was declaring himself to be "I AM," the God of Abraham, Isaac and Jacob.[13]

---

[13] James E. Talmage adds the following helpful commentary: "*Jehovah* is the Anglicized rendering of the Hebrew, *Yahveh* or *Jahveh*, signifying the *Self-existent*

The Old Testament teaches that one of the titles of the God of Israel is the "Rock" of Israel. (See, e.g., 2 Samuel 23:3; Deuteronomy 32:3-4; and Psalm 18:31 &46.) The apostle Paul taught that Jesus Christ was the God of Israel when he alluded to the time when the Lord caused water to run out of the rock that Moses struck (Exodus 17:6 and Deuteronomy 8:15). Paul wrote to the Corinthians that the "spiritual Rock" of the Israelites "was Christ" (1 Corinthians 10:4).[14]

Accordingly, if Israel is to return to the true and living God, they will return to Jesus Christ. And the gathering of Israel will be brought about by the servants of God who preach the gospel of Jesus Christ to the world.

b.   *In the Last Days Jesus Will Gather His Elect.* Jesus taught that in the last days he would "gather together his elect" (Matthew 24:31). Comparing his "elect" to "eagles," Jesus said that the "eagles" would be "gathered together" when the Second Coming bursts upon the world (Matthew 24:28). Jesus said that the gospel would "be preached in all the world for a witness unto all nations; and then shall the end come" (Matthew 24:14). In these verses Jesus makes it clear that he will

---

One, or *The Eternal*. This name is generally rendered in our English version of the Old Testament as LORD, printed in capitals. . . . The central fact connoted by this name *I AM*, or *Jehovah*, the two having essentially the same meaning, is that of existence or duration that shall have no end, and which, judged by all human standards of reckoning, could have had no beginnings; the name is related to such other titles as *Alpha and Omega*, the first and the last, the beginning and the end.... The Jews regarded *Jehovah* as an ineffable name, not to be spoken; they substituted for it the sacred, though to them the not-forbidden name, *Adonai* signifying *the Lord*. The original of the terms *Lord* and *God* as they appear in the Old Testament, was either *Yahveh* or *Adonai*." James E. Talmage, *Jesus the Christ* (Salt Lake City: Deseret Book Co., 1916, 1972), pp. 36-37.

"LORD" and "JEHOVAH" are both titles, and they have been used to identify God the Father as well as Jesus. (See, e.g., Psalm 110:1 and Matthew 22:42-46.)

[14] That Jesus was the "rock" or "stone" of Israel was further taught by Paul when, in writing to the Ephesians, he alluded to the prophecy of the Psalmist that the "stone" that the "builders refused" would become the "head stone of the corner" (Psalm 118:22). Paul wrote that Jesus Christ himself [is] the chief corner stone" (Ephesians 2:20). Jesus and Peter similarly taught that Christ fulfilled the Psalmist's prophecy (Matthew 21:42-44 and Acts 4;10-12).

accomplish the gathering of his elect in the last days by the preaching of his gospel. The gathering spoken of by Jesus is one and the same as the gathering of Israel spoken of by Moses. It will be accomplished by the preaching of the gospel of Jesus Christ.

5. The Gathering of Israel Is Not Limited to the Gathering of Literal Descendants of Israel.

Just as the gospel of Jesus Christ is preached and made available to every living soul, so likewise every living soul is invited to join the House of Israel and to covenant with the true and living God to serve Him and to keep His commandments. Though an individual may be a "gentile" (one who is not a blood-descendent of Israel[15]), by accepting the gospel of Jesus Christ he becomes adopted into the house of Israel. (See Galatians 3:7-9, 14, 26-29; and Romans 9:4, 25-26.)

One who is born of the water and of the Spirit becomes a spiritual son or daughter of Jesus Christ—becomes an heir to salvation. At the same time, in a similar, figurative sense, he or she becomes an adopted child of Abraham. Paul taught: And if ye be Christ's, then are ye Abraham's seed, and heirs according to the promise" (Galatians 3:29). Thus, by covenanting with God through the ordinance of baptism to serve Him and keep His commandments, both Jew and gentile alike become Abraham's seed and play a part in the spiritual and physical gathering of Israel.

---

[15] Sometimes "gentile" is used to mean an Israelite who is not of the tribe of Judah.

CHAPTER 4

The God of Heaven Shall Set Up a Kingdom

A. Daniel Prophesied that in the Last Days, Prior to the Second Coming, God Would "Set Up a Kingdom" on Earth.

One of the best-known biblical prophecies about the last days came about in a most unusual way. In about 600 B.C. Babylon conquered Judah, uprooted thousands of Jews, and deported them to distant lands. One of the largest Jewish exile colonies was established in Babylon, the capital city of Babylonia. While the Jews lived there in captivity, the prophet Daniel was a young man. He became known among both Jews and Babylonians to be brilliant, and his advice was even sought by the leaders of Babylon on important matters. In this setting, the following story unfolds.

Nebuchadnezzar, King of Babylon, had a dream. It impressed him as being very important, but two things bothered him about it: First, he didn't know what it meant; and second, he couldn't even remember what he dreamed. He called his wise men to help him, but their efforts to discover and interpret the dream were futile. They complained that this was a difficult task he had asked of them, but this only made King Nebuchadnezzar angry, and he ordered all the wise men in the kingdom to be destroyed. When Daniel learned that his life was also being sought because of the failure of the Chaldean wise men, he immediately sought an audience before the King. Audience was granted, and Daniel went before the King and asked for time, promising to interpret the dream. The King granted his request, and Daniel returned to his friends, who prayed with him that God would make the dream and its meaning known to Daniel. God did reveal the dream and its meaning to Daniel in "a night vision" (Daniel 2:19). Daniel then returned to the King and made his report.

The King asked Daniel, "Art thou able to make known unto me the dream which I have seen, and the interpretation thereof?" (Daniel 2:26). Daniel replied:

> [T]here is a God in heaven that revealeth secrets, and maketh known to the King Nebuchadnezzar what shall be in the latter days. . . .
>
> Thou, O King, sawest, and behold a great image. This great image, whose brightness was excellent, stood before thee; and the form thereof was terrible.
>
> This image's head was of fine gold, his breast and arms of silver, his belly and thighs of brass,
>
> His legs of iron, his feet part of iron and part of clay.
>
> Thou sawest till that a stone was cut out without hands, which smote the image upon his feet that were of iron and clay, and brake them to pieces.
>
> Then was the iron, the clay, the brass, the silver and the gold broken to pieces together, and became like the chaff of the summer threshingfloors; and the wind carried them away, that no place was found for them; and the stone that smote the image became a great mountain, and filled the whole earth. (Daniel 2:28, 31-35)

As for the interpretation, Daniel said that the God of heaven revealed that King Nebuchadnezzar was the head of gold, and that after him would arise three other kingdoms that would rule over the earth, followed by a day when there would be multiple kingdoms ruling the world, some of which would be strong and some of which would be weak. Daniel said:

> And in the days of these kings [the kings of the multiple kingdoms] shall the God of heaven set up a kingdom which shall never be destroyed: and the kingdom shall not be left to other people, but it shall break in pieces and consume all these kingdoms, and it shall stand forever. (Daniel 2:44)

Daniel said that "in the latter days" (Daniel 2:28) God himself would "set up a kingdom," which he said "shall stand for ever" and "shall never be destroyed" (Daniel 2:44).

When will this Kingdom of God be set up? It will be in a day when multiple kingdoms rule the world. Daniel wrote that "the Ancient of days" would present this kingdom to the Lord at the Second Coming. Daniel said:

> [O]ne like the Son of man [Christ] came with the clouds of heaven, and came to the Ancient of days, and they brought him near before him.
>
> *And there was given him* dominion, and glory, and *a kingdom* . . . that which shall not be destroyed. (Daniel 7:13-14 [emphasis added])

The apostles John and Paul both said that at his Second Coming, Christ would come with the clouds (Revelation 1:7 and 1 Thessalonians 4:17), just as he was taken up to heaven in a cloud before the eleven apostles at his ascension (Acts 1:9-11). The kingdom spoken of by Daniel will be set up before the Lord's Second Coming because it is to be given to Him when He comes. But when before the Second Coming will it be set up? Some Bible students argue that the prophecies of Daniel and of John the Revelator pinpoint a precise year when this will happen. But such interpretations that I have considered are too strained and contain too many assumptions to suit me. However, I do contend that the prophecies do give us enough information to identify a time period when God would set up his kingdom. According to Daniel, this would be during a time of many kings and kingdoms, some of which would be strong and others weak. I understand this to identify a time after the fall of the Roman Empire.

Tracing the main rulers of the world from the days of King Nebuchadnezzar until today is not difficult. (See figure on next page.) Nebuchadnezzar was King of the Babylonian Empire from 606 to 561 B.C. He is the head of gold (Daniel 2:38). His son, Belshazzar, ruled after Nebuchadnezzar's death. During his reign, Belshazzar convened a royal party for all the lords in the kingdom and their wives and concubines. At this royal feast, Belshazzar brought out the holy vessels that Nebuchadnezzar had taken from the temple of the Lord at Jerusalem. Then Belshazzar and his party used these vessels as they feasted and praised idols. This was a blasphemous and mocking action on the part of Belshazzar. The party was suddenly interrupted by the appearance of a hand that made a curious writing on the wall. The sight of the hand without a body disturbed the king so much that "the joints of his loins were loosed, and his knees smote one against the other" (Daniel 5:6).

Belshazzar, like his father, first sought an interpretation of the heavenly communication from his wise men, astrologers and soothsayers. And, as was the case with his father, when they failed to interpret the communication, Daniel was brought in to interpret the message. God revealed to Daniel the meaning of the writing, which Daniel related to the king as follows:

"MENE; God hath numbered thy kingdom and finished it. TEKEL; Thou art weighed in the balance, and art found wanting. PERES; Thy kingdom is divided, and given to the Medes and the Persians" (Daniel 5:26-28). That night the prophecy of the handwriting was fulfilled as Belshazzar was slain and Darius, the Median, conquered Babylon and took over the rule of the world (Daniel 5:30-31). The Medo-Persian Empire is the breast and arms of silver in Nebuchadnezzar's dream.

Beginning with King Darius, the Medo-Persian Empire ruled the world until 330 B.C., when Alexander the Great conquered the world for the Greeks. Daniel specifically identified "Grecia" as the world power that would succeed the Medo-Persian Empire (Daniel 8:5-8, 20-21). The Greco-Macedonian kingdom controlled the world until around 160-168 B.C. The Greco-Macedonian Empire is the belly and thighs of brass is Nebuchadnezzar's dream.

In 168 B.C. The Roman Empire came into power and ruled the world alone until approximately 476 A.D. (600+ years). (See Chester G. Starr, "Roman Empire," *World Book Encyclopedia*, 1969 ed.) The Roman Empire is the legs of iron in Nebuchadnezzar's dream.

After the end of the Roman rule, there has been no other long and dominant ruler of the world. For the last 1500 years a mixture of weak and strong nations have ruled the world at the same time—these could be the feet of iron and clay in Nebuchadnezzar's dream. Spain and England each had periods of dominance, especially in connection with the discovery and colonizing of the new world. France, under Napoleon, attempted to rule the world. And, of course, Hitler attempted this and failed. But no one nation has indisputably ruled the world since then—world rule has been shared by a number of nations at a time.

World Powers Represented by the Body Parts
of the Image in Nebuchadnezzar's Dream:

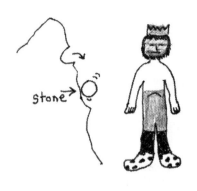

Head of Gold—Assyrio-Babylonish
Monarchy (6th & 5th centuries B.C.)

Breast and Arms of Silver—Medo-
Persian Empire (538-330 B.C.)

Belly and Thighs of Brass—Greco-
Macedonian Kingdom (330-160 B.C.)

Legs of Iron—Roman Empire
(160 B.C. — 476 A.D.)

Feet of Iron & Clay Mixed—
Multiple Kingdoms

For an additional discussion of this prophecy, see Roberts,
"Introduction." HC, vol. I, pp. xxxiv-xxxix.

As you can see, this only helps us to identify the post 476 A.D. era
as the time when God would set up his kingdom for ever.

The setting up of Christ's Church around 30 A.D. Was the setting
up of a kingdom, but I don't understand it to be the setting up of the
kingdom spoken of by Daniel. The timing does not coincide with
Daniel's description of the dream. Rome ruled the world in 30 A.D.
But Daniel said the kingdom would be set up in a day when multiple
kingdoms ruled the world "in the latter days" (Daniel 2:28). Thus, we
must look for the Lord to do this great work after the Romans ruled
the world.

Once again, I would refer to Isaiah's prophecies to help pinpoint
the time of fulfillment of Daniel's prophecy. Daniel and Isaiah both
used the "mountain" image in their prophecies, and they both used
it to mean the kingdom of God. Daniel said that the kingdom would
start out small—like a stone—but that the stone rolled forth and
"became a great mountain, and filled the whole earth" (Daniel 2:35).
In this same vein, Isaiah wrote that "in the last days, the mountain of
the LORD's house shall be established in the tops of the mountains"

(Isaiah 2:2). Isaiah's many references to "Mount Zion" and to the "mountain of the Lord's house," and to the setting up an "ensign" and a "banner" on a mountain, show that he uses the word "mountain" literally and as a symbol for the kingdom of God (Isaiah 2:2-3; 4:5; 10:12; 11:9; 18:3 & 7; 24:23; 25:6-12; 29:8; 52:7; 65:25 & 66:20). And you may recall from a few pages earlier, that a major theme in Isaiah's prophecies was *the restoration and gathering of Israel* to the "ensign" or to the "mountain of the Lord's house" (Isaiah 2:2-3; and 11:12). Thus, by using Isaiah's prophecies with Daniel's prophecy we can infer that the kingdom Daniel spoke of has to do with the gathering of Israel, and that God would set up his kingdom at the time of the restoration and gathering of Israel in the last days.

We can see from the return of the Jews to Palestine, and from the recent establishment of the nation "Israel" in 1948, that some of the gathering of Israel is now taking place. So, we know that the stone must have already been cut out of the mountain prior to that time, since God will be the one to get the stone started and rolling. And, I would suggest, on the other end, that we can look to the establishment of the United States in 1776 as a time before which this did not happen. The "Mountain" place of gathering prophesied by Isaiah (e.g., Isaiah 2:2-3) sounds very much like the United States of America. Certainly, God's kingdom will grow from a small stone to a large mountain by *gathering* together the people of God. This suggests that the time of God's cutting the stone out of the mountain could coincide with the founding of the American nation. Isaiah wrote this:

> [I]n the last days, . . . the mountain of the LORD's house shall be established in the tops of the mountains, . . . and all nations shall flow unto it.
> . . . people shall go and say, Come ye, and let us go up to the mountain of the LORD, to the house of the God of Jacob; and he will teach us of his ways, and we will walk in his paths: for out of Zion shall go forth the law, and the word of the LORD from Jerusalem. (Isaiah 2:2-3)

Bordered by mountains on its east and west coasts, America fits the geographic description of the place where people will come to serve the Lord. All nations have come to America. No other nation in the world has ever had the appeal that America has had to all peoples. People have come here to worship God in freedom, both now and from the earliest days after the discovery of America. Isaiah refers to this mountainous place as "Zion," and he says the "law shall go forth from Zion." This has been fulfilled through the establishing of the U. S. Constitution, which has now been a model for other nations around the world for 230 years.

Isn't it reasonable to look for the kingdom of God, the "ensign to the nations," the "mountain of the LORD's house," and the "stone" that becomes a "mountain" to be set up in the United States of America— the land to which people from all nations have gathered.

I submit that a reasonable interpretation of these prophecies is that the early years of the American nation is the time when Daniel's prophecy would begin to be fulfilled—the time when God would set up the small kingdom upon the earth, which in time would roll forth and fill the whole earth.

B.   Daniel Prophesied that God Would Reveal the "Words" of a "Sealed" "Book" at the Last Days.

Daniel had several dreams and revelations about the last days. In one of them God showed him a vision of the resurrection of the dead and of other future happenings. Then God told Daniel:

> But thou, O Daniel, shut up the words, and seal the book even to the time of the end: many shall run to and fro, and knowledge shall be increased. . . .
>
> And he said, Go thy way, Daniel: for the words are closed up and sealed till the time of the end. (Daniel 12:4 & 9)

Since the Lord "closed up and sealed" these "words" until "the time of the end," no one will be able to tell us in advance, before the book is revealed what its words will be. But we do know that at "the time of the end" the message of this "book" will be unsealed and made known.

C. Daniel Prophesied that One Called "the Ancient of Days" Will Come to the Earth Just Prior to the Second Coming.

We mentioned above that the kingdom spoken of by Daniel will already be on earth when the Lord comes "with the clouds of heaven." But note that Christ will come to "the Ancient of days," who will then turn the kingdom over to Christ (Daniel 7:13-14). Daniel said that "the Ancient of days" would come at a time when nations were warring against the saints and were prevailing over them. Daniel said that when "the Ancient of days" comes the tide would turn in favor of the saints (Daniel 7:22).

This prophecy, then, tells of another messenger to come prior to the Second Coming. I understand "the Ancient of days" to be a descriptive title for the oldest man, the patriarch of all mankind, Adam. His coming will apparently be just prior to the Lord's return to the earth.

D. The Kingdom of God on Earth Will Be the Church of Jesus Christ, having Living Apostles and Prophets as Its Earthly Leaders.

Prior to the coming of "the Ancient of days," how will this kingdom be administered? Certainly the kingdom will exist to do God's will. I would suggest that God will reveal his will to his prophets—the earthly leaders of his kingdom. This has always been God's manner of dealing with his people. Shouldn't we expect that this kingdom spoken of by Daniel will be the Church of Christ, having apostles and prophets to direct it. Just as Amos declared that God would always reveal his secrets to his servants the prophets, so did the Apostle Paul declare that apostles and prophets were essential to the on-going operation of Christ's church:

> And he gave some, apostles; and some, prophets; and some, evangelists; and some, pastors and teachers;
>
> For the perfecting of the saints, for the work of the ministry, for the edifying of the body of Christ:
>
> Till we all come in the unity of the faith, and of the knowledge of the Son of God, unto a perfect man, unto the measure of the stature of the fulness of Christ:
>
> That we henceforth be no more children, tossed to and fro, and carried about with every wind of doctrine, by the sleight of men, and cunning craftiness, whereby they lie in wait to deceive. (Ephesians 4:11-14)

That apostles and prophets were essential to the Church of Christ in Paul's day cannot be questioned. Paul states that they are necessary for "the work of the ministry." If apostles and prophets were necessary then, wouldn't they be necessary to work in God's ministry today? Of course they would. And Paul declares that apostles, prophets, evangelists, pastors and teachers will always be necessary until we come to a "unity of the faith," and to a "unity . . . of the knowledge of the Son of God," until we come "unto a perfect man, unto the measure of the stature of the fulness of Christ."

The disciples of Christ have never yet "come to a unity of the faith"; neither have they attained "the measure of the stature of the fulness of Christ"; neither has the "perfecting of the saints" been accomplished. All of these purposes for which apostles and prophets were put in Christ's church remain unfulfilled. The need for apostles and prophets has remained. According to Paul, they will always be needed in Christ's work until it is completed. Nowhere in the Bible is this doctrine rescinded or modified.

In some respects, God's kingdom is the Church of Jesus Christ.

God's kingdom will be directed by living apostles and prophets in communion with God, just as has always been the pattern. Just as Amos said: "Surely the Lord God will do nothing, but he revealeth his secret to his servants the prophets" (Amos 3:7).

E. The Foundation of Apostles and Prophets in the Church of Christ is a Foundation of Living Apostles and Prophets.

No Christian disputes the words of Paul that Christ's church is "built upon the *foundation of apostles and prophets,* Jesus Christ himself being the chief corner stone; In whom all the building fitly framed together groweth unto an holy temple in the Lord" (Ephesians 2:20-21 [emphasis added]). But does this foundation refer only to the original twelve apostles and the prophets of the Bible, or does it refer to living apostles and prophets who would continue to be in Christ's church? I submit that a full consideration of this question will lead to the conclusion that continuing, living apostles and prophets are the foundation of Christ's church. There are three scriptural evidences that establish this truth.

First, after Judas Iscariot betrayed Jesus and killed himself—leaving only eleven apostles—the remaining apostles chose and ordained Matthias to replace Judas and to be "numbered with the eleven apostles" (Acts 1:22-26)—bringing the number of apostles up to twelve again. The fact that the apostles had the power to and did appoint a replacement for the dead apostle shows their understanding that there were to be living apostles in the foundation of Christ's church, and it is evidence that they acted to keep the number of their quorum at twelve.

Second, Paul, Barnabas and James (the brother of Jesus) all later became apostles (Acts 14:14 & Galatians 1:19). The Bible does not specifically state whether or not they were numbered among the "twelve" when they were called to be apostles. But there is some evidence that they became members of the quorum of twelve apostles. In the case of Paul and Barnabas, they were not referred to as apostles until 45 A.D., about three years after the apostle James was beheaded by Herod (Acts 12:2). It is possible that Paul and Barnabas were called to replace James and another deceased apostle. In the case of James, the brother of Jesus, we do not know of him being referred to as an apostle until Paul makes mention of it in his epistle to the Galatians, written in 55-58 A.D.

The word "apostle" comes from the Greek language and denotes "person sent forth" (Webster's Dictionary). In the general sense, apostle is synonymous with "messenger." And in this sense, any witness of Jesus Christ is sometimes referred to as an "apostle." In the general sense, Paul may have been an apostle after the Lord appeared to him on the road to Damascus. But Paul's *calling* as an apostle did not come until later. Nowhere is he referred to as an apostle until ten years later (Acts 14:14—about 45 A.D.) In 55-57 A.D. Paul referred to himself as "the least of the apostles" in one of his epistles (1 Corinthians 15:9). By his comment, he affirms that he, too, was one of the twelve living apostles; by ranking himself as "least" among the apostles, he both expresses his humility and establishes that he was indeed one of the apostles, albeit he may be the newest or the least deserving of the group.

Paul's calling as an apostle is particularly significant because he was not an eyewitness of Jesus' death and resurrection, as Matthias and the eleven were (Acts 1:22). Nevertheless, Paul was a special witness of Christ's resurrection because of his personal revelations from the Lord. Thus, we learn that apostles were not limited to the saints who eye-witnessed Jesus' resurrection. And thus, we see how the Lord could continue to call living apostles to direct his church to replace those who would die. The apostles had the power to replace those of their number. They exercised this power and transferred their apostleship to others. Theoretically, the authority of the apostles could have continued on the earth from that day to this.

The Bible does not specifically state that the number of apostles was limited to twelve. But the Bible undisputedly establishes that in the original Church of Christ new apostles were called after the death of the original twelve.

Third, Paul taught that Christ placed apostles in the church "first," and prophets "secondarily" (1 Corinthians 12:28). This scripture shows that Paul did not consider the prophets of the Old Testament to be the "foundation" of Christ's church. If Paul *had* meant that, he would have said prophets were "first" and apostles "second." But Paul was not speaking in a chronological sense; rather, he was speaking in terms of importance and authority. Paul did not refer to dead apostles and prophets as the foundation for Christ's church—rather he referred to living ones, including himself, Matthias, Barnabas and James, the brother of Jesus. When these men were called to the apostleship by God and ordained by existing apostles, they became apostles just as much as if Jesus had ordained them himself.

When Paul taught that apostles and prophets were the foundation of Christ's church, he listed apostles first, then prophets (Ephesians 2:20). Similarly, when Paul taught that apostles and prophets performed essential services in Christ's church, he mentioned apostles before prophets (Ephesians 4:11). This fact, coupled with the context of these passages, refutes any notion that the "prophets" referred to were the Old Testament prophets of the past. The New Testament is replete with visions, revelations and prophecies of the apostles. The plain meaning of "foundation" as Paul used it (in stating that apostles and prophets were the foundation of Christ's church) is that *living* apostles and prophets in communion with the Lord, Jesus Christ are the continuing foundation of Christ's church.

That apostles and prophets have been long absent from the Christian scene cannot be disputed. In fact, some have claimed that God no longer reveals himself to man; that revelation stopped with the biblical apostles and prophets. Yes, apostles and prophets were absent from Christianity for hundreds of years—but not because that's what God wanted. God always gives men their free agency to either obey him or to disobey him. And God's prophets were repeatedly rejected throughout the Old Testament. Things were no different for Jesus and the New Testament apostles and prophets. Many of Christ's original twelve apostles suffered martyrs' deaths. Their disappearance from Christ's church was not because of revelation from God that said they were no longer needed. They disappeared from the church because they and Christ were rejected. Their disappearance coincided with the early Christians' turning from truth to fables (2 Timothy 4:4). The "mystery of iniquity" that Paul said "doth already work" (2 Thessalonians 2:7), was not checked; it ran its course. And, as Paul prophesied, "after [his] departing . . . grievous wolves [did] enter in . . . not sparing the flock" (Acts 20:29).

The absence of apostles and prophets from the church after the first century is one of the most obvious signs that it had become corrupted. Instead of having inspired apostles and prophets to lead it, the apostate church began to promulgate a new and convenient doctrine that there was to be no more revelation from God. The Bible did not teach this, but then few people had their own scriptures to enable them to refute it. But now that Bibles are easily accessible to all, the counterfeit can now be exposed; uninspired men changed many of the Christian ordinances and doctrines. And when uninspired men replaced apostles and prophets as the foundation of Christ's church, the edifice did not "grow[] unto an holy temple in the Lord" (Ephesians 2:21), but rather it became an unholy temple for the adversary, who set himself up to reign there instead. Paul's prophecy was fulfilled:

> Let no man deceive you by any means: for that day [the Second Coming] shall not come except there come a falling away first, and that man of sin be revealed, the son of perdition;
>
> Who opposeth and exalteth himself above all that is called God, or that is worshipped; so that he as God sitteth in the temple of God, shewing himself that he is God. (2 Thessalonians 2:2-3)

Certainly the "restoration of all things" will include a reestablishment of apostles and prophets in God's church and kingdom. The kingdom that Daniel said God would set up in the last days will be the Church of Jesus Christ, with living apostles and prophets as its foundation.

CHAPTER 5

Summary: The Bible Teaches that God Will Reveal New Scripture in the Last Days

In chapters 2, 3 and 4, we reviewed a number of biblical prophecies of messages and messengers that God would send to the earth in the last days. Some of these messengers will be angels from heaven. Others will be mortal servants of God.

God has always worked through living prophets, even though the people usually rejected them while they were yet living. Jesus himself was rejected by most of the Jews when he ministered among them. But notwithstanding the continual rejection of God and of his prophets by the people, He continues to reach out to teach and to help his children—and always by his chosen servants, the prophets.

After calling His twelve apostles, Jesus commanded them to go and preach His word. And he told them, "He that receiveth you receiveth me (Matthew 10:40). And conversely, he told them: "And whosoever shall not receive you, nor hear your words, . . . It shall be more tolerable for the land of Sodom and Gomorrah in the day of judgment, than for that city" (Matthew 10:14-15). God destroyed the cities of Sodom and Gomorrah by sending down brimstone and fire out of heaven (Genesis 19:24).

It is beyond dispute for Christians to acknowledge that the word of God came to the world through the mouths of Peter and Paul and other servants of the Lord. The Lord has never altered this pattern. The prophet Amos wrote: "Surely the Lord GOD will do nothing, but he revealeth his secret unto his servants the prophets" (Amos 3:7). The biblical prophecies that we have discussed confirm that God will deal with his children through prophets in the latter days, just as he has always dealt with his children in all ages of the world. Today we can also look for God to give the world his messages through his chosen prophets. When God's messengers do appear and deliver messages, it will be up to us to discern whether they are true or false prophets—this has always been the lot of man. And those who declare that there will be no messengers from God in these last days are themselves false prophets—they teach a doctrine that is contrary to the Bible and a doctrine that hinders many people from considering, evaluating, accepting and obeying the messages that will come from God's prophets.

Do not these prophecies we have reviewed unitedly affirm that God will reveal more of his word to the world in the last days? Malachi said that the Lord would send a "messenger" to the earth before his Second Coming (Malachi 3:1). Do you believe this prophecy? If the Lord will send a "messenger," then there will necessarily be a "message" from God that he will deliver. Do you look for the coming of this "messenger"? Would you tell this "messenger" that the world doesn't need his message because we already have the Bible? Will you choose to ignore, reject or explain away Malachi's prophecy because you believe the Bible teaches that there will be no divine messengers after John the Revelator penned his final words?

Jesus said that "Elias truly shall first come and restore all things" before the Second Coming (Matthew 17:11). Do you believe this? What does it mean to "restore all things"?

Joel prophesied that in the last days the Spirit of God would be poured out upon all flesh and that "your sons and your daughters shall prophesy, your old men shall dream dreams, your young men shall see visions" (Joel 2:28). All of these dreams, visions and prophecies will be given by God long after God gave John his revelations. Will these dreams, visions and prophecies be any less of the word of God just because they are to occur *after* the New Testament was written? Obviously not! Joel didn't discount their value, and neither did the apostle Peter. In fact, according to Peter, the spiritual outpouring prophesied by Joel will be just like the heavenly manifestations that occurred on the Day of Pentecost (Acts 2:16-18). Do you believe this prophecy of Joel?

Do you believe John's prophecy of the angel he saw coming with a message to declare to all the inhabitants of the earth? (Revelation 14:6-7.) The apostle Paul warned that even if an angel should come and declare a false gospel, that we should not believe such an angel (Galatians 1:8). But does this warning require us to reject John's prophecy in Revelation that an angel from God will come and declare the gospel? Of course not. And why? Because the angel that John wrote about would declare the true gospel, not a false one; the angel's message would be in harmony with the Bible and with the Spirit of God. Of course John's prophecy will be fulfilled. Of course we should look for the coming of this angel. When John prophesied that anyone who would "add unto" or "take away from" his words would be punished (Revelation 22:18-19), he was not renouncing his prophecy that the lord would send an angel to proclaim the gospel to the world. Rather, John affirmed that there will be heavenly messages for the world in the last days.

Jesus warned that there would appear false Christs and false prophets in the last days who would deceive many (Matthew 24:5 & 11). But never did he say that there would be no more prophets any more than did he declare that he would not come again. But Jesus did declare that he would return (Matthew 24:30-31), and he likewise declared that he would send an "Elias" to prepare the way before his return. He told the apostles that "Elias indeed shall first come and restore all things" (Matthew 17:11). Jesus said this when his apostles inquired of him whether the prophecies in the third and fourth chapters of Malachi had been fulfilled by the appearance of Moses and Elijah on the Mount of Transfiguration. Jesus affirmed that "Elijah" the prophet and the "messenger" spoken of by Malachi would yet come—later, before the Second Coming. Jesus explained that in one sense, John the Baptist had already come as an "Elias" in fulfillment of Malachi's prophecy. But he reaffirmed that an "Elias" would also come before the Second Coming to "restore all things." This future "Elias" would have God's authority and would speak God's word just as much as John the Baptist did before Jesus' first coming.

What does it mean to "restore all things"? Does not "restore" mean to bring back or to put back in the original condition that which has been either taken away or tarnished? Shouldn't we look for this "Elias" to bring back something that was lost or to put something back in its original condition? And what will "Elias" restore? Jesus said he would restore "all things." That is a lot; that means that Elias' work of restoration will be broad and all-encompassing. We're talking about a *major* work of restoration.

Peter echoed Jesus' prophecy when he said that there would be a "restitution of all things" before Jesus comes again (Acts 3:20-21). And Paul described this day of restitution as "the dispensation of the fulness of times" (Ephesians 1:10). Paul's use of the word "dispensation" indicates his understanding that there would be a special dispensing of God's authority by revelation to man in the last days. Do you believe that God will reveal a special dispensation to man in the last days?

Were you aware of these prophecies? And now that you are, do you believe them? Or will you now try to interpret them away? There is no way around these prophecies. As long as the King James Version of the Bible is the word of God, then we must look for the coming of a "messenger," for the coming of an "angel," and for the coming of an "Elias" who will "restore all things." Will you look for their coming? Or will you deny their coming because you prefer to believe that there will be no more prophets and revelations from God after the writing of the Book of Revelation?

You believe Elijah the prophet will return again, don't you? (Malachi 4:5-6.) If you were to witness his return, wouldn't you tell it to the other devout Christians, if not to the whole world? Certainly someone will tell about Elijah's return when that prophecy is fulfilled. And some hearers will believe the report, and some won't. But Elijah will return some time, won't he? And when he does, the testimony of those to whom he comes will be true. And it will fall upon those who do not personally witness his return to believe the witnesses' testimony.

Daniel prophesied that one called "the Ancient of days" would come in the last days, at the time of a war against the saints, which the saints would be losing (Daniel 7:21-22). Who will this person be? Will he be a messenger from heaven? Why does Daniel call him "the Ancient of days"? With the coming of this person, the tide of the battle will turn in favor of the saints, who will then prevail over their enemies. You do believe "the Ancient of days" will come, don't you?

Isaiah prophesied that in a time of hypocrisy God would bring forth a "book" through the work of an "unlearned" man (Isaiah 29:10-12 & 18). At least part of this book will be "sealed" (verse 11). And Isaiah said that its words would "speak out of the ground" and "whisper out of the dust" (verse 4). The book will contain the words of a people who would "be brought down" to the grave and whose record would be buried with them, to be brought forth by God at a later time. Isaiah said that the book would come from a people who came from "Ariel, the city where David dwelt" (i.e., Jerusalem) (verse 1). What do you think about this prophecy? Were you aware of it?

In connection with the coming forth of this book, Isaiah said that it would cause "the wisdom" of the "wise men" to "perish" and that it would cause the "understanding" of the "prudent men" to be "hid" (verse 14). What does this mean? Doesn't it at least mean that its message will be at odds with the world's wisdom? When Isaiah said that the words of this book would cause the deaf to hear and the blind to see (verse18), isn't he making an analogy of how the spiritual message of this "book" will bring people of the world out of spiritual deafness unto sound, and out of spiritual darkness unto light? Isn't it the word of God that heals spiritual deafness and spiritual blindness?

What book is this? Is this the same "sealed" book spoken of

by Daniel, whose words will be revealed at "the time of the end" (Daniel 12:4 & 9)? We know that the book spoken of by Isaiah will be spiritually powerful, just like the Bible. And yet, this book is not the Bible; Isaiah's description of this book does not fit the Bible? The Bible is not sealed. The Bible did not come forth in a day of spiritual darkness, as this book is to do (verses 10-11). We have had the Bible with us for 3500 years—beginning with the writings of Moses (about 1500 B.C.) and including the writings of prophets and apostles which were added to it during a period of 1600 years. But the Bible was already with us when Isaiah made his prophecy. You would have to strain and stretch the words of Isaiah in order to make the Bible fit his prophecy. It just doesn't fit! Clearly there is to be another book that God will bring forth as He proceeds to do "a marvellous work and a wonder" among the people (verse 14). Do you see that the Bible prophesies of and endorses the divinity of another book of scripture? Despite these biblical prophecies, now that you know the Bible prophesies that someday there will be another book of scripture, do you still deny these prophecies?

To what was Ezekiel referring when he prophesied of two "sticks" with "writing" on them that would be used to gather scattered Israel? He said the "sticks" would be held together in one hand "before their eyes" (Ezekiel 37:20). If Israel is to be gathered by returning to the true and living God, as Moses prophesied (Deuteronomy 30:1-3 & 10), then doesn't it make sense that the Bible—the writings of the descendants of Judah—would be used to bring the people to worship the true and living God? Of course it does? The Bible is used throughout the world to bring people to God. Paul taught that by accepting the gospel of Jesus Christ we become a part of the house of Israel (Galatians 3 and Romans 9). Preaching the word of God from the Bible will help to gather Israel.

Clearly, the Bible is the "stick of Judah" spoken of by Ezekiel; it helps bring people to the true and living God, and thereby it assists in gathering scattered Israel. But there are to be two "sticks." The other "stick" is the stick of "Joseph" or "Ephraim" (Ezekiel 37:16 & 19). What is the "stick of Joseph" that you can hold in your hand with the Bible to help gather scattered Israel? Won't it also be a book of scripture? Won't it be written by the descendants of Joseph, just as the Bible was written primarily by the descendants of Judah? Won't it also contain the word of God, just like the Bible? Could the "stick of Joseph" be the "book" spoken of by Isaiah?

Surely, the Lord will come again—and soon. And just as surely, his Second Coming will be preceded by messages from God for us, both from angelic messengers and from contemporary prophets of God. Disciples of Christ will look for divine messengers as a vital part of the great and glorious work of God in the latter days.

In light of these prophecies, do you believe that the Bible is the last and final word of scripture for the world? Where did the notion come from that the Bible is the last and final word of scripture for the world? It did not come from the prophets and apostles who wrote the Bible. No reasonable interpretation of the Bible supports it. Those who cling to this unfounded belief are building a delusion into their faith—a delusion that will eventually destroy their faith in the true and living God, if they do not root it out.

Let's now turn to the contention that the Bible is the last and final word of God for the world. Let's see whether or not that's what the Bible really says.

CHAPTER 6

The Bible Is Not the Last Word

Some people reject the idea that today God would give us messages of equal stature with biblical messages. In support of this notion, they point to a scripture in the Book of Revelation that they interpret to say that there will never be any written book of scripture other than the Bible. This passage is the next to last verses in the Bible (in the 22nd chapter of Revelation), which read as follows:

> For I testify unto every man that heareth the words of the prophecy of this book, If any man shall add unto these things, God shall add unto him the plagues that are written in this book:
> And if any man shall take away from the words of the book of this prophecy, God shall take away his part out of the book of life, and out of the holy city, and from the things which are written in this book. (Revelation 22:18-19)

The argument is made by some that John is saying in verse 18 that God will not give man any additional revelation after this book. In support of this interpretation they refer to 2 Timothy 3:15, which states that "the holy scriptures . . . are able to make thee wise unto salvation." Therefore, they urge that this is *all* we need to know to obtain salvation,[16] and that therefore we do not need any more of the word of God—that we should content ourselves with abiding by the principles taught in the Bible and not delude ourselves into thinking that God has other commandments for us to obey when we are still working at obeying the commandments taught in the Bible. Some argue that by regarding some other book to be of equal stature with the Bible we harm ourselves spiritually because in adhering to some other book we are taking ourselves away from the word of God. However, on close examination, none of these arguments is correct.

John's warning in the final verses of the Book of Revelation is evidence of his concern that his words not be altered through either additions, deletions or explanations. No one was authorized to change his words. Perpetrators of such abominations will bring upon themselves the judgment of God at the last day. Moses similarly warned the people not to alter his words in the Fourth chapter of Deuteronomy: "Ye shall not add unto the word which I command

---

[16] Orson Pratt said the following about this argument: "A saying of Paul to Timothy is sometimes referred to by the enemies of new revelation and applied in the most deceptive manner, in order to strengthen the world in the fatal delusion that God will no more speak with man: it reads as follows—'From a child thou hast known the holy scriptures, which are able to make thee wise unto salvation.' (2 Timothy iii:15). The objector to new revelation argues, from this passage, that the scriptures with which Timothy was acquainted in his childhood, were abundantly sufficient to make him wise unto salvation, and consequently *there was no need of any more.* If this conclusion be correct, it would do away with all the scriptures of the New Testament; for Timothy when a child was only acquainted with the scriptures of the Old Testament, the scriptures of the New Testament not being yet written. Thus, again, the enemy of new revelation in his fanatical zeal to close up the volume of inspiration, has done away the very scriptures which he pretends so firmly to belief." Orson Pratt, *Divine Authenticity* (Liverpool, 1850), p. 5.

The existence of fundamental differences in belief among Christian denominations today as to what one must do to be saved, highlights the need for additional, clarifying revelation from God settling these differences of opinion. Certainly, new revelation from God would help unify Christians around the truth; it would help dispel confusion and expose false doctrines.

you, neither shall ye diminish ought from it, that ye may keep the commandments of the LORD your God which I command you" (Deuteronomy 4:2). The words of John give a similar commandment, plus they warn of a judgment to come upon whosoever makes a counterfeit of his words. The apostle Paul also warned of severe consequences for anyone who would alter the Gospel of Jesus Christ. In the First chapter of Galatians we wrote: "But though we, or an angel from heaven, preach any other gospel unto you than that which we have preached unto you, let him be accursed" (Galatians 1:8).

The warning contained in each of these scriptures were of prophetic importance for the people at that time. John's warning in Revelation 22:18-19 was not merely a possibility—men had already begun to change the words of the prophets; they had already begun to wrest the scriptures to their own condemnation.

That false teachings were manifesting themselves anciently was one of the very reasons some of the epistles were written. For example, the early Jewish-Christians had to be taught that the law of circumcision was done away in Christ—that the law of Moses was "a shadow of good things to come" and that it had now been fulfilled (Hebrews 10:1). Many of the epistles addressed the need to recognize that it was faith in the Lord Jesus Christ, rather than the works of the law of Moses that brought salvation to an individual. (See, e.g., Romans 10, Ephesians 2, and Hebrews 9-11.) The opposite problem also manifest itself among the early saints—that is the belief of some that salvation came by merely professing with words that one believed in the Lord. This false belief was also addressed and corrected in the epistles. (See, e.g., James 2, 2 Peter 2, and the entire First Epistle of John. See also chapter 16, below.)

In summary, the fear that John had that the prophetic words of his book would be altered, was a concern shared by many of the Lord's prophets in many dispensations. And John gives a stern warning to any would-be-alterers, hopefully to discourage the altering of his text in any way.

But where does the apostle John, or any other prophet, say that there will be no other scripture given after the Bible? By what authority can one broaden the meaning of John's words in verses 18 and 19 to mean that the Bible is the one, the only, and the last word of God ever to be given to man in written form? The answer is that there is no scripture anywhere that says that no other scripture will be given after the Bible. On the contrary, the Bible refers to other books of scripture which are not in our Bible, and the Bible teaches that God will continue to speak to man through prophets, just as he has always done. And it must be expected that these prophets would also write the words of God; and the reading of those words is something that every disciple of Christ would want to do as he attempts to "live by every word that proceedeth from the mouth of God" (Matthew 4:4).

Isn't it ironic that Christian denominations with contradictory doctrines seek to be unified, but they reject the only belief that can bring them to a unity of the faith—the belief that God can resolve the doctrinal disputes that divide Christianity today through direct revelation to man.

What serious, courageous seeker for the truth will fall for the totally unsupported notion that the Bible is the one and only book containing the word of God? The Bible doesn't say this. And again, what scripture is most cited to support such a blinding notion?—Revelation 22:18-19, where John warned against adding to or taking away from the words of his book.

Scholars date the writing of the Book of Revelation to be no later than 96 A.D.[17] Of course, the New Testament had not been compiled by that time. Surely John did not mean that no other writings should be added to his book in the sense of compiling books together. And, of course, the Bible is just that—a compilation or collection of 66 books—not just one book. "Bible" is the Greek word for "book<u>s</u>."

Edgar J. Goodspeed, the noted biblical scholar and translator, wrote that the compiling of the 27 books in the New Testament was not complete until well into the Fourth Century. The compiling began with the gospels, which the early saints used. Soon after 90 A.D., nine

---

[17] Edgar J. Goodspeed, "New Testament," *American People's Encyclopedia*, 1956 ed., 14:582-9; W. E. Garrison, "Bible," *American People's Encyclopedia*, 1956 ed.; and Frederick G. Grant, "Revelation," *World Book Encyclopedia*, 1969 ed.

of Paul's epistles, plus the Book of Acts and the Book of Revelation and other letters were added, bringing the collection to 22 books. Goodspeed said that it was perhaps as late as 367 A.D. when the Greek and Latin churches settled on the collection of 27 books which now constitutes our New Testament (Goodspeed, 14:583). There can be no dispute that books were "added" to the New Testament collection after John wrote the Book of Revelation. Obviously, John did not mean for verses 18 and 19 to prohibit such a compilation nor to condemn it.

There have also been a number of books which have been taken from the Bible that the early Christian church used. For the 300 years before the present collection of 27 New Testament books was decided upon, a number of other books were added to and taken away from the collection of books that the early saints considered to be scripture. Around 200 A.D. Clement of Alexandria accepted 30 books to be part of his New Testament.[18] Some of the books that were in, but which were taken out by the end of the Fourth Century included the Apocalypse of Peter, the Epistle of Barnabas, the Epistle of Clement, and the Preaching of Peter (*Id.*). And still other books have been deleted from the Bible in the last two hundred years. The fourteen books called the Apocrypha[19] have been deleted from Protestant

---

[18] Clyde L. Manschreck, *A History of Christianity in the World*, 2d ed. (Englewood Cliffs, NJ: Prentice Hall, 1985) p. 33, cited by Daniel C. Peterson and Stephen D. Ricks, "Comparing LDS Beliefs with First-Century Christianity," *Ensign*, March, 1988, p. 9.)

[19] The Apocrypha consists of fourteen books of ancient Hebrew writing which were included in the Bible used by the early Christians. These books are: (1) and (2) The First and Second Books of Esdras; (3) The Book of Tobit; (4) The Book of Judith; (5) Additions to the Book of Esther; (6) The Wisdom of Solomon; (7) Ecclesiasticus or the Wisdom of Sirach; (8) The Book of Baruch; (9) The Story of Susanna; (10) The Song of the three Children (11) The Prayer of Manasseh; and (13) and (14) The First and Second Books of Maccabees.

These books were a part of a Greek version of the Bible called the Septuagint, which was used by the early Christians for over 300 year. Beginning in about the year 400 A.D., a Latin version of the Bible, called the Vulgate, became the authorized text for the church. In editing this version of the Bible, St. Jerome found that these books were not a part of the Hebrew Bible, so he named these books "Apocrypha," which means "hidden" or "secret" books. These fourteen books were scattered through both the Septuagint and the Vulgate Bibles.

Bibles since 1827, even though they constituted a part of the Bible for at least fourteen hundred years prior to that. (The books of Apocrypha have continued to be a part of the Catholic Bible.)

Was the removal of the Apocrypha from the Bible an act condemned by God? The overwhelming consensus among Protestants has been and continues to be that the Apocrypha is not scripture—that it is not the divine word of God, of the same spiritual caliber as the other books of the Bible. It is unheard of today for Christians to condemn the deletion of these books. Surely John's warning not to take away from the words of his book was not meant to prohibit the deletion of the Apocrypha from the Bible. Clearly, John's warning applied only to his book of Revelation.

It should also be noted that several of the books in our current New Testament were written after John's book of Revelation. Surely John's warning not to add to his words was not meant to keep these books out of the Bible. Edgar J. Goodspeed dates the writing of the Gospel of John and of John's three epistles to be after he wrote the book of Revelation. (Goodspeed, "New Testament," 14:585-9.) Clearly John did not intend for verses 18 and 19 to prohibit him from writing additional scripture. Goodspeed also dates the writing of I and II Timothy and Titus to be after the writing of Revelation (*Id.* 14:587-8). Both Goodspeed and W. E. Garrison date the writing of the epistle of Jude to be after the writing of the Book of Revelation (*Id.* 14:589; and Garrison, "Bible"). No Bible believer would suggest that verses 18 and

---

However, in 1534, Martin Luther separated these books into a separate section after the Old Testament in his German translation of the Bible. Similarly, the next year (1535) in the first printed edition of the English Bible, Coverdale put these books in a separate section after the Old Testament. These books were also a part of the first edition of the King James Version in 1611. However, the Puritans and other Christian denominations disapproved of these books. Finally, in 1827, both the British and American Bible Societies (comprised of Protestants) took stands against the publication of the Apocrypha, and since then these books have been left out of Protestant Bibles. They continued to be included in Catholic Bibles. Edgar J. Goodspeed (translator), "Preface," *The Apocrypha, an American Translation* (New York: Vintage Books, 1959) pp. vii-xi.

19 were intended to condemn all of these epistles that were written after Revelation.

Regardless of the order of writing of the books of the New Testament, the plain meaning of verses 18-19 is that John was warning against adding to or taking away from the revelations he had written in his book—John was not saying that God would not later give additional revelations to man that would also be the word of God and that could be added to the Bible.

And what about those other writings of the prophets and apostles which are mentioned in the Bible, but which are not a part of our Bible—are they any less the word of God because they are not in our Bible? Does the fact that a writing was found and added to the compilation of books by 367 A.D. give it validity as the word of God, while a writing that is not found by 367 A.D. must automatically be rejected as God's world? The Bible's writers themselves seemed to regard other books as containing the word of God. To quote from Orson Pratt:

> Would not the prophecy of Enoch, with which the Apostle Jude was familiar, and from which he makes a quotation relative to the second coming of Christ [Jude 14],—be as sacred as any other prophecy of the Bible? Would not the book of Iddo the seer [2 Chronicles 12:15]—the book of Nathan the prophet [1 Chronicles 29:29]—together with some twelve or fifteen other books and epistles, written by inspired prophets, seers, and apostles, and referred to in scripture, be as worthy of a place in the Bible as any that human wisdom have already compiled. (Orson Pratt, *Divine Authenticity* [Liverpool, England, 1850] p.4.)

There are twenty scriptural writings referred to in the Bible which are not included there:

Name of Book	Biblical Reference
Book of the Covenant	Exodus 4:4 & 24:7
Book of the Wars of the Lord	Numbers 21:14
Book of Jasher	Joshua 10:13 and 2 Samuel 1:18
Book of the Acts of Solomon	1 Kings 11:41
Book of Gad the Seer	1 Chronicles 29:29
Book of Nathan the Prophet	1 Chronicles 29:29
Book of Ahijah	2 Chronicles 9:29
Book of Shemaiah	2 Chronicles 12:15
Visions of Iddo the Seer	2 Chronicles 9:29
Book of Iddo the Seer	2 Chronicles 12:15
Story of the Prophet Iddo	2 Chronicles 13:22
Book of Jehu	2 Chronicles 20:34
Acts of Uzziah (by Isaiah)	2 Chronicles 26:22
Sayings of the Seers	2 Chronicles 33:19
Missing Prophecy of Jeremy	Matthew 27:9-10
Missing Epistle of Paul	1 Corinthians 5:9
Missing Epistle of Paul	Ephesians 3:3
Missing Epistle of Paul	Colossians 4:16
Missing Epistle of Jude	Jude 3
Prophecy of Enoch	Jude 14

Of these 20 writings, we now have discovered a Book of Jasher, whom the prophets Joshua and Samuel identified as a book of scripture.[20] And several Enoch manuscripts[21] have been discovered in the last 150 years which originated from an ancient writing of the Patriarch Enoch (whom the Lord took into heaven). Not only did Jude authenticate the divinity of a book of Enoch, but from these recently

---

[20] *Book of Jasher*, translation from Hebrew (Salt Lake City: J. H. Parry & Co., 1887).

[21] Hugh Nibley, *Enoch the Prophet* (Salt Lake City: Deseret Book Co., 1986). (Supporting sources are cited in his text.) While the scholars acknowledge the Enoch books to pre-date the writing of the New Testament books, few scholars have yet to embrace the belief that the prophet Enoch actually wrote it.

discovered texts we have now learned that Enoch was quoted at least 128 times in the New Testament.[22] Biblical scholars acknowledge that the Book of Enoch was regarded by the early Christians as treasured scripture.[23] So, why is it not in our Bible today? Why? Because later Christians decided it should be deleted.[24]

In addition to the books of Jasher and Enoch, hundreds of ancient, scriptural texts have been discovered in the middle-east in the mid 1940s. Ancient writings of a Christian community in Egypt were discovered at Nag Hammadi in 1945; and hundreds of other scriptural texts have been found among the Dead Sea Scrolls, which were found in 1947. Many of these writings have now been translated and published. Among these are writings purportedly by or about the ancient prophets Enoch, Melchizedek and Seth, and by or about apostles Peter, James, John and Thomas. Admittedly, some of the writings may be pseudepigrapha (i.e., intentionally given the name of a famous prophet, other than the author of the text). Nevertheless, by the nature and location of these discoveries, it appears that some of these texts could be divine scripture.[25]

---

[22] *Id.*, 8 and 95. The influence of the Book of Enoch on many of the New Testament books has been well established in recent years. See, e.g., Dr. Charles E. Potter, *Did Jesus Write This Book?* (Greenwich, CT: Fawcett World Library, 1965; and E. Isaac, "I (Ethiopic Apocalypse of) Enoch," in *The Old Testament Pseudepigrapha*, ed. J. H. Charlesworth, 2 vols. (Garden City, NY: Doubleday, 1983) 1:10, quoted in Daniel C. Peterson and Stephen D. Ricks, "Comparing LDS Beliefs with First-Century Christianity," *Ensign*, March, 1988, p. 9.)

[23] Nibley, 95-99.

[24] Hillery, Jerome and Augustine, all of whom admitted that earlier Christians held different beliefs than theirs, deleted Enoch from their Bibles. *Id.*, 95-99, and sources cited therein. See also, Potter, 21-22.

[25] Of the recent translations of many of these writings, I have found that titles to the following texts to be most intriguing:
The Apocryphon of John;
Melchizedek;
The letter of Peter to Philip;
The Apocalypse of Peter;
The Second Treatise of the Great Seth;
The Apocalypse of Adam;
The First Apocalypse of James;

No Bible scholar will dispute that John foretold that a future angelic messenger would come to the earth. (See Revelation 14:6-7 and the discussion above.) Would not his words also be the word of God? Of course they would; they would also be scripture. Was John declaring that no other words of God would ever be written down after his book? No, that doesn't make sense either. What does make sense is that John's warning in Revelation 22:18-19 is that no one should alter his words in any way, either by addition or deletion. John's words were not meant to refer to a compilation of 27 epistles and books, some of which did not then exist and to which he did not refer. Neither did John say that there would be no more revelation from God after his book was written. Rather John foresaw and foretold of additional revelations that would occur in the latter days.

The Second Apocalypse of James;
The Apocalypse of Paul;
The Gospel of Thomas;
The Gospel of Philip; and
The Apocryphon of James.
The translation of these texts and others are found in the following two books:
James M. Robinson, ed., *The Nag Hammadi Library* (New York: Harper & Row, Publishers, Inc., 1981) and Theodor H. Gaster, ed., *The Dead Sea Scriptures* (Garden City, NY: Anchor Press/Doubleday, 1976) 3rd ed.

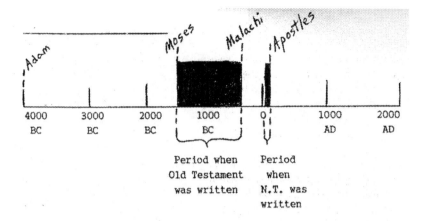

The authors of the Old Testament wrote between approximately 1500 B.C. (Moses) and 400 B.C. (Malachi), covering 1100 years.

The authors of the New Testament wrote between 33 A.D. and around 100 A.D., covering approximately 100 years.

In the 6,000 years since the fall of Adam, the writers of the Bible live in only 1200 of those years--only 20% of the time.

The authors of the Old Testament wrote between approximately 1500 B.C. (Moses) and 400 B.C. (Malachi), covering 1100 years.

The authors of the New Testament wrote between 33 A.D. and around 100 A.D., covering approximately 70 years.

In the 6,000 years since the fall of Adam, the writers of the Bible lived in only 1200 of those years—only 20% of the time.

DID GOD PROHIBIT HIS PROPHETS FROM WRITING SCRIPTURE, EXCEPT DURING A 1200-YEAR PERIOD?

THE FULFILLMENT

PART I

A MESSAGE FROM CHRIST IN 1820

I t is not the convincing words of man nor the rationalization of clever thinkers that convinces one of the truthfulness of the word of God, but rather it is the Spirit of God that carries the conviction of truth directly into the souls of men—a direct witness from God. And thus, the faith of every individual can and must rest squarely and solely upon that person's own witness from God, and must not be founded upon some mortal person or upon man's reasoning alone.

The Apostle Paul clearly taught this principle to the Corinthians, when he wrote in the second chapter of First Corinthians:

> And I, brethren, when I came to you, came not with excellency of speech or of wisdom, declaring unto you the testimony of God. . . .
>
> And my speech and my preaching was not with enticing words of man's wisdom, but in demonstration of the Spirit and of power;
>
> That your faith should not stand in the wisdom of men, but in the power of God. (1 Corinthians 2:1, 4-5)

So it is today. The Spirit of God manifests to the souls of men the truthfulness of the word of God when those words are communicated to them. In this light, I invite you to consider in the next chapters the fulfillment of biblical prophecies about the coming of divine messengers and about the establishment of the Kingdom of God in preparation for Christ's triumphal reign on earth.

CHAPTER 7

Joseph Smith's First Vision

In 1820, the Lord called a 14-year-old young man named Joseph Smith to be a prophet. After a few introductory comments, I will give an account of his prophetic calling.

From the time of his prophetic calling until his death, 24 years later, Joseph Smith was a bold and valiant witness that Jesus Christ is our Lord and Savior; that he suffered in Gethsemane and on the cross for the sins of the world; that on the third day after his death he resurrected from the dead; that through Christ's grace all mankind will likewise be resurrected; and that through Christ's grace those who have faith in him can return to dwell with God in the world to come.

Joseph Smith was a dynamic individual who had a keen mind and a magnetic personality. He loved people, and he was greatly loved by thousands who believed his testimony. The boldness of his message and the successes of his efforts also spawned jealousy and animosity among some people. Satan is furious at the work done by Joseph Smith, and the devil works relentlessly to disparage, defeat and destroy The Church of Jesus Christ of Latter-day Saints.

Joseph Smith was persecuted almost constantly from the time he first proclaimed his prophetic calling at the age of 14 until he was murdered at the age of 38 (1844) by an angry mob in Illinois (while he was a prisoner of the State, waiting to be tried on a trumped up treason charge). In all, Joseph Smith was arrested on false charges over 30 times in his life. He was tarred and feathered; he was beaten; he and his believers were persecuted and driven from Ohio, Missouri and Illinois. In fact, on October 27, 1836, Missouri Governor Lilburn W. Boggs, issued an executive order stating that: "The 'Mormons' must be treated as enemies, and must be exterminated or driven from the State...." (HC 3:426). All of this occurred in the United States of America, in bold defiance of the freedoms guaranteed by our Constitution. Perhaps the saddest irony pertaining to the persecution of Joseph Smith is that so much of it was incited and led by Christian ministers and by government officials.

As I have investigated the life and teachings of Joseph Smith, and as I have considered the criticisms leveled at him by his adversaries, in most instances I have found them biased, full of mistakes and falsehoods, and often patently deceptive. I have found that his loudest critics are often motivated by a grudge and a raging personal obsession to destroy Joseph Smith and the cause he espoused. To one who is familiar with the work and writings of Joseph Smith, the maliciousness of his critics is very clear. It often occurs in the combined form of misinterpretations, misrepresentations, quoting out-of-context, and out-and-out lying. And even though in most instances the spreader of such falsehoods attempts to present himself to be objective, if not also loving and understanding, the lies and misrepresentations that come from their mouths and pens reveal their true character and the true source and motivation of their criticisms.

It is perhaps a little unorthodox to include a defense of Joseph Smith before even presenting his testimony. But in view of the flood of malicious and erroneous information that has been published and broadcast nationally against Joseph Smith, I feel it is best to put the propaganda on the table right up front. If the reader has prejudged Joseph Smith and Mormonism before hearing Joseph Smith's side of the matter, then have the fairness and the courage to identify what you know and what you don't know about Mormonism; for the time being set aside the conclusions you may have made about Mormonism that are based on biased or unreliable information. If the reader is not now aware of these criticisms, he or she will undoubtedly be made aware of them in the future—especially if the word gets out that he or she is investigating the message of The Church of Jesus Christ of Latter-day Saints. Many times, after others learn that an individual is studying Mormonism, there will follow a flood of material heaped upon that person, the design of which is to challenge and attempt to disprove the messages brought by Joseph Smith. I want the reader to know that I am aware of many of these materials, and that there are answers to every such accusation and criticism that I have ever heard.

Quite often these anti-Mormon materials attempt to persuade people not to fully investigate Joseph Smith and Mormonism, using arguments such as: Joseph Smith taught doctrines that are false and of the devil, and therefore one should not even subject himself to the influence of studying such material. Thus, such lying propagandists hope that the investigator will accept their conclusions about Mormonism without making his own investigation and drawing his own conclusions.

Courageous truth seekers will not be diverted by scare tactics that claim it is spiritually dangerous to make an independent investigation of Mormonism. Independent investigation will manifest that the principles taught by Joseph Smith are good, pure and virtuous, and are from God.

Any evaluation of Joseph Smith and his work should start with his own story, from his own mouth, and not with the unreliable hearsay versions of his proclaimed enemies.

The testimony of Joseph Smith is of unsurpassed importance to all the world. The work of God in the last days is taking an axe to the root of the devil's kingdom; and Satan doesn't like it. He is fighting with all of his might and with all of his power against God and God's servants. Whenever a person investigates the doctrines and teachings of Joseph Smith and The Church of Jesus Christ of Latter-day Saints, Satan will exert influences to try to block and stop it. Just as superficial signs and miracles were wrought by Satan in the days of Moses to confuse the people, so he also employs these deceptive tactics today for the same purposes. In fact, the devil will rage and show his power against this work in every way he can to attempt to dissuade the sincere seeker from accepting the truth of divine messages. A wicked and adulterous generation of sign-seekers will be captivated by signs and wonders wrought by Satan. But the elect will not be deceived.

So, do not be surprised if you also witness such things. And do not despair either, for the power of God is greater than the power of the adversary, and God does not work in darkness and deception. But God works in love and plainness and truth; and he works in power unto those who exercise faith in Him; and when he works in power he works for the benefit of people—to uplift and edify and enlighten. Normally, God does not employ miracles to persuade people to believe in Him, but rather he brings miracles to bless and benefit those who already believe in Him and who desire to be of service to their fellow man.

Now, without further introduction, here is the story of Joseph Smith's being called of God to be the Lord's chief prophet in presiding over the restoration of all things in preparation for the Savior's Second Coming.

A. God Called Joseph Smith to Be His Prophet.

When the American nation emerged as a free and independent state in 1776, there existed among the people a powerful feeling of both political liberty and a divine destiny. In the history of the world there was never before a nation that had burst on the world stage as a champion of individual political liberty and religious freedom. There was a sense of divine empowerment that swept the nation—God was with the Americans, and they knew it. This was the spark that ignited the Revolution in 1775 and 1776. This was the burning fire that sustained and strengthened Washington and his troops during the difficult and trying years of the war, until the British troops surrendered at Yorktown, Virginia in 1781. This was the inspiration that caused the thirteen diverse colonies to unite in support of the Constitution in 1787, and to defeat the British troops at New Orleans in 1815. This pervasive, inspired feeling that was shared by the new American citizens had a strong spiritual component. The freedom that they demanded was their God-given right; and they knew that God was on their side. And they also knew that it was their duty to worship God and do His will.

This American spirit was unique in history, and it resulted in a nation of millions of people who were turning to God, and seeking to do his will. Historians identify the time period of 1790-1830 as the Second Great Awakening. It was accompanied by a national movement to place a Bible in every home in America, and the movement was considerably successful in accomplishing this. By 1830, there had been one million Bibles printed and distributed among the ten million Americans (and by 1848, the number of Bibles distributed in America had increased to 5.8 million). The American spirit was a combination of political determination to enjoy liberty and the moral imperative to serve God.

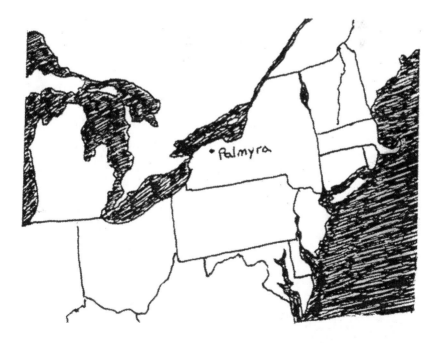

Joseph Smith grew up in this national environment. Economic hardship caused Joseph's family to move to Palmyra, New York in 1815. Palmyra was one of several towns on the Erie Canal, which was in the process of being built, which connected Albany, New York with Lake Ontario—which became the economic engine of prosperity, growth and development of not only upstate New York, but also of the fast-growing areas of Ohio, Indiana, Illinois and Michigan. Palmyra, like most of the towns along the canal, was a fertile place for farming, but the Erie Canal led to the success of multiple industries and business along that corridor. The move of the Smith family to Palmyra made a lot sense.

The town of Palmyra was a typical canal town in almost every respect, including the religious fervor that it maintained. The main intersection in Palmyra was anchored by four churches that represented the four primary Christian denominations in most of America at that time: Methodists, Presbyterians, Episcopalians and Baptists. (Catholicism had a much lesser presence in most of America in 1820.) These four denominations shared a common foundation, in that each had broken away from the Roman Catholic Church—protested, if you will—taking the common position that the Catholic Church had fallen away from the pure gospel of Jesus Christ. The need to reform the church had led to the formation of these Protestant churches, and there existed many people who were looking for God to do a great work in preparing for the Millennial reign of Christ. As more and more Americans were reading the Bible (one of the few books that was available to read), the nation became more familiar with biblical prophecies of latter-day messages and miracles, and of a restoration of all things spoken of by Jesus himself. Nevertheless, there were many ministers and religionists who denied that God continued to be a God of miracles in 1820; many taught that God had done his work, and that He no longer spoke to living prophets, as He had done in biblical times.

It was in this environment that Joseph Smith grew to be a young teenager. His family had faithfully and regularly read the Bible together. His family was devout in their worship of God, although they were not united in deciding which of the four denominations they should join.

With this backdrop, in the spring of 1820, one morning, Joseph walked from his log cabin home (about two miles south of Palmyra), and made his way into a nearby grove of trees. There he prayed to God to ask which church he should join. Joseph told of this event in these words (from Joseph Smith—History 1:8-19):

> During this time of great excitement my mind was called up to serious reflection and great uneasiness. . . . In process of time my mind became somewhat partial to the Methodist sect,. . . but so great were the confusion and strife among the different denominations, that it was impossible for a person young as I was . . . to come to any certain conclusion who was right and who was wrong. . . .
>
> In the midst of this war of words and tumult of opinions, I often said to myself: What is to be done: Who of all these parties are right; or, are they all wrong together? ...
>
> While I was laboring under the extreme difficulties cause by the contests of these parties of religionists, I was one day reading the Epistle of James, first chapter and fifth verse, which reads: "*If any of you lack wisdom, let him ask of God, that giveth to all men liberally, and upbraideth not, and it shall be given him.*"
>
> Never did any passage of scripture come with more power to the heart of man than this did at this time to mine. It seemed to enter with great force into every feeling of my heart. I reflected on it again and again, knowing that if any person needed wisdom from God, I did . . . .
>
> At length I came to the conclusion that I must either remain in darkness and confusion, or else I must do as James directs, that is, ask of God. . . .
>
> So, in accordance with this, my determination to ask of God, I retired to the woods to make the

attempt. It was on the morning of a beautiful, clear day. . . .

After I had retired to the place where I had previously designed to go, having looked around me, and finding myself alone, I kneeled down and began to offer up the desire of my heart to God. I had scarcely done so, when immediately I was seized upon by some power which entirely overcame me, and had such an astonishing influence over me as to bind my tongue so that I could not speak. Thick darkness gathered around me, and it seemed to me for a time as if I were doomed to sudden destruction.

But, exerting all my powers to call upon God . . ., at the very moment when I was ready to sink into despair . . .—just at this moment of great alarm, I saw a pillar of light exactly over my head, above the brightness of the sun, which descended gradually until it fell upon me.

It no sooner appeared than I found myself delivered from the enemy which held me bound. When the light rested upon me I saw two Personages, whose brightness and glory defy all description, standing above me in the air. One of them spake unto me, calling me by name and said, pointing to the other—*This is My Beloved son. Hear Him!*

. . . No sooner, therefore, did I get possession of myself, so as to be able to speak, than I asked the Personages who stood above me in the light, which of all the sects was right—and which I should join.

I was answered that I must join none of them, for they were all wrong; and the Personage who addressed me said that all their creeds were an abomination in his sight; that those professors were all corrupt; that: "they draw near to me with their lips, but their hearts are far from me, they teach for doctrines the

commandments of men, having a form of godliness,
but they deny the power thereof."

Joseph said that the Lord said He had a work for Joseph to do which would be made known to him at a later time. We will later discuss additional directions that God gave to Joseph. But initially consider the several very significant truths that Joseph learned in 1820. This message taught that God continues to speak to man; that God has the power to and does answer prayers today, as he did in times of old. The message also taught Joseph that God did not endorse any existing Christian organization. Another important message was that God had called Joseph Smith to be his prophet. These truths are of vital importance for the world today. But the most fundamental truth that Joseph learned from this vision was what God revealed about his nature and personality. The significance of these truths will be discussed in the next chapter.

CHAPTER 8

The Nature and Personality of God

In 1820 no church correctly taught the truth about God. It required a revelation from God to correct the erroneous notions about Him that had become embedded in the official creeds of the major Christian denominations of that day.

After the death of Jesus' apostles, false beliefs about the nature of God took hold in Christianity. During the reign of Emperor Constantine, the Catholic Church and the Roman Empire combined their influence to establish a false and incomprehensible doctrine about the nature of God—a doctrine that forever after has been adopted by most of organized Christianity as an acceptable and even cherished "mystery"—the great mystery of the Trinity.

Because of the continuing pervasiveness of this false doctrine, let us first review what it is and how it came to be. Then we will examine what Joseph Smith taught about God and compare it with the teachings of the Bible.

A. The Making of the Mystery of the Trinity.

Constantine, the Roman Emperor who made Christianity the

official Roman religion, played a key role in establishing an erroneous definition of God in Christianity. Historians do not deny the sin and treachery of Emperor Constantine (4th Century), who made Christianity an arm of the state, and who changed it from a persecuted to a persecuting religion. Constantine (who refused baptism until on his death bed, so that he could live a life of sin with impunity, feeling that he could wash away his sins later on) was a hypocrite, a political manipulator and a murderer. Among others, he put to death his wife's father, Maximilian Herculius; his sister's husband, Bassianus; his own son, Crispus; his wife, Fausta; the husband of one of his sisters, Licinius; and the eleven-year-old son of Licinius, a lad named Licinianus (Roberts, "Introduction," HC 1: lviii).

In 313 A.D. Constantine and his once-colleague Licinius, saved the Christians from persecution by issuing the Edict of Milan, which established religious liberty in the empire (*Id.*, at lxi). But only twelve years later, he decreed that all Christians must conform to one particular belief in God, or else be banished from the empire (*Id.*, at lxv).

And what was this particular belief in God? It was the Nicene Creed, a declaration or definition of God, prepared by some of the Christian leaders of the empire in 325 A.D. Constantine directed that a council be convened to resolve a heated dispute in the empire concerning God's nature. Constantine had no ecclesiastical authority to convene such a council—but he did it anyway. Because of his improper usurpation of authority in spiritual matters, many of the priests in the empire refused to attend the council. For political reasons, a resolution of this dispute was important to Constantine; he attended some of the daily debates of the council and made his presence felt as those in attendance deliberated on what they felt the nature of God was and was not. The result of the debate was the adopting of a resolution or "creed" approved by a majority of those present. Such a resolution was a wholly unsatisfactory manner to resolve the fundamental doctrine of what God's nature is (*Id.*, at lxxxiii-lxxxiv). Where were the apostles and prophets to speak up boldly, without compromise, to set the matter straight? Well, there were none present, because there just weren't any apostles or prophets involved with this organization at that time.

And just as the Nicene Council lacked both the knowledge and the authority to decide what God's nature was, so the definition that they decided upon was flawed. Before giving the text of the creed, it is important to understand that the principal dispute that gave rise to the council was the question of in what respect God the Father and Jesus were one: Was Jesus of the "same" essence or substance as God the Father? Or was Jesus another distinct being of "similar" substance? Arius, a priest of Alexandria held for the doctrine that Jesus and God the Father were two distinct beings of "similar" substance. However, Arius also believed that Jesus only began to exist at his birth. The other side prevailed on both of these points. The council voted that God the Father and Jesus were of the "same" substance, and that those who said otherwise (such as Arius) were to be excommunicated. (*Id.*, at lxxxiii-lxxxiv; and Fulton J. Sheen, "Nicene Councils," *The World Book Encyclopedia*, 1969 ed.) Here is the text of the creed:

> We believe in one God, the Father Almighty, creator of all things visible and invisible; and in one Lord Jesus Christ, the Son of God, only begotten of the Father, that is, of the substance of the Father, God of God, Light of Light, very God of very God, begotten, not made, being of the same substance with the Father, by whom all things were made in heaven and in earth, who for us men and for our salvation came down from heaven, was incarnate, was made man, suffered, rose again the third day, ascended into the heavens, and He will come to judge the living and the dead; and in the Holy Ghost. Those who say there was a time when He was not, and He was not before He was begotten, and He was made of nothing (he was created), or who say that He is of another hypostatis, or of another substance (than the Father), or that the Son of God is created, that he is mutable, or subject to

change, the Catholic church anathematizes. (Roberts, "Introduction," p. lxxxiv, quoting from *Hist. Christian Councils* [Hefele], p. 294.)

(Note that there are differing translations of the original creed. Also, in subsequent years the Catholic Church modified the creed.)

The doctrine stated in the Creed is fatally flawed. It established a confusing and erroneous definition of God in three ways: (1) By denying the separateness of Jesus' person from the person of God the Father; (2) By making Jesus equal with God the Father, rather than subordinate to him;[26] and (3) By denying that God the Father and Jesus have tangible bodies of flesh and bone. The word "substance," as used in the Creed, means "lacking tangible substance," which is opposite of the meaning we usually give to the word today. Edgar T. Lyon explains that as used in the Creed, "substance" means "*immaterial essence,* the underlying *immaterial nature of reality,* the *force behind nature, immaterial spirit,* and similar illusive interpretations." Edgar T. Lyon, *Apostasy to Restoration* (Salt Lake City: Deseret Book Co., 1960), 151.

This incomprehensible doctrine about God took hold and flourished. In defense of this definition, people have said that it is a divine "mystery" that we are not meant to understand. One man, in describing the mystery of the Trinity to me, said that we cannot understand how the Trinity are one and yet at the same time how they are three. And, he said, "That's the beauty of it!" But it isn't beautiful. It is erroneous and sad. It is a tragedy that people will blindly believe that it is beautiful not to understand what God is like and to fight against the notion that God would reveal additional information about himself to the world.

In years subsequent to the Council of Nicaea, other creeds and explanations have been promulgated to clarify and expand upon the Nicene Creed, but never rooting out the fatal flaws of the

---

[26] "Councils," *Encyclopedia Britannica* 6:634. In 381 A.D. at the First Council of Constantinople, the Catholic leaders declared that the Holy Ghost was also equal with the Father and the Son. This declaration is regarded as ending "a long debate on the trinitarian doctrine." *Id.*

immateriality of God and the indivisibility of Jesus and God the Father. For example, in more recent years, Bruno, in *Catholic Belief*, at page 1, says that church's belief in God is: "There is but one God, the creator of heaven and earth, the supreme incorporeal, uncreated being who exists of Himself and is infinite in all his attributes" (quoted in Roberts, "Introduction," p. lxxxv). This definition says that God is "incorporeal"—that is, he has no substance. The Church of England gives a similar description of God as a being without substance: "[T]here is but one true God everlasting, without body, parts, or passions, of infinite power, wisdom and goodness" (*Decline and Fall*, xxi, quoted in Roberts, "Introduction," HC 1:lxxxv-lxxxvi).

The seriousness of these erroneous teachings about God cannot be passed over lightly. To know and to worship the true and living God was the first commandment given to Moses (Exodus 20:3); it was labeled by Jesus as the first and great commandment (Matthew 22:36-38); and Jesus further said that it was the purpose of this life for us to know God the Father and Jesus Christ (John 17:3). The belief in a god whose nature is different from that of the true and living god is belief in a false god and is a violation of the commandment that we should have no other gods before us.

B. The Testimony of Joseph Smith: God the Father and Jesus Christ Are Separate and Distinct Persons with Immortal Bodies.

The vision of God the Father and of his Son, Jesus Christ, to Joseph Smith was an extraordinary occurrence. The King James Version of the Bible only records one other incident where God the Father and Jesus Christ were seen together at the same time; that was at the time of the martyrdom of Stephen (Acts 7), who, "being full of the Holy Ghost, looked up stedfastly into heaven, and saw the glory of God, and Jesus standing on the right hand of God, And said, Behold, I see the heavens opened, and the Son of man standing on the right hand of God" (Acts 7:55-56).

At the baptism of Jesus, as well as on the mount of transfiguration, the voice of God the Father was heard bearing record that "this is my beloved Son, in whom I am well pleased" (Matthew 3:17; and 17:5). The scriptures do not state that God the Father was seen on these two occasions.

Some people say that the testimony of Joseph Smith cannot be true because it is inconsistent with two verses in the King James Version that declare, "No man hath seen God at any time" (John 1:18 and 1 John 4:12). (See discussion below.) However, these two verses are inconsistent with over 30 other passages in the Bible that declare that God has been seen by his prophets. (See Sections E-H, below.) As we just read, Stephen saw God the Father and Jesus, and the Bible records several visits of the resurrected Savior to his disciples. Nothing that Joseph Smith related about his vision of God the Father and Jesus Christ is inconsistent with the Bible.

Joseph Smith's experience was not common place and ordinary; it was extraordinary and miraculous. And it was necessary! The knowledge of the true character and nature of God had been lost from the organized Christian religions. The preachers and teachers of Christianity did not teach the truth about God. They taught a mixture of truth and error. For the most part, God did not manifest his power through them. Joseph Smith was acquainted with a religious society similar to that which Jesus ministered during his mortal life (Matthew 15:7-9)—a people that the Lord said, "draw near me with their mouth, and with their lips do honour me, but have removed their heart far from me, and their fear toward me is taught by the precept of men" (Isaiah 29:13).

Not only was the Christian world of Joseph Smith's day polluted with many hypocritical ministers, but the great majority of those ministers also denied the power of God to work miracles. The words of Jesus to Joseph Smith, that he should not join with any of the sects of his day echoed the words of Apostle Paul's prophecy of the last days, wherein he advised to "turn away" from those "having a form of godliness, but denying the power thereof" (2 Timothy 3:5).

What did Joseph Smith learn about God from this vision? He learned that God the Father and the Son Jesus Christ were two, separate and distinct beings, each having immortal bodies of flesh and bones, as tangible as man's. He learned that Jesus Christ, who had been resurrected 1800 years before, was resurrected still. And Joseph Smith learned from this and subsequent events that the Holy Ghost, also a member of the Godhead, was merely a personage of spirit, without a tangible body of flesh and bones.

C. The Concept of God Taught by Joseph Smith is Fully Supported by the Bible.

Following Joseph's first vision, his understanding of God was different from that of the ministers of his day. And even though there is full biblical support for Joseph Smith's testimony of God's nature,[27]

---

[27] B. H. Roberts gives the following recitation of scriptures that set forth the separate and distinct nature of God the Father and His Son Jesus Christ, as taught in the New Testament. This is an excellent, comprehensive summary: "He (Jesus) declares the fact that God was His Father, and frequently calls Himself the Son of God. (See John 10; Matt. 27; and Mark 14:61-62.) After His resurrection and departure into heaven, the Apostle taught that He, the Son of God, was with God the Father in the beginning; that he, as well as the Father, was God; that under the direction of the Father He was the Creator of worlds; that without Him was not anything made that was made. (See John 1:1-4, 14, Heb. 1:1-3; Matt. 23:18.) That in him dwelt all the fulness of the Godhead bodily (Col. 1:15-19; 2:9); and that He was the express image of the Father's person (Heb. 1:2-3). Jesus Himself taught that He and the Father were one (John 10:30; 17:11-22); that whosoever had seen Him and seen the Father also (John 19:9); that it was part of His mission to reveal God, the Father, through His own personality; for as was the Son, so too was the Father (John 19:1-9; John 1:18). Hence Jesus was God manifested in flesh—a revelation of God to the world (1 Tim. 3:16). That is, a revelation, not only of the *being* of God, but of the *kind* of being God is. "Jesus also taught (and in doing so showed in what the 'oneness' of Himself and His Father consisted) that the disciples might be one with Him, and also one with each other, *as* He and the Father were one (John 14:10, 11, 19, 20; also, John 17). Not one in person—not all merged into one individual, and all distinctions of personality lost; but one in mind, in knowledge, in love, in will—one by reason of the indwelling in all of the one spirit, even as the mind and will of God the Father was also in Jesus Christ (Ephesians 3:14-19).

"The Holy Ghost, too, was upheld by the Christian religion to be God. (Acts 5:1-14.) . . . Jesus ascribed to Him a distinct personality . . . .

nevertheless, he was strongly criticized by his contemporary Christian ministers for what he taught. That criticism has continued until today. And while I have heard people criticize what Joseph Smith taught about God, I have never heard anyone explain any other belief in God that was as complete and that made more sense than that taught by him. And, though the scriptures support what Joseph Smith taught, it should be remembered that when Joseph Smith began to declare what he knew about God's nature, it was not conclusions that he had reached after interpreting multiple biblical passages (though he later came to learn that there was such support). God taught Joseph Smith what he was like and what his attributes were. Joseph's knowledge of God did not come from hearsay, nor from a poll of religious leaders, nor from a man's personal interpretation of the Bible—God revealed himself to Joseph Smith; and that is what Joseph taught.

Nothing is more important for us to do in this life than to come to know God. The apostle John records that Jesus stated the following words in praying to God, his Father: "And this is life eternal, that they might know thee the only true God, and Jesus Christ whom thou hast sent" (John 17:3). That we should know God was not an isolated teaching of the Savior's, but rather was one that he taught repeatedly. (See chapter 19, below.) He often used it in pointing out to his critics that their chief condemnation was that they did not know Him. (See John 5:36-47; 7:28; 8:19, 54-59; 14:21-23; 15:21; 16:3; see also 1 John 3:1-6; and 4:7-8.)

"The distinct personality of these three individual Gods (united however into one Godhead, or Divine Council), was made apparent at the baptism of Jesus; for as He, God the Son, came up out of the water from His baptism at the hands of John, a manifestation of the presence of the Holy Ghost was given in the sign of the dove which rested upon Jesus, while out of the glory of heaven the voice of God the Father was heard saying, 'This,' referring to Jesus, 'is my beloved Son, in whom I am well pleased.' The distinctness of personality of each member of the Godhead is also shown by the commandment to baptize those who believe the Gospel equally in the name of each person of the Holy Trinity. That is, in the name of the Father, and of the Son, and of the Holy Ghost (Matt. 28:19-20). And again, also in the Apostolic benediction, viz., 'The grace of the Lord Jesus Christ, and the love of God, and the communion of the Holy Ghost, be with you all.' (2 Cor. 13:14.)" (Roberts, "Introduction," HC 1:lxxix-lxxxi)

The Bible teaches that God the Father, Jesus Christ and the Holy Ghost are all three members of the Godhead. Thus, these three are often referred to today as the "Trinity," even though that term does not appear in the Bible. All three are identified at the baptism of Jesus (Matt. 3:16-17; Mark 1:10; and Luke 3:22) and at the stoning of Stephen (Acts 7:55-56). Jesus taught the distinction and relationship between the three as follows:

> And I will pray the Father, and he shall give you another Comforter, that he may abide with you for ever . . . .
>
> But the Comforter, which is the Holy Ghost, whom the Father will send in my name, he shall teach you all things, and bring all things to your remembrance, whatsoever I have said unto you. (John 14;16 & 26)

> But when the Comforter is come, whom I will send unto you from the Father, even the Spirit of truth, which proceedeth from the Father, he shall testify of me. (John 15:26)

In addition to these scriptures that distinguish all three members of the Godhead, there are other scriptures that clearly show the nature of God the Father and of Jesus Christ, and which distinguish the two. Probably the most obvious scriptures that show these two beings to be separate and distinct are those about Jesus praying to his Father, and those in which Jesus refers to his Father as a being separate and distinct from himself. (See, e. g., John 5:17-29, 36-47; 8:16-19, 38, 42, 54-55; 11:41-42; 12:28-30; 14; 15; 16 and 17.)

The Bible teaches that Jesus resurrected with a body of flesh and bones. Luke records that Jesus appeared to his eleven apostles and said to them: "Behold my hands and my feet, that it is I myself: handle me, and see; for a spirit hath not flesh and bones, as ye see me have" (Luke 24:39). Then Luke records that Jesus ate a piece of broiled fish and a honeycomb (Luke 24:42-43). Joseph Smith's testimony verifies the reality of the immortal resurrection—that Jesus continues to live as a being of flesh and bone.

The Bible teaches that God the Father is greater than His Son, Jesus (John 14:28); that God the Father is the father of all of our spirits (Hebrews 12:9 and Job 38:7); but that God the Father has begotten only one child in this mortal life—His Beloved Son, Jesus Christ—His "only begotten Son." The scriptural support of this great truth—that God the Father is the physical father of Jesus—is well supported in the Bible. (See, e. g., John 1:3, 14; 3:16; 5:17, 18-24; Hebrews 1:1-4; 1 John 5:1; and Luke 2:32-35.) Notwithstanding the substantial and uncontradicted scriptural support for this truth, many people still choose to deny this truth, claiming it to be vulgar and demeaning to God. Nevertheless, the truth is not altered by the opinion of man. And, I submit that the plain meaning of the words "the only begotten Son" gives increased power and beauty to the oft-quoted Christmas passages from Matthew and Luke about the birth of Jesus. (See Luke 1:26-38 and Matthew 1:18-25.[28])

The Bible teaches that Jesus inherited from his Father the power to resurrect himself. Jesus plainly taught this truth on at least two occasions. In the fifth chapter of John, Jesus said: "For as the Father hath life in himself; so hath he given to the Son to have life in himself." And in the tenth chapter of John, Jesus said: "Therefore doth my Father love me, because I lay down my life, that I might take it again. No man taketh it from me, but I lay it down of myself. I have power to lay it down, and I have power to take it again. This commandment have I received of my Father" (John 10:17-18). So, just as all mankind was created in the image and likeness of God (Genesis 1:26-27), so Jesus

---

[28] The passage in Matthew 1:18 says that Mary "was found with child of the Holy Ghost." However, Luke's account gives a fuller explanation of the role played by the Holy Ghost in Mary's conception. Luke records that the angel told Mary: "The Holy Ghost shall come upon thee, and the power of the Highest shall overshadow thee" (Luke 1:35). This means that Mary was to be transfigured or glorified by the Holy Ghost, and that thereafter the power of the Highest (God the Father) would cause her to conceive. Thus, as Luke records, the child would be "the Son of God" (Luke 1:32 & 35). The Holy Ghost is not the father of Jesus. (See also appendix D, "The Virgin Birth vs. The Divine Sonship of Christ.")

was in the express likeness of his Father, being the Only Begotten Son of God. Paul, so eloquently described this special relationship in the opening verses of the Epistle to the Hebrews:

> God, who at sundry times and in divers manners spake in time past unto the fathers by the prophets,
>
> Hath in these last days spoken unto us by his Son, whom he hath appointed heir of all things, by whom also he made the worlds;
>
> Who being the brightness of his glory, and the express image of his person, and upholding all things by the word of his power, when he had by himself purged our sins, sat down on the right hand of the majesty on high.
>
> Being made so much better than the angels, as he hath by inheritance obtained a more excellent name than they.
>
> For unto which of the angels said he at any time, Thou art my Son, this day have I begotten thee? And again, I will be to him a Father, and he shall be to me a Son.
>
> And again, when he bringeth in the firstbegotten into the world, he saith, And let all the angels of God worship him. (Hebrews 1:1-6)

In light of all of these teachings, there is no reason for any man to cling to the belief that we do not know or even cannot know the nature of God. Of course, we cannot fully comprehend God's nature and attributes. But the Bible teaches the basic truths about Him, which truths are uplifting and inspiring to us, as they teach of our divine heritage and our glorious eternal potential.

D.   Jesus Christ Is Also God.

Having discussed the separate and distinct nature of each of the three members of the Godhead, we should point out that the fact of Jesus' being separate and distinct from God the Father does not mean that Jesus is not God. On the contrary, the Bible teaches that Jesus is also God.

That Jesus is God is taught many places. In the first chapter of John, that apostle says that Jesus was the "word" and that "the word was God" (John1:1 & 14). When doubting Thomas first saw the resurrected Savior, he addressed him; "My Lord and my God" (John20:28). Writing to the Philippians, Paul wrote of Jesus: "who, being in the form of God, thought it not robbery to be equal with God" (Philippians 2:6). Paul also wrote that Jesus represented the "Godhead" (Colossians 2:9). And we have previously discussed some of the biblical passages that teach that Jesus Christ is Jehovah, the God of Israel. (See chapter 3.) In the Old Testament, when Isaiah prophesied of Christ's birth, he said that Jesus would be called "the mighty God" (Isaiah 9:6) and "Immanuel" (Isaiah 7:14), which means "God with us" (Matthew 1:23).

Two biblical passages that have been interpreted to deny the Godhood of Jesus are the following: "[T]here is but one God, the Father, of whom are all things, . . . and one Lord Jesus Christ, by whom are all things" (1 Corinthians 8:6); and "[T]his is life eternal that they might know thee, the only true God, and Jesus Christ whom thou hast sent" (John 17:3). In light of the other scriptures that state that Jesus Christ *is* God, I believe that these scriptures that describe God the Father as the only God are referring to the supreme sovereignty of God the Father, rather than to teach that it is wrong to call Jesus "God." It is to God the Father, alone, that we should pray, in the name of His Only Begotten Son, Jesus Christ. God the Father is the presiding member of the Godhead; but Jesus Christ and the Holy Ghost also perform Godly functions in the council of three that makes up the "Godhead."

While God the Father is the supreme being, the ultimate creator and the author of the plan of salvation, he is assisted in his work by Jesus Christ and the Holy Ghost. Jesus carries out the Father's plan; Jesus created the world as God's chief administrator (John 1:1-3; 14;

Colossians 1:16; and Hebrews 1:2); Jesus is our Redeemer and Savior; he is the sole "mediator" between us and God the Father (John 14:6; and 1 Tim. 2:5). All of these functions are part of Jesus' Godly mission, and in that respect the Bible properly refers to him as "God." Similarly, the Holy Ghost is sometimes referred to as "God" or the "Spirit of God" because of the Godly mission he performs; and that mission is to witness to the souls of men that God lives, that Jesus Christ is the Savior of mankind, and to reveal all truth to the souls of men (John 14:26; 15:26; & 16:13).

Jesus commanded his apostles to baptize in the name of the Father, the Son, and the Holy Ghost (Matthew 28:19). John wrote that the witness of all three members of the Godhead is recorded in heaven (1 John 5:7). And then John taught, these three form one Godhead; and in this sense they may also be said to be "one God."

Moses' account of the creation of the world and of Adam and Eve also teaches of a plurality in the Godhead: "And God said: Let *us* make man in *our* own image, after *our* likeness." (Genesis 1:26 [emphasis added].) "And the LORD God said, Behold the man is become as one of *us*." (Genesis 3:22 [emphasis added].) Undoubtedly the "us" and "our" included both God the Father and Jesus Christ, since Christ carried out the Father's plan to create the world (John 1:1; Colossians 1:16; and Hebrews 1:2).

Thus, while the Bible teaches of a plurality of three Gods, in the sense that I have explained,[29] it repudiates the worship of any other gods, such as the Greek idols and gods that Paul condemned while preaching in Athens (Acts 17. But see also the discussions in sections I and J, below, in this chapter and chapters 14 and 15.)

E. God Has Been Seen by His Prophets Throughout the Ages.

Some people assert that Joseph Smith's account of his vision could not be true because of what is written in the King James Version of the

---

[29] See also Psalm 82:1 & 6; Deuteronomy 10:17; and John 10:33-36.

Gospel of John and in the First Epistle of John, where it states that "no man hath seen God at any time" (John1:18 and 1 John 4:12). In further support of this assertion is the verse found in Exodus 33:20, which states that "Thou canst not see my face; for there shall no man see me, and live." However, in contradiction of these three scriptures, there are numerous biblical accounts of prophets who have seen God. Just a few verses later in Exodus the Lord told Moses that he would shortly appear to him and let him see his back parts. The Lord said: "I . . . will cover thee with my hand while I pass by: And I will take away mine hand, and thou shalt see my back parts: but my face shall not be seen" (Exodus 33:22-23). Before the Lord told Moses that no man would see his face, they had been speaking to each other "face to face, as a man speaketh to his friend" (Exodus 33:11). The implication from this verse is that Moses did see God's face at that time. Verse 20 had reference to a future appearance of God to the children of Israel, when they and Moses would be shown God's back parts, but because of their transgressions they would not be shown God's face. (See Isaiah 59:2.) That the face of God can be seen and should be sought was taught by the Psalmist, who wrote: "Thy face, Lord will I seek" (Psalm 27:8). John the Revelator wrote that at the Second Coming "they shall see his face" (Revelation 22:4). And the Lord himself told the prophet Hosea: "I will go and return to my place, till they acknowledge their offence, and seek my face" (Hosea 5:15).

Moses wrote that the "LORD appeared unto Abram" (Genesis 12:7). Isaiah testified that he, too, had seen the Lord. He wrote: "[M]ine eyes have seen the King, the LORD of hosts" (Isaiah 6:1 & 5). There are at least a couple of dozen additional passages in the Old Testament that report appearances of God to his prophets.[30] And there are many

---

[30] Genesis 15:1; 17:1; 18:1; 26:24; 32:30; 35:1 & 9; Exodus 3:6 & 16; 4:1-2 & 5; 6:2-3; 16:10; 24:9-11 & 15-18; 33:20-23; 34:28-35; Leviticus 9:23; Numbers 12:6 & 8; 14:13-14; 20:6; Deuteronomy 5:4 & 24; 31:17-18; 34:10; Judges 6:22-23; 2 Chronicles 1:7-12; 3:1; 7:12 & 14; Psalm 105:4; Daniel 10:6; Luke 24:13-32 & 36-43; John 20:11-17, 19-23 & 24-29; John 21:1-14; Acts 7:55-58; 1 Corinthians 15:4-8; and Revelation 1:10-18 and 19:11-16.
The following additional passages teach that God can be seen, and many of these passages teach conditions to be met in order to see God: Exodus 19:9-25;

additional passages that teach that God can be seen, and that teach conditions to be met in order to see God.[31]

The New Testament witnesses that the Lord appeared unto many people after his resurrection—on one occasion to over 500 brethren (1 Corinthians 15:4-8). One of the most notable of these appearances is that reported by Luke of the Savior's appearance to his apostles after his resurrection:

> And as they thus spake, Jesus himself stood in the midst of them, and saith unto them, Peace be unto you.
>
> But they were terrified and affrighted, and supposed that they had seen a spirit.
>
> And he said unto them, Why are ye troubled? And why do thoughts arise in your hearts?
>
> Behold my hands and my feet, that it is I myself: handle me, and see; for a spirit hath not flesh and bones, as ye see me have.[32] (Luke 24:36-39)

The notion that the Bible is infallible and without any error leads some people to invent new, false doctrines about God as they attempt to interpret these scriptures in a way that would explain away the errors and contradictions.

The Lord revealed to Joseph Smith that alterations had been made to all three of these verses (John 1:18, 1 John 4:12 and Exodus 33:20)

Deuteronomy 4:27-29; 1 Chronicles 16:11; Psalm 24:6 and 27:8; Isaiah 59:1-2; "Ezekiel 20:35; Hosea 5:15; Matthew 5:8; John 6:46 and 14:21 & 23; Hebrews 12:14; 1 John 3:2-3 & 6; 3 John 11; and Revelation 22:4.

[31] *Id.*

[32] Some contend that Jesus did not retain his resurrected body forever, but that he only temporarily takes upon himself the form of a man on special occasions. But this interpretation is not supported by scripture—it is a doctrine of man's creation. The very essence of the resurrection is its eternal duration; otherwise, it would not be the victory over death that Isaiah prophesied it would be (Isaiah 25:8). Also, John the Revelator prophesied that "there shall be no more death" after "death and hell deliver[] up the dead" in the resurrection (Revelation 21:4 & 20:13). (see also 1 Corinthians 15 and 1 John 3:2-3.)

from what the prophets originally had written. I will give you the correct rendition of each of these shortly. But before doing so, let us consider the implications of the notion that there should exist errors in the Bible.

F.   Some Errors Exist in the Bible.

There are those who hold tenaciously to the belief that the Bible is without any error of any kind or nature whatsoever—that the printed words in the King James Version of the Bible (or of whatever other version they have) is as pure as the original words spoken or written by the prophets. Where such a notion originated, I do not know. One's faith in Christ should not be so insecure as to be dependent upon the notion that the Bible must be free of any typographical errors, misspellings, omissions, mistaken repetitions, as well as free from all alterations in meanings (including idiomatic expressions) in the process of translation. Scholars have now substantiated that some intentional changes have also been made in biblical texts. (See, e.g., Potter, 10, 21-22, 31, 54, 94-97 & 106; and Nibley, 95-99.)

How does someone who believes the Bible is without error reconcile the rendition of biblical passages taken from the ancient Dead Sea Scrolls which differ from current translations of the Bible? And how does someone of this opinion reconcile contradictions within the Bible? Did the men who were with Saul hear the voice or didn't they? (Acts 9:7 and 22:9). Did Peter deny knowing Jesus three times before the cock's first crow (as Matthew, Luke and John report), or before the cock crowed twice (as Mark reported)? (Matthew 26:26-75; Mark 4:16-22; Luke 22:54-62; and John 18:15-27).

While some errors in the Bible are of little import, they nevertheless do exist, and they demonstrate that man has imperfectly recorded the word of God in the Bible.

Frankly, there is no need for the narrow view that the Bible is free of any and all errors. Such a view promotes narrow-mindedness and hinders one from growing in truth and knowledge. Such a view can lead one to twist and manipulate the normal meaning of words in the

Bible, in an overzealous and unnecessary effort to prove the Bible to be error-free. The resulting, strained interpretations only exacerbate the problems caused by the errors in the first place.

Errors have made their way into our current translations of the Bible—errors that have occurred over the centuries—as original texts have been copied and translated. No serious biblical scholar denies the existence of such errors.[33] In fact, even the existence of so many different versions of the Bible necessarily establishes that errors exist. But the existence of mistakes in our Bible does not make the message of the Bible of any less validity or importance. Certainly, faith in the Lord Jesus Christ is not or at least should not be founded on the infallibility of the Bible; rather our faith in the Lord Jesus Christ should rest directly and squarely upon Him. Indeed, the very purpose of the Bible is to bring all mankind to Christ—to teach us to have faith in Him. The Bible does not teach that we should put our faith in man's rendition of God's word. We can do better than putting our faith in a book; we can put our faith in the true and living God. A book can have flaws; but God is flawless. Of course, the Bible's value to us is exceedingly great; but there is no need to worship *it* out of

---

[33] See, e. g., H. G. G. Herklots, *How Our Bible Came to Us* (New York: Oxford UniversityPress, 1954). This text is an excellent introduction to the history of how our Bible, especially the New Testament, came to be compiled. It summarizes the works of the principal translators and the principal texts from which our Bible has come. The author also discusses findings from the Dead Sea scrolls. At pages 148-153, Herklots summarizes the nature and extent of discrepancies between some of the Dead Sea scrolls and existing versions of the Bible. He makes no attempt to establish one particular version over another. He considers the known errors to be minor and in no way detracting from the central message of the Bible.

Discoveries of the Dead Sea scrolls in 1947 and of the Nag Hammadi documents in 1945 have given the world hundreds of new, ancient documents of Jewish scripture. Every book in the Bible has been discovered among the Dead Sea scrolls except the Book of Esther. These documents are significant because they are older manuscripts than those from which the Bible had previously been translated. None of our current versions of the Bible was translated from original Bible texts. There exist no original texts of any book of the Bible. All modern versions of the Bible are revisions and/or translations of other translations or revisions.

an overzealous reverence for the book. Remember that Jesus and his apostles taught the word of God "without purse or script" before the New Testament was even written.

G.   Inconsistent Passages about God in the Bible.

Having laid this groundwork, we must start with the observation that the apparent meaning of the words in the King James Version renditions of John 1:18 and 1 John 4:12 is inconsistent with numerous other biblical passages recounting appearances of God to his prophets. As written, they are contradictory. They cannot be reconciled, and no attempt should be made to reconcile them as written, for they contain errors.

When the prophet Joseph Smith inquired of the Lord regarding these passages, the Lord revealed that both of these verses were incomplete and incorrect. The Lord also revealed that Exodus 20:33 was not complete as written in the King James Version. The Lord rendered these scriptures to Joseph Smith as follows:

> John 1:18: *"And* no man hath seen God at any time, *except he hath borne record of the Son*; for except it is through him no man can be saved."

> 1 John 4:12: "No man hath seen God at any time, *except them who believe.* If we love one another, God dwelleth in us, and his love is perfected in us."

> Exodus 33:20: "And he said unto Moses, *Thou canst not see my face at this time, lest mine anger be kindled against thee also, and I destroy thee, and thy people*; for there shall no man among them see me *at this time*, and live. *And no sinful man hath at any time, neither shall there be any sinful man at any time that shall see my face and live.*

The revisions that the Lord inspired Joseph Smith to make in

these three verses are completely in harmony with other passages
that have treated this subject, and which show that God can indeed
be seen—but only by the pure in heart. For example, consider the
following:

> Blessed are the pure in heart: for they shall see
> God. (Matthew 5:8)

> Follow peace with all men, and holiness, without
> which no man shall see the Lord. (Hebrews 12:14)

> [W]hen he shall appear we shall be like him; for
> we shall see him as he is.
> And every man that hath this hope in him
> purifieth himself, even as he is pure. . . .
> [W]hosoever sinneth hath not seen him neither
> known him. (1 John 3:2-3 & 6)

> Then my anger shall be kindled against them in
> that day, and I will forsake them, and I will hide my
> face from them. . . . And I will surely hide my face
> in that day for all the evils which they shall have
> wrought. (Deuteronomy 31:17-18)

> But your iniquities have separated between you
> and your God, and your sins have hid his face from
> you, that he will not hear. (Isaiah 59:2)

> He that hath my commandments and keepeth
> them he it is that loveth me: and he that loveth me
> shall be loved of my Father, and I will love him, and
> will manifest myself to him. (John 14:21)

These scriptures make it unquestionably clear that GOD CAN
BE SEEN. The Bible recounts that God has been seen by his prophets
throughout the ages.

Before leaving these three verses, there is another argument that we should consider that is sometimes proffered in support of the notion that these three verses are correct as written. The argument is that in these verses the word "God" refers to "God the Father," and not to the Lord Jesus Christ. Thus, it is reasoned, though our Lord Jesus Christ *can* be seen, God the Father *cannot* be seen. If the word "God" were intended to be restricted in meaning only to "God the Father," this interpretation *would* resolve some contradictions with other scriptures, but not all of them. It fails to reconcile Stephen's testimony that he saw "Jesus standing on the right hand of God" (Acts 7:55-56). Neither is this interpretation reconcilable with the words of Jesus: "Not that any man hath seen the Father, save he which is of God, he hath seen the Father" (John 6:46). Jesus declares that not just anybody can or has seen the Father, only "he which is of God . . . hath seen the Father." Jesus made it clear that God the Father *can be seen* by Godly people. Thus, the notion that God the Father cannot be seen is directly contradicted by Jesus. Accordingly, I reject such an attempt to reconcile these three scriptures without admitting of any error in them.

Nevertheless, it is true that almost all of the biblical references to seeing God refer to seeing the Lord Jesus Christ, who is JEHOVAH, the God of Israel. (See discussion and references in chapter 3, section 4, above.) Appearances of God the Father are indeed few. He appeared to Adam; and Stephen saw him (Acts 7:55-56); and his voice was heard on a few occasions. (See, e. g., Matthew 3:17; 17:5; and John 12:28.) For the most part, God the Father has appeared and spoken to man only to introduce his only begotten son, who is the mediator between us and God the Father, and through whom we can obtain salvation and return to live with our Father in Heaven. Still, God the Father has been seen on occasion. And in the case of Joseph Smith in 1820, that appearance was necessary to restore to the earth the truth about the nature of God.

H.   Godly People Can See God.

Since we are on the subject of seeing God—how one can see God, and who cannot see God—here is some additional information that the Lord revealed to Joseph Smith on how Moses was able to see God. The Lord revealed to Joseph Smith some writings of Moses which had been lost from the Old Testament, of which the following is a part:

> But now mine own eyes have beheld God; but not my natural, but my spiritual eyes, for my natural eyes could not have beheld, for I should have withered and died in his presence; but his glory was upon me; and I beheld his face, for I was transfigured before him. (*Pearl of Great Price*, Moses 1:11)

As this writing explains, Moses was able to withstand the presence of God only because of a change, or transfiguration, that happened to him. With regard to this necessary change, the Lord told Joseph Smith in November, 1831: "For no man has seen God at any time in the flesh, except quickened by the Spirit of God" (*Doctrine and Covenants* 67:11). In December, 1832, the Lord revealed another message to Joseph Smith pertaining to seeing God:

> [C]all upon me while I am near—
> Draw near unto me and I will draw near unto you; seek me diligently and ye shall find me; ask and ye shall receive; knock and it shall be opened unto you.
> Whatsoever ye ask the Father in my name it shall be given unto you, that is expedient for you;
> And if ye ask anything that is not expedient for you, it shall turn unto your condemnation. . . .
> And if your eye be single to my glory, your whole bodies shall be filled with light, and there shall be no

darkness in you; and that body which is filled with light comprehendeth all things.

Therefore, sanctify yourselves that your minds become single to God, and the days will come that you shall see him; for he will unveil his face unto you, and it shall be in his own time, and in his own way, and according to his own will. (*Doctrine and Covenants* 88:62-68)

Finally, we should note one other fact about the nature of God to consider as we seek to understand what the scriptures teach about Him. We previously pointed out that Jesus Christ is Jehovah, the God of Abraham, Isaac and Jacob. (See chapter 3, section 4, above.) Most of the references to "God," "Lord" and "LORD" in the Old Testament are to Jehovah, not to God the Eternal Father. And until Jesus' birth at Bethlehem he (Jehovah) did not yet have a body of flesh and blood—he existed as a spirit being, waiting to come to earth to obtain a body, to become the "Only Begotten Son" of God the Father. Thus, those prophets who saw God in Old Testament times saw Jesus as a glorious spirit. Accordingly, on these occasions when God was seen, He was seen by man's spiritual eyes, not by man's natural eyes (*Pearl of Great Price*, Moses 1:11). Thus, until Jesus' birth, anyone who saw him, saw him as a spirit.

Jesus explained this truth when he appeared to the Brother of Jared over 2,000 years before his birth (as recorded in *The Book of Mormon*): "Behold, this body which ye now behold, is the body of my spirit; and man have I created after the body of my spirit; and even as I appear unto thee to be in the spirit will I appear unto my people in the flesh" (*Book of Mormon*, Ether 3:16). Prior to his birth, anyone who saw Jehovah/Jesus saw him as a spirit. But after Jesus' resurrection, anyone who saw him saw him as a being of flesh and bones. (See, e. g., Luke 24:36-43.) Of course, the scriptures teach that one must still be pure and holy in order to see Him after his resurrection, just as before his birth.

I.   The Nature of Spirits.

Before leaving the Brother of Jared's account of seeing the Lord, let's dwell a minute on what the Lord taught about the nature of spirit beings.[34] As a spirit being, Jesus looked just like he was to later look as a mature man. Since all mankind, including Jesus, are spirit children of God the Father (Hebrews 12:9 and Acts 17:28-29), it follows that all of us likewise are now spiritual beings clothed in mortal bodies which (except for individuals with handicaps and deformities) come to look just like our spirits when we reach physical maturity.[35] (Our resurrected bodies will have no deformities or handicaps.) This is a beautiful and important truth to contemplate as we consider who we are and what our eternal destiny is.

J.   Heirs of God.

There is more than mere symbolism in the words of the Apostle Paul: "The spirit itself beareth witness with our spirit, that we are the children of God. And if children, then heirs; heirs of God and joint-heirs with Christ; if so be that we suffer with him, that we may be also glorified together" (Romans 8:16-17). It is literally true that through the gospel of Jesus Christ we can become God's heirs. The eternal potential of man is not only to return and live with God, but to be "heirs of God, and joint-heirs with Christ." (See also Galatians 3:29; & 4:7; Titus 3:7; Hebrews 1:2 & 14; and James 2:5.) To be an heir is better than to be a servant or a guest; heirs have dominion, heirs inherit. To become God's heir is to become like God. Jesus himself

---

[34] What is the nature of a spirit being? A spirit being is a being of a material nature. Regarding spirit matter, the Lord revealed to Joseph Smith: "All spirit is matter, but it is more fine or pure, and can only be discerned by purer eyes; We cannot see it; but when our bodies are purified we shall see that it is all matter" (*Doctrine and Covenants* 131:7-8).

[35] Jesus' statement that God is "a spirit" (John 4:24) need not be and should not be interpreted to mean that God does not also have a tangible, physical tabernacle for his spirit.

taught this when he quoted approvingly the Psalm which proclaimed that children of Israel were "gods" (John 10:33-36 and Psalm 82:6). (The psalmist had written: "Ye are gods, and all of you are children of the most High." See chapters 14 and 15 for further discussion of this.)

John taught that "when he [Jesus] shall appear, we shall be like him" (1 John 3:2). Possessed of immortal bodies in the resurrection, of course we will be like him in this respect. But the great challenge of life is for us to purify and perfect our characters to the greatest extent possible so that we can become godly in character as well. This is the challenge that John identified when he said that "every man that hath this hope in him purifieth himself, even as he is pure" (1 John 3:3). (See also, Matthew 5:48 & 7:21.) Through the grace of Christ, an Eternal inheritance has been prepared for us (Revelation 21:7); it is ours for the taking if we will have faith in Christ and obey his gospel.

K.   Summary.

The teachings of Joseph Smith about the nature of God and how He may be seen, were not merely the result of his own power of reasoning—they were based upon his first-hand experiences as a prophet of God, as God appeared to him and revealed His word to him. Not only are the teachings of Joseph Smith on this subject both plausible and consistent with the Bible, but I humbly submit that they are also inspiring, as the word of God always is.

What then is the great significance of the fact that no organized religion in 1820 taught the truth about God? It demonstrates that the true Gospel of Jesus Christ was not on the earth. There remained only partial truths mixed with falsehoods.

There is no more fundamental and important truth for us to understand than the true nature of God. Based upon it we build our faith. Based upon it we learn who we are and that we have the potential to become like God, our Father in Heaven. Joseph Smith learned in 1820 that Christianity had departed from an understanding of the truth about God. The churches had departed from the true and living God. They believe in Jesus Christ, but their doctrines and creeds about God's nature contained mistakes and falsehoods.

The restoration of the truth about the nature and attributes of God is one of the most important and fundamental truths restored to the earth in the latter days.

CHAPTER 9

Status of Christianity in 1820

You will recall that Joseph Smith's purpose in going into the grove of trees to pray was to learn which of the churches he should join—the Methodists? The Presbyterians? The Baptists? Or what? Each of the denominations with which he was familiar claimed to be the true church of Christ. The fourteen-year-old youth simply wanted to know which organized church he should join. And that is what he asked the Savior.

In response to his question, the Lord told Joseph not to join any church. He said they were all corrupt—that "all their creeds were an abomination in his sight" Joseph Smith—History 1:18) and that their ministers were "corrupt." Jesus said that "they draw near to me with their lips, but their hearts are far from me, they teach for doctrines the commandments of men, having a form of godliness, but they deny the power thereof" (*Id.*, at 19).

This statement by the Savior to Joseph Smith is a forceful but sad commentary on organized Christianity. It meant that the divine church of Christ was not on the earth in 1820. It meant that there had been a great apostasy from the doctrines and ordinances of Jesus Christ. But although it meant that "all" existing, organized churches had become corrupted, it did not mean that all Christians were corrupt.[36] For years many valiant Christians had acknowledged the corruption that had taken hold in organized Christianity.

A.   Evidences of Apostasy from the Gospel of Jesus Christ.

Joseph Smith was not the first person to declare that Christianity had become corrupted; Christian reformers had been saying this for 300 years before Joseph Smith was even born. In fact, the corruption of Christianity had been foretold in the Bible. There are numerous passages of scripture that foretell of an apostasy from the true gospel before Christ's Second Coming. One of these was made by the Apostle Paul, who wrote to the Thessalonians:

> [B]e not soon shaken in mind, or be troubled, neither by spirit, nor by word, nor by letter as from us, as that the day of Christ is at hand.
>
> Let no man deceive you by any means: for that day shall not come, except there come a falling away first, and that man of sin be revealed, the son of perdition;
>
> Who opposeth and exalteth himself above all that is called God, or that is worshipped; so that he as God sitteth in the temple of God, shewing himself that he is God. . . .
>
> And then shall that Wicked be revealed, whom the Lord shall consume with the spirit of his mouth, and shall destroy with the brightness of his coming:
>
> Even him, whose coming is after the working of Satan with all power and signs and lying wonders,

---

[36] In the sense that "church" means the collective group of all believers in Christ, there is no question that the church of Christ has continued, uninterrupted on the earth since the time of Christ. But in the sense that "church" means the divine organization that Christ established, this "church" disappeared from the earth shortly after the death of the apostles.

> And with all deceivableness of unrighteousness
> in them that perish; because they receive not the love
> of truth, that they might be saved.
> And for this cause God shall send them strong
> delusion, that they should believe a lie:
> That they all might be damned who believed
> not the truth, but had pleasure in unrighteousness.
> (2 Thessalonians 2:2-12)

In this passage, not only does Paul state that a "falling away" will occur before the Second Coming of the Lord, but he states that this "mystery of iniquity doth already work"—In other words, it was already under way. Paul stated that when this "falling away" does occur, Satan would place a counterfeit religion in place of the truth and set himself up to the world, "shewing himself that he is God." This means that the falling away would not cause the knowledge of Jesus and of his gospel to be eliminated, but only to be altered. And this tells me that Satan will have control over many edifices and congregations who profess to be Christian. And Paul warned that Satan will perform powerful "signs and lying wonders" to deceive the people.

The New Testament contains many additional prophecies of an apostasy, as well.[37] As unsettling as such prophecies may be, they must nevertheless be fulfilled. Undoubtedly the great Christian reformers recognized their fulfillment in the abominations that crept into the Christianity and that they attempted to reform. And many of the reformers were also aware of the biblical prophecies of a restoration that were discussed in chapters 2-5. In fact, it is only logical that a "falling away" would occur prior to a restoration; what was not lost

---

[37] Other prophecies of an apostasy include: Acts 20:29-30; 1 Timothy 4:1-3; 2 Timothy 3:1-9; and 4:3-4; 2 Peter 2:1-3; Jude: 3-4; 1 John 2:18 and Revelation 2:4-5. For an excellent discussion of these and many other scriptures pertaining to an apostasy from the gospel of Jesus Christ, see Kent P. Jackson, "Early Signs of the Apostasy," *Ensign*, December, 1984, pp. 8-16. See also, Roberts, "Introduction," pp. xl-xlvii.

could not be restored. And the apostles of Jesus prophesied that both an apostasy and a restoration would occur.

B.   Christian Reformers.

1. Recognizing Corruption in Christianity.

Martin Luther (1483-1546) recognized the corruption that had taken hold in the church's leaders and doctrines.[38] But when he sought to teach doctrine in the church that conformed with the Bible, the Catholic Church excommunicated him. Martin Luther wrote this:

> I have sought nothing beyond reforming the Church in conformity with the Holy Scriptures. The spiritual powers have been not only corrupted by sin, but absolutely destroyed; so that there is now nothing in them but a depraved reason and a will that is the enemy and opponent of God. I simply say that Christianity has ceased to exist among those who should have preserved it. (*In Galat.* (1535) *Weins IX, P.I.* 293, 24-27, p. 50, *Luther and His Times*, p. 509, *Martin Luther*, p. 188—as quoted in "The Falling Away and Restoration of the Gospel of Jesus Christ Foretold," [Salt Lake City: The Church of Jesus Christ of Latter-day Saints, 1976] p. 3.)

---

[38] Protestant and Catholic historians confirm the fact that corrupt leaders controlled the church beginning after the days of the apostles. But while the religious historians describe the decadence, they usually maintained that Christianity continued to survive in spite of it. However, the widespread corruption that went unabated for centuries is clearly an evidence of the apostasy from the true gospel of Jesus Christ. Did hypocrites preserve Christianity or did they pervert it? (B. H. Roberts discusses the writings of many of these historians in Roberts, "Introduction," pp. xlvii-lxxvi.)

The sale of Indulgences,[39] the Inquisition,[40] and the forbidding of lay people to read the Bible are just three of many blatant transgressions of which the Catholic Church was guilty.

Who would be offended at Martin Luther's bold words? Only those who were built upon the sandy foundation of sin and error. But, of course, there were many who were offended. And so they persecuted Luther. Today, however, Luther's valiant zeal for the truth is a monument to all Christians. We all thank him for the role he played in helping to put purity back in Christianity. We thank God for his courage.

Another of the early reformers who spoke out plainly against the evils that had ravished the church of Christ was John Wesley (1705-1791). He was a force behind the formation of the Methodist Church that separated from the Church of England. Part of his frank teachings included the following:

> It does not appear that these extraordinary gifts of the Holy Ghost were common in the Church for more than two or three centuries. We seldom hear of them after the fatal period when the Emperor Constantine called himself a Christian; . . . From this time they almost totally ceased; . . . The Christians had no more of the Spirit of Christ than the other heathens. . . . This was the real cause why the extraordinary gifts of the Holy Ghost were no longer to be found in the Christian Church; because the Christians were turned Heathens again, and had only a dead form left. (*Wesley's Works*, vol. 7, Sermon 89, pp. 26-27, quoted in "The Falling Away and Restoration of the Gospel of Jesus Christ Foretold," p. 4.)

Though his words were offensive to some, they were not offensive

---

[39] For definitions of "Indulgences" and the "Inquisition," see footnotes in chapter 10, section C (at page 148).
[40] *Id.*

to sincere seekers of truth. Salvation does not come through a vain belief in superstition or erroneous tradition. To one who will not face up to the hard truth, that truth becomes an insurmountable obstacle. It is only when one courageously acknowledges truth that God can turn an apparent obstacle into a great stepping stone and blessing. John Wesley's forthright preaching played an important role in preparing the world for the restoration of the Gospel of Jesus Christ in its fullness, just a few years after his death.

2. Looking for God's Messengers.

Another courageous reformer, and one of the early colonizers of Massachusetts and Rhode Island was Roger Williams (1604-1684). He was not blinded to the corruption of Christianity either. But neither was he despondent about it. He foresaw the Lord's sending new apostles to the earth in preparation for His Second Coming. He said: "There is no regularly constituted church on earth, nor any person authorized to administer any church ordinance; nor can there be until new apostles are sent by the Great Head of the Church for whose coming I am seeking" (*Picturesque America*, p. 502, quoted in LeGrand Richards, *A Marvelous Work and A Wonder* (Salt Lake City: Deseret Book Co., 1950, 1976) p. 27). Williams was convicted of heresy and banished from Massachusetts because he preached doctrine that was offensive to the Puritans. He moved to Rhode Island and there started the first Baptist church in America. Later, he left that church and became an Independent. ("Roger Williams," *American Peoples Encyclopedia*, 1956 ed.) Roger Williams wrought a great work for the Lord, as a colonizer, a champion of religious freedom for all, and as a forthright advocate for the truth.

Do you think any of these three reformers would have been offended at Joseph Smith's declaration that the church of Christ had been corrupted and that none of the existing Christian denominations found favor in the eyes of God? I think that these reformers would have admitted this truth. Roger Williams, for one, was already "seeking" the coming of God's messengers to usher in a divine work.

Of course, none of these great disciples lived to see the fulfillment of Roger Williams' vision. But they all played a part in preparing the world for it. So, too, the establishment of the United States of America, with a Constitution that provides for freedom of worship, played a role in preparing the world for the divine restoration of the gospel. The American Revolution was instigated and backed by educated, noble, idealistic men who worked and fought to create a nation where people could enjoy a life of liberty. Their success in this noble endeavor created a nation where the gospel of Jesus Christ could survive and then flourish. Unlike their mother countries, the new nation, America, made its laws to protect freedom of worship, rather than to persecute those who chose to worship in a manner different from the majority.

One of these founding fathers, Thomas Jefferson (1743-1826), made the following observations about Christianity:

> The religion builders have so distorted and deformed the doctrines of Jesus, so muffled them in mysticisms, fancies and falsehoods, have caricatured them into forms so inconceivable, as to shock reasonable thinkers. . . . Happy in the prospect of a restoration of primitive Christianity, I must leave to younger persons to encounter and lop off the false branches which have been engrafted into it by the mythologists of the middle and modern ages. (*Jefferson's Complete Works*, vol. 7, pp. 210, 257, cited in "The Falling Away and Restoration of the Gospel of Jesus Christ Foretold," p. 6.)

Reasonable men would not be, were not, and are not offended at the declaration of Joseph Smith that Christ's church was no longer on the earth in 1820. In the early 1800s many sincere seekers of truth acknowledged this to be the case; they awaited the restoration foretold in the bible to occur prior to the Lord's glorious reign on earth, which restoration was to be performed by divinely commissioned servants of God.[41]

In summary, what was the status of the Church of Christ in 1820? The organization that Christ established in the meridian of time was no longer on the earth. But God promised to shortly reestablish it.

---

[41] See historical notes at the end of chapter 12, about some men who were looking for a restoration.

THE FULFILLMENT

PART II

◆

MESSAGES FROM CHRIST 1823-1829

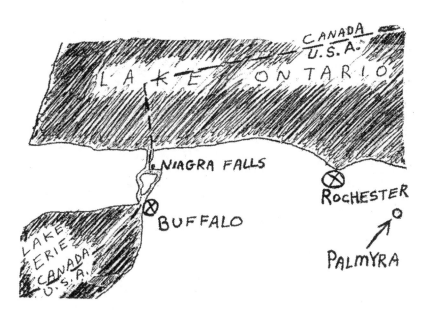

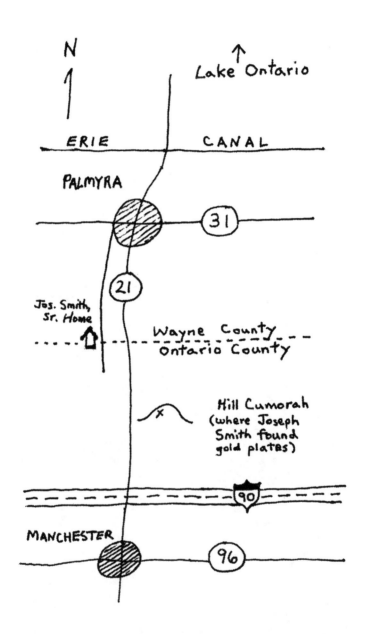

CHAPTER 10

Angelic Messengers Restore the Gospel of Jesus Christ

A. Origin of the Book of Mormon.

Although the Lord told Joseph Smith at the age of fourteen that he was to be the Lord's servant in accomplishing a future work, no specific task was given to Joseph to perform at that time. But beginning from that moment he was aware that the Lord expected him to conduct his life worthily and to prepare himself for the later-to-be-revealed work.

Following Joseph's vision in 1820, he related that experience to others a number of times and found that rather than its being received with gladness, it was greatly criticized and condemned by many people. This was surprising to Joseph, who said that he suffered "severe persecution at the hands of all classes of men, both religious and irreligious" because he asserted that he had seen a vision (Joseph Smith—History 1:27). Then, three years later, on the night of September 21, 1823, he said, "I betook myself to prayer and supplication to Almighty God for forgiveness of all my sins and follies, and also for a manifestation to me, that I might know of my state and standing before him; for I had full confidence in obtaining a divine manifestation as I previously had one" (*Id.*, v. 29). While praying, Joseph said that a brilliant personage appeared to him, standing in the air by his bed. Joseph said that the messenger said that he was "sent from the presence of God" and that his name was Moroni, and "that God had a work for [Joseph] to do; and that [his] name should be had for good and evil among all nations, kindreds, and tongues, . . . among all people" (*Id.*, v. 33).

Moroni told Joseph that "there was a book deposited, written upon gold plates, giving an account of the former inhabitants of this continent, and the source from whence they sprang. He also said that the fulness of the everlasting Gospel was contained in it, as delivered by the Savior to the ancient inhabitants" (*Id.*, v. 34). Moroni also told Joseph that buried with the plates were two stones in silver bows, which is called the Urim and Thummim, "and the possession and use of these stones were what constituted "seers" in ancient or former times; and that God had prepared them for the purpose of translating the book" (*Id.*, v. 35).

After this, Moroni quoted several biblical prophecies to Joseph, which prophecies Moroni explained were about to be fulfilled. These prophecies included: Malachi chapters 3 and 4; Isaiah chapter 11; Acts 3:22-23; and Joel 2:28-32. Joseph said that while listening to Moroni a "vision was opened to my mind that I could see the place where the plates were deposited, and that so clearly and distinctly that I knew the place again when I visited it" (*Id.*, v. 42). The vision/visitation came to an end, but then the same vision unfolded to Joseph two additional times, taking up most of the night. Then the next morning, Joseph was exhausted. As he attempted to work in the field with his family, Joseph's father saw that something was wrong with Joseph, and he sent him home. But on the way home Joseph collapsed, and then Moroni appeared to him again, and for the fourth time presented the same information to him. This time, Moroni told Joseph "to go to [his] father and tell him of the vision and commandments which [he] had received" (*Id.*, v. 49). Joseph said: "I returned to my father in the field, and rehearsed the whole matter to him. He replied to me that it was

of God, and told me to go and do as commanded by the messenger"
(*Id.*, v. 50).

Joseph then went to the place that had been shown him in vision.
He proceeded to a hill about three miles from his home. The hill was
only about 110 feet higher than the surrounding areas, but it was
the most elevated hill in the area. "On the west side of this hill, not
far from the top, under a stone of considerable size, lay the plates,
deposited in a stone box" (*Id.*, v. 51). Joseph used a lever to dislodge
the stone and uncover the stone box, underneath. There, Joseph found
the gold plates, the Urim and Thummim, and a breastplate. Joseph
attempted to pick up the plates, but Moroni appeared and stopped
him. Moroni directed Joseph to return there in precisely one year, and
to receive additional instruction (*Id.*, v. 53).

Joseph Smith said that he did as instructed and visited that same
place on the same day the next year (1824), and then for the next three
years after that (1825, 1826 and 1827). Joseph said that each time he
"found the same messenger there, and that he received instruction and
intelligence from him at each of our interviews, respecting what the
Lord was going to do, and how and in what manner his kingdom was
to be conducted in the last days" (*Id.*, v. 54). Finally, on September 22,
1827, when Joseph Smith was 21 years old, he went again to the hill.
This time the messenger did deliver the plates to Joseph, and gave him
a strict charge that "I should be responsible for them; that if I should
let them go carelessly, or through any neglect of mine, I should be cut
off; but that if I would use all my endeavors to preserve them, until
he, the messenger, should call for them, they should be protected"
(*Id.*, v. 59).

Thereafter, Joseph Smith translated a portion of these gold plates
by the gift and power of God. The translation was completed in 1829,
and the first printing of the translation was completed in 1830. The
work was entitled *The Book of Mormon.*

The Book of Mormon tells the story of a group of Israelites, led by a
prophet named Lehi, who was commanded by the Lord to take his
family and another family and leave the area of Jerusalem, to be led
to a promised land. The account begins about 600 B.C., during the

first year of the reign of King Zedekiah, just prior to the Kingdom of Judah being taken captive by the Babylonians. The families traveled southward, through the Arabian Desert. They brought with them certain plates of brass that contained the genealogy, prophecies and history of their ancestors—the tribes of Ephraim and Manasseh (the two sons of Joseph). This record contained many of the same writings that are now found in the Old Testament, including the writings of Moses, Isaiah and other prophets, down through prophecies of Jeremiah.

The Lord commanded this people to also record their own history, their teachings and their prophecies on plates. This they did. They recorded their journey through the wilderness and how the Lord instructed them in building a ship and crossing the ocean, leading them to a promised land, which is called today North and South America. Upon arriving in the Americas, they divided into two groups, referred to in the Book of Mormon as Nephites and Lamanites.

The prophet-leaders of this people continued to engrave their history and many of their prophecies and teachings upon metal plates for about a thousand years. During that time the civilization spread throughout the Americas. In about 385 A.D., the prophet Mormon completed an abridgement of the many records that covered this thousand-year period. Mormon engraved this abridgement upon gold plates in a reformed Egyptian language. In about 421 A.D., Mormon's son, Moroni, completed the abridgement project and added to the plates a summary of the history of another group of people (called the Jaredites) that had also been led by the Lord to the Americas at the time of the tower of Babel. The Jaredite civilization existed here from an estimated 2200 B.C. to about 300 B.C. Moroni also included with the plates a number of plates that were "sealed." Moroni then buried the plates in a hill in what is now western New York State, near the present town of Palmyra, about 25 miles south of Lake Ontario and east of Rochester. In 1827, 1400 years later, Moroni, then a resurrected being, appeared to Joseph Smith and delivered these plates to him.

The most significant part of this record is the account that it gives of a visit by the resurrected Lord to some of his disciples on the

American Continent after his crucifixion and his ascension to heaven. This ancient record is a witness to the world, together with the Bible, that Jesus Christ is the Savior of the world, that he died for our sins, and that if we believe in him and keep his commandments we can be saved and return to live with him in the hereafter.

Moroni was the last person to write on the gold plates. He witnessed and described a great war, lasting many years, which resulted in the death of hundreds of thousands of people and the annihilation of all Christians who would not deny the Christ. Moroni wrote that he would not deny the Christ, and therefore he was forced to live in hiding for many years. Moroni recorded the destruction of his people, the Nephites, by the Lamanites, and he wrote some prophecies to the future people who he knew would later obtain this record. Finally, in about 421 A.D. he buried the plates in a stone box, to be hid from the world until 1823.

Moroni wrote a preface to the records, the translation of which is found today on the title page of *The Book of Mormon*. In it he says that the purpose of the book is for "the convincing of the Jew and Gentile that JESUS is the CHRIST, the ETERNAL GOD, manifesting himself unto all nations."

Joseph Smith completed his translation in June of 1829, which resulted in a book in English of over 500 pages. Moroni told Joseph that he was not to translate the "sealed" portion of the plates, but that the sealed plates would be translated and brought forth at a later time. With the translation completed, Moroni took the plates back into his custody. Then, in Fayette, New York, Moroni appeared in vision to Joseph and three men, Oliver Cowdery, David Whitmer and Martin Harris, and showed them the gold plates. This was a glorious manifestation, where they heard the voice of God declare to them that the translation of the plates was true, and commanding them to bear this witness to the world. The testimony of these three witnesses in printed in every copy of *The Book of Mormon*.

A short time later, in Palmyra, New York, Joseph was permitted to show the plates to eight additional men, who hefted the plates and turned the metal pages. These eight men prepared and signed a written testimony of their experience in viewing and handling the plates, which testimony is also printed in every copy of *The Book of Mormon*. The names of these men are: John Whitmer, Christian Whitmer, Jacob Whitmer, Peter Whitmer, Jr., Hiram Page, Hyrum Smith, Samuel H. Smith, and Joseph Smith, Sr. (The latter three were two of Joseph's brothers and his father.) Following this showing of the plates, Moroni retrieved the plates and continues to have custody of them until the time comes for the sealed portion to be brought forth to the world.

To my knowledge, none of these eleven witnesses ever denied his testimony as subscribed to in *The Book of Mormon*, even though more than half of these men later disassociated themselves with Joseph Smith and Mormonism. Thus, the existence of the gold plates can be proven by the testimony of Joseph Smith and eleven others. But proving that Joseph's translation of those records is the word of God is a separate matter. The ultimate test for whether *The Book of Mormon* is the word of God is whether the Spirit of God manifests the truthfulness of it to the souls of those who ask God. My witness is that the Holy Ghost does bear witness of this, as He does of all truth (John 16:13).

The purpose of *The Book of Mormon* is to invite and encourage all mankind to come unto Christ. *The Book of Mormon* confirms the words of Jesus that the purpose of this life is to come to know God (John 17:3). The Lord has brought forth *The Book of Mormon* in these last days to be used with the Bible to gather the elect of God to prepare them to receive Jesus Christ when he comes for His Millennial reign on earth. This gathering of Israel is accomplished as people accept Jesus Christ as their Savior and are baptized by his actual authority into Christ's Church, which would be restored in 1830.

B.   The Restoration of the Priesthood.

In the spring of 1829, Joseph and Emma Smith were residing in the small town of Harmony, Pennsylvania. There, Joseph was working with his scribe, Oliver Cowdery, translating the gold plates; Oliver would write down the words that Joseph would dictate to him. While doing this work, on May 15, 1829, they had a question about baptism. They went to the Lord in solemn prayer about baptism, and in response they were visited by an angelic messenger, who identified himself as John, the same man who had baptized Jesus. John the Baptist (now resurrected from the dead) laid his hands upon Joseph and Oliver, and ordained them, saying this:

> Upon you my fellow servants, in the name of Messiah, I confer the Priesthood of Aaron, which holds the keys of the ministering of angels, and of the gospel of repentance, and of baptism by immersion for the remission of sins; and this shall never be taken again from the earth until the sons of Levi do offer again an offering unto the Lord in righteousness. (Joseph Smith—History 1:69)

The messenger said that the priesthood he had bestowed on them did not give them the power to confer the gift of the Holy Ghost by the laying on of hands, but that this power would be conferred upon them later by Peter, James and John. John commanded them to then baptize one another, which they did.

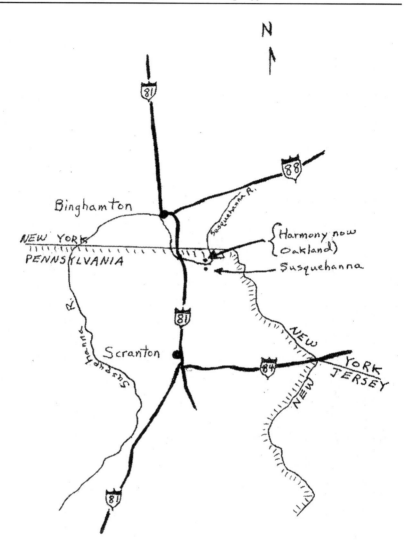

John also directed them to ordain one another to the Aaronic Priesthood after being baptized, which they did. Both Joseph and Oliver reported experiencing a great outpouring of the Spirit on this occasion. Joseph wrote this:

> Immediately on our coming up out of the water after we had been baptized, we experienced great

and glorious blessings from our Heavenly Father. No sooner had I baptized Oliver Cowdery, than the Holy Ghost fell upon him, and he stood up and prophesied many things which should shortly come to pass. And again, so soon as I had been baptized by him, I also had the spirit of prophecy, when, standing up, I prophesied concerning the rise of this Church, and many other things connected with the Church, and this generation of the children of men. We were filled with the Holy Ghost, and rejoiced in the God of our salvation. (Joseph Smith—History 1:73)

This heavenly manifestation reaffirms the indispensability of baptism and the necessity for the one administering the ordinance to have actual authority from God to do it. When Jesus visited the ancient Americans, he told them that baptism was essential for salvation and that it must be performed by immersion and by one having authority from Him. (See also chapter 17.) It was perhaps in the course of translating this part of the gold plates that Joseph and Oliver prayed for enlightenment on the question of baptism, in response to which they were visited by John the Baptist. The importance of administering the ordinance of baptism in the exact manner prescribed by the Savior may not have been abundantly clear prior to the reading of this passage. Baptism is a gospel ordinance that had been changed, so that in 1829 there did not exist one group of Christians that practiced it as Jesus commanded it to be done. The Lord made it clear that there was only one way to perform baptisms; and he also made it clear that authority was necessary on the part of one performing this ordinance. He also taught that baptism was for those who are accountable for their actions, but not for little children. (See also, footnote 61 at page 239.)

It is significant to note that Joseph and Oliver did not take it upon themselves to perform baptisms until God's angelic messenger actually conferred such authority upon them by the laying on of hands.[42] Since there was not then upon the earth any person having authority to act in the name of God, it was necessary that God send messengers from heaven to restore this authority again to the earth.

Shortly after the visit of John the Baptist, Peter, James and John did appear to Joseph and Oliver and conferred upon them the higher Priesthood, the same power and authority possessed by the apostles of old, including the power to bestow the Gift of the Holy Ghost by the laying on of hands.[43] From that time until this, apostles and prophets have again been on the earth with authority to baptize and to direct the affairs of the work of God.

Why did the Lord send Peter, James and John to perform this holy ordination? Because it was essential that Joseph and Oliver have this power and authority in doing the Lord's work; and, because there was no one then on earth having this authority. God sent angelic messengers to the Prophet Joseph Smith to restore His authority to the earth.

After receiving the Gift of the Holy Ghost, the minds of Joseph and Oliver were enlightened. Joseph records that: "[W]e began to have

---

[42] The Lord taught Joseph that a desire to preach the gospel was not sufficient to authorize one to do God's work. A short time after the visitation of John the Baptist, Joseph's brother Hyrum asked Joseph if he could go and preach the restored gospel. Through the Urim and Thummim, Joseph received a revelation instructing Hyrum as follows:

> Behold, I command you that you need not suppose that you are called to preach until you are called.
>
> Wait a little longer, until you shall have by word, my rock, my church, and my gospel, that you may know of a surety my doctrine.
>
> And then, behold, according to your desires, yea, even according to your faith shall it be done unto you. (*Doctrine and Covenants* 11:15-17)

At the time of Hyrum's inquiry, the translation of the Book of Mormon was not yet complete, the Melchizedek Priesthood had yet to be restored, and the Church of Jesus Christ was not to be organized for another 10 or 11 months. Later, the Lord revealed to Joseph that no one is authorized to preach the gospel or to perform the gospel ordinances unless "he be ordained by some one who has authority" (*Doctrine and Covenants* 42:11).

[43] There is a distinction between the authority to baptize and the authority of the apostles to confer the Gift of the Holy Ghost, as is demonstrated by the following biblical passages: John 1:27, 33; and Acts 8:13-16.

the scriptures laid open to our understandings, and the true meaning and intention of their more mysterious passages revealed unto us in a manner which we never could attain to previously, nor ever before had thought of" (*Pearl of Great Price*, Joseph Smith—History 1:74).

C.   Significance of These Messages for the World.

The Lord revealed truths to Joseph and Oliver line upon line, precept upon precept. They then understood that the apostasy from the true gospel of Christ must have occurred shortly after the death of Christ's apostles. The apostle Paul clearly taught that the Church of Jesus Christ was built upon the "foundation of the apostles and prophets, Jesus Christ himself being the chief corner stone" (Ephesians 2:20). And Paul taught that apostles and prophets were there for a purpose: "For the perfecting of the saints, for the work of the ministry, for the edifying of the body of Christ; Till we all come in the unity of the faith, and of the knowledge of the Son of God, unto a perfect man, unto the measure of the stature of the fulness of Christ" (Ephesians 4:12-13). But what apostles and prophets remained in the church after the first century? What apostles and prophets were there in the second, third and fourth centuries? The answer to this question is not a matter of debate; it is undisputed that after the apostle John disappeared, in the early second century, there were no more apostles or prophets in the church. Did apostles and prophets continue to be the foundation of the church during the days of Emperor Constantine or during the years of the Inquisition,[44] or when Indulgences[45] were sold to the church? Of course not. There were no apostles or prophets then. After the first century, the foundation of the Church of Christ was gone; the Lord no longer guided and directed the affairs of that organization by revelation, as he had done when the apostles and prophets were there.

How can one look at the history of Christianity—look at its changes; look at its problems; look at its reformations; and look at its multiple divisions and denominations today—and not admit that these aberrations indicate serious and extensive problems in Christianity? If the Lord desires his disciples to be one, he must not be happy with the numerous differences and divisions in doctrines and practices. Of course he desires to bring all of his disciples to "a unity of the faith." And how would He accomplish that? Wouldn't it be by calling a prophet—the same as He has always done throughout the ages. "Surely the Lord GOD will do nothing," Amos wrote, "but he revealeth his secret unto his servants the prophets" (Amos 3:7).

And what scriptural basis is there for the belief that apostles and prophets are no longer needed? There is none.

So when the proclamation is made by Joseph Smith that God has sent angelic messengers to him—Peter, James and John—who conferred upon him the same authority they possessed in their day,

---

[44] The INQUISITION was an effort by the Roman Catholic Church to force people to conform their religious beliefs to that of the Catholic Church. Thousands of people who refused to change their beliefs were put to death in the name of God, under the Inquisition. Beginning with the reign of Constantine (306-337 A.D.), heresy became an offense against the state as well as the church. In 1231, Pope Gregory IX convened courts to carry out the Inquisition. The Inquisition continued to operate into the 1500s in France, Germany, Italy and Spain, where it was turned against the Protestants. (Raymond H. Schmandt, "Inquisition," *World Book Encyclopedia*, 1969 ed.)

[45] INDULGENCE is a Roman Catholic doctrine which signifies the remission of the temporal punishment for sin after eternal punishment for it is removed by confession. "Many glaring abuses were practiced in the distribution of indulgences, particularly the 'sale' of them for money offerings, until the Catholic Reformation of the Council of Trent [1563]." ("Indulgence," *The American People's Encyclopedia*, 1956, ed.)

should not our hearts rejoice to hear this glad news? Should not our hearts be receptive and open to hear the word of the Lord again from the mouths of His apostles and prophets?

Certainly it is not unheard of for God to call an unsophisticated youth to be his prophet. God has done this before. Certainly God would not call as his prophet one of the "pastors that destroy and scatter the sheep of [his] pasture" (Jeremiah 23:1). Neither would he select a prophet from among those who had "transgressed the laws, changed the ordinance, broken the everlasting covenant" (Isaiah 24:5). Neither would he select a prophet from among the proud or the worldly. Neither would he select one who merely honors God with his mouth, but whose heart is far from Him—of course not.

How would God correct the apostasy problem? Isaiah described just such a problem where:

> the priest and the prophet have erred through strong drink, they are swallowed up of wine, they are out of the way through strong drink; they err in vision, they stumble in judgment.
>
> For all tables are full of vomit and filthiness, so that there is no place clean.
>
> Whom shall he teach knowledge? and whom shall he make to understand doctrine? them that are weaned from the milk, and drawn from breasts.
>
> For precept must be upon precept, precept upon precept; line upon line, line upon line; here a little, and there a little. (Isaiah 28:7-10)

Would God attempt a patch-work reparation of his Church in order to make it good once again? Probably not. Jesus taught:

> No man putteth a piece of new cloth unto an old garment, for that which is put in to fill it up taketh from the garment, and the rent is made worse.

> Neither do men put new wine into old bottles:
> else the bottles break, and the wine runneth out, and
> the bottles perish: but they put new wine into new
> bottles, and both are preserved. (Matthew 9:16-17)

Might not we expect God to raise up a prophet from his youth, like Moses or Joseph or Samuel or John the Baptist? Certainly God could train and prepare a prophet to do his work today, just as much as in ancient times. God frequently chooses the weak to confound the wise and the mighty (1 Corinthians 1:27). Those who come unto Christ in meekness and faith, them will He make strong and mighty (2 Corinthians 12:9).

In these latter days God has chosen the meek and the humble to do a marvelous work and a wonder among the world. The young man, Joseph Smith, was called in his youth and prepared by the Lord and by angelic messengers and by the Holy Ghost to restore the pure gospel of Jesus Christ again to the earth.

The Lord does desire that all of his disciples unite—but he desires that they unite around the truth, not around a mixture of part truth and part fables and falsehoods.

The claims of visions and heavenly manifestations made by Joseph Smith are astounding, that's for sure. But is not Joseph Smith's testimony reminiscent of how God dealt with his ancient prophets—Moses, Abraham, Elijah, Isaiah, and Daniel? Of course it is. Joseph Smith's testimony is a magnificent witness to the world that the power of God is being manifest today in fulfilling the great prophecies of the restoration of all things in the latter days. The God of Abraham, Isaac and Jacob lives today, and is revealing his secrets to his servants, his prophets. The pure and undefiled gospel of Jesus Christ has been restored to the earth. God has cut the stone out of the mountain, and it is now rolling forth, beginning to fill the whole earth. That stone is The Church of Jesus Christ of Latter-day Saints—the kingdom of God on earth.

CHAPTER 11

The Book of Mormon—Another Testament of Jesus Christ

A. Publication of the Book of Mormon.

In 1829 Joseph Smith completed the translation of the gold plates. About the translating process, Joseph said that the plates were translated by the gift and power of God, through his use of the Urim and Thummim that had been placed in the stone box with the gold plates.[46] In translating, Joseph would dictate the translated messages to a scribe. Oliver Cowdery acted as scribe for almost all of the translation.

After the translation was completed, Joseph arranged for it to be printed by Egbert B. Grandin, of Palmyra, New York. Martin Harris mortgaged his farm to pay for the printing costs. Five thousand copies were printed for $3,000. The printing was completed in 1830. The book was published with the title: *The Book of Mormon*. Later the descriptive subtitle was added: *Another Testament of Jesus Christ*.

The name "Mormon" was used in the title because the gold plates

---

[46] This is a different Urim and Thummim from the one possessed by Moses and Aaron (Exodus 28:30; and *Book of Mormon*, Ether 3:23).

were anciently designated the "Plates of Mormon." Mormon was the father of Moroni—both were prophets of God. Mormon is the one who made the gold plates, and he is the principal writer on the plates; he made an abridgement of the historical and religious records of his people, which covered a thousand-year period of history of his people. Mormon died shortly after 385 A.D. His son, Moroni, completed the abridgement and hid it in the stone box where Joseph Smith later retrieved it.

B. How to Prove Whether or Not the Book of Mormon Is the Word of God.

Jesus taught that the Comforter, whom he would send after his departure, would testify of him and would help us discern truth from falsehood (John 15:26). More than once Jesus referred to the Comforter as "the Spirit of truth," and he taught that "when he, the Spirit of truth, is come, he will guide you into all truth, . . . and he will shew you things to come" (John 16:13). Shortly after the ascension of Jesus, on the Day of Pentecost, about three thousand souls were baptized and added to the disciples of Christ after they listened to the preaching of Peter and were "pricked in their heart[s]" by the Holy Ghost, who came as Jesus had promised (Acts 2:37).

Just as these souls knew that the words of Peter were true because of the witness of the Spirit of God, so we can know the divinity of a message by the accompanying, confirming witness of the Holy Ghost.

But, of course, sometimes people reject the witness of the Holy Ghost, just as the Jews did after Stephen had called them to repentance. "Ye do always resist the Holy Ghost," Stephen told the multitude (Acts 7:51). But they still rejected his words, wrongfully accused him of sin, and moved by the spirit of the devil, they stoned him to death.

The test for us is identical to the one faced by those who listened to Peter and to Stephen. In both instances the Holy Ghost bore witness of the divinity of the words spoken by God's messengers. Some people gladly accepted the message, while others resisted the Holy Ghost.

To this point, I have been speaking about a person's testing the message to determine whether or not it is divine. But, of course, from God's perspective it is we that are being tested, not him and not his message. Jesus did not fail when many people rejected him and his message. Of course not! It was the people who failed by rejecting him.

Is it not a sad irony that the people who rejected, condemned and executed Jesus (for committing blasphemy, for declaring himself to be the Son of God [John 19:7]), were God's chosen people—the very nation that had guarded and preserved the holy scriptures. Jesus brought this hypocrisy directly to their attention when he said:

> And ye have not his word abiding in you: for whom he hath sent, him ye believe not.
>
> [Ye] search the scriptures; for in them ye think ye have eternal life: and they are they which testify of me.
>
> And ye will not come to me, that ye might have life. (John 5:38-40)

Jesus then went on to tell the Jews that they really did not believe Moses. How offensive this must have been to the studious Jews, who knew the letter of the law so well and who could cite chapter and verse from the scriptures to support and rationalize their erroneous beliefs. But, of course, as this incident demonstrates, a mere knowledge of the scriptures without an understanding of them by the Spirit of God is not sufficient. As Peter taught, we must understand the scriptures by the Holy Ghost, the same power that moved the prophets to write scripture (2 Peter 1:20-21).

Today, as in Jesus' day and as in the days of Peter and Stephen, it is we the people who are being tested. As foretold by the prophets, the word of the Lord is coming to us today through God's messengers. By our accepting and obeying it we follow Him; but by rejecting and disobeying it we refuse Him. As Jesus instructed his twelve disciples at the beginning of their ministries: "And whosoever shall not receive you, nor hear your words, ... It shall be more tolerable for the land of Sodom and Gomorrha in the day of judgment, than for that city. . . .

He that receiveth you receiveth me" (Matthew 10:14-15 & 40). If we accept and believe Jesus, we will accept and believe his servants. While those who reject and disbelieve Jesus' servants, reject and disbelieve Him.

It is true that while we are judging God's messengers, we are also being judged. We know that by what judgment we judge, we shall be judged; and with what measure we mete, it shall be measured to us again (Matthew 7:1-2). Nevertheless, we still must judge and choose; we cannot escape this test of our own faith and courage. But, fortunately, the way to judge is clear—we must prove all things by the Spirit of God. The ultimate test of truth is whether the Spirit of God bears witness to our souls that it is true. By this standard we know the testimony of the Bible is true; and by this standard we can test the truthfulness of any purported message from God. We must not be like the Jews of old who knew the letter of the scriptures, but who rejected the Spirit of God. We must be like the prophets of old and understand the scriptures by the very power that moved men to write them (2 Peter 1:20-21).

C. The Words of Christ in America.

The Book of Mormon records that heavenly signs appeared in the Americas to announce the birth of the Savior of the world in the land of Jerusalem. One of these signs was a new, bright star. Thirty-three years later the American prophets recorded a cataclysmic destruction that took place throughout their land. Many cities were burned; others disappeared into the sea; and others were buried by upheavals of the earth. A short time after this destruction, to a group of survivors who had gathered at the temple in the city called "Bountiful," the resurrected Savior descended from heaven and appeared to over two thousand people. He showed them the marks in his hands and feet and side. He healed the sick among them and blessed their children. He taught them for several days. This important testament of Jesus Christ is recorded in *The Book of Mormon*. If you do not have a *Book of Mormon*, you should obtain one. And if you have one you should read this account. Judge by the Spirit whether or not the words reported there are the words of Christ.

D.   The Words of Christ Delivered by His Prophets in Ancient America.

---

1. Moroni Saw Our Day in 421 A.D.

After Jesus ended his visit to the ancient Americans, they continued to have prophets to lead them. One of these prophets, Moroni, wrote on the gold plates a prophecy about our day and wrote some counsel for us. Below is a selection of some of his words. Judge by the Spirit whether or not these words are inspired of God:

Just before hiding up the gold plates in the hill in New York, Moroni gave an admonition and challenge to us, the people to whom *The Book of Mormon* would be delivered:

> Behold, I would exhort you that when ye shall read these things, if it be wisdom in God that ye should read them, that ye would remember how merciful the Lord hath been unto the children of men, from the creation of Adam even down unto the time that ye shall receive these things, and ponder it in your hearts.
>
> And when ye shall receive these things, I would exhort you that ye would ask God, the Eternal Father, in the name of Christ, if these things are not true; and if ye shall ask with a sincere heart, with real intent, having faith in Christ, he will manifest the truth of it unto you, by the power of the Holy Ghost.
>
> And by the power of the Holy Ghost ye may know the truth of all things.

And whatsoever thing is good is just and true; wherefore, nothing that is good denieth the Christ, but acknowledgeth that he is.

And ye may know that he is by the power of the Holy Ghost. . . .(*Book of Mormon*, Moroni 10:3-7)

And now I speak unto all the ends of the earth— that if the day cometh that the power and gifts of God shall be done away among you, it shall be because of unbelief.

And wo be unto the children of men if this be the case; for there shall be none that doeth good among you, no not one. For if there be one among you that doeth good, he shall work by the power and gifts of God. . . . (*Book of Mormon*, Moroni 10:24-25)

And again I would exhort you that ye would come unto Christ, and lay hold upon every good gift, and touch not the evil gift, nor the unclean thing. . . .

Yea, come unto Christ, and be perfected in him, and deny yourselves of all ungodliness; and if ye shall deny yourselves of all ungodliness and love God with all your might, mind and strength, then is his grace sufficient for you that by his grace ye may be perfect in Christ; and if by the grace of God ye are perfect in Christ, ye can in nowise deny the power of God.

And now I bid unto all, farewell. I soon go to rest in the paradise of God, until my spirit and body shall again reunite, and I am brought forth triumphant through the air, to meet you before the pleasing bar of the great Jehovah, the Eternal Judge of both quick and dead. Amen. (*Book of Mormon*, Moroni 10:30, 32 & 34)

Those who truly thirst to hear the word of God will become immersed in reading *The Book of Mormon* as their thirst is being quenched. The reading of that book has transformed the lives of millions of people as the Spirit enlightens their minds and makes their souls yearn to serve God and their fellow man.

Those who hunger and thirst to hear more of the word of God will find *The Book of Mormon* to be a hard book to put down. A friend of mine who was recently introduced to it read it steadily for hours, until he completed it three days later. When he emerged from the experience, his desires had been sanctified and he had become committed to put away his sins and to dedicate his life to doing God's will.

2. Nephi Saw Our Day in 556 B.C.

Of course, not everyone is anxious to read *The Book of Mormon*. Some people even receive it with anger and contempt. To them the prophet Nephi addressed this message, as he foresaw in vision the cold reception that the book would receive by many who should have cherished and embraced it:

> [B]ehold, I prophesy unto you concerning the last days; concerning the days when the Lord God shall bring these things forth unto the children of men. . . .
> And the Gentiles are lifted up in the pride of their eyes, and have stumbled, because of the greatness of their stumbling block, that they have built up many churches; nevertheless, they put down the power and miracles of God, and preach up unto themselves their own wisdom and their own learning, that they may get gain and grind upon the face of the poor. (*Book of Mormon*, 2 Nephi 27:14 & 20)

> For it shall come to pass in that day that the churches which are built up, and not unto the Lord, . . .
> For behold, at that day shall he [the devil] rage in the hearts of the children of men, and stir them up to anger against that which is good. . . .

Yea, wo be unto him that hearkeneth unto the precepts of men, and denieth the power of God, and the gift of the Holy Ghost!

Yea, wo be unto him that saith: We have received, and we need no more!

And in fine, wo unto all those who tremble, and are angry because of the truth of God! For behold, he that is built upon the rock receiveth it with gladness; and he that is built upon a sandy foundation trembleth lest he shall fall.

Wo be unto him that shall say: We have received the word of God, and we need no more of the word of God, for we have enough!

For behold, thus saith the Lord God: I will give unto the children of men line upon line, precept upon precept, here a little and there a little; and blessed are those who hearken unto my precepts, and lend an ear unto my counsel, for they shall learn wisdom; for unto him that receiveth I will give more; and from them that shall say, We have enough, from them shall be taken away even that which they have. . . . (*Book of Mormon*, 2 Nephi 28:3, 20 & 26-30)

Thou fool, that shall say: A Bible, we have got a Bible, and we need no more Bible. Have ye obtained a Bible save it were by the Jews?

Know ye not that there are more nations than one? Know ye not that I, the Lord your God, have created all men, and that I remember those who are upon the isles of the sea; and that I rule in the heavens above and in the earth beneath; and I bring forth my word unto the children of men, yea, even upon all the nations of the earth?

Wherefore murmur ye, because that ye shall receive more of my word? Know ye not that the testimony of two nations is a witness unto you that I am God, that I remember one nation like unto another? Wherefore, I speak the same words unto one nation like unto another. And when the two nations shall run together the testimony of the two nations shall run together also.

And I do this that I may prove unto many that I am the same yesterday, today, and forever; and that I speak forth my words according to mine own pleasure. And because that I have spoken one word ye need not suppose that I cannot speak another; for my work is not yet finished; neither shall it be until the end of man, neither from that time henceforth and forever.

Wherefore, because that ye have a Bible ye need not suppose that it contains all my words; neither need ye suppose that I have not caused more to be written. (*Book of Mormon*, 2 Nephi 29:6-10)

And now, my beloved brethren, and also Jew, and all ye ends of the earth, hearken unto these words and believe in Christ; and if ye believe not in these words believe in Christ. And if ye shall believe in Christ ye will believe in these words, for they are the words of Christ, and he hath given them unto me; and they teach all men that they should do good.

And if they are not the words of Christ, judge ye— for Christ will show unto you, with power and great glory, that they are his words, at the last day; and you and I shall stand face to face before his bar; and ye shall know that I have been commanded of him to write these things, notwithstanding my weakness. (*Book of Mormon*, 2 Nephi 33:10-11)

LAKE ONTARIO

ROCHESTER

o Palmyra
✝ Hill Cumorah

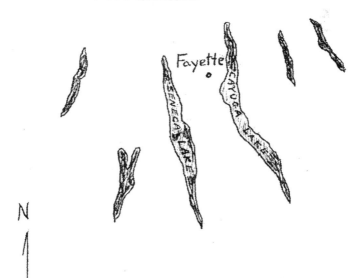

Fayette
o

SENECA LAKE

CAYUGA LAKE

N

THE FULFILLMENT

PART III

MESSAGES FROM CHRIST 1830-1836

CHAPTER 12

God Sets Up His Kingdom on Earth

In giving an inspired interpretation of King Nebuchadnezzar's dream of a stone "cut out of the mountain without hands" (Daniel 2:45), Daniel prophesied that "in the latter days" "shall the God of heaven set up a kingdom, which shall never be destroyed, . . . and it shall stand for ever" (Daniel 2:28 & 44). Although the stone or kingdom would start small, Daniel saw that in the dream it rolled forth and "became a great mountain, and filled the whole earth" (Daniel 2:35).

You may recall that we discussed another aspect of the prophecy about this kingdom in pointing out that God would send to the earth "the Ancient of days" and other messengers to work in this kingdom prior to Jesus' Second Coming. (See Daniel 7:22 and chapters 2 and 4, above.) *Has Daniel's prophecy of God's setting up a kingdom in the latter days been fulfilled? If so, what events fulfilled it?*

The part of Daniel's prophecy about God's setting up a kingdom has been fulfilled. The part of that prophecy about the kingdom's filling the whole earth has not been fulfilled, but is in the process of being fulfilled.

A. Messages from God Announce the Setting Up of the Kingdom of God on Earth.

Messages from God to Joseph Smith in 1820, 1823-27 and 1829 told him of the forthcoming establishment of the Church and kingdom of God through his instrumentality. The translation and publication of *The Book of Mormon* and the restoration of the Priesthood of God to the earth were essential prerequisites to God's establishing his kingdom on earth; and in one sense these events were also a part of the setting up of the kingdom of God. However, the formal organizing of that earthly kingdom did not occur until 1830.

In April of 1830, the Lord commanded Joseph Smith to organize the Church of Jesus Christ again upon the earth, and the Lord designated April 6, 1830 as the day to do it (*Doctrine and Covenants*, 20:1). Later, the Lord revealed that the church should be called "The Church of Jesus Christ of Latter-day Saints" (*Doctrine and Covenants* 115:4).

In obedience to the commandment of God and by virtue of the authority God had given him, Joseph convened the first meeting of the Church at the home of Peter Whitmer, Sr., in Fayette, New York, a town 25 miles southeast of Palmyra. There were six original members, plus a number of their friends and relatives present at the first meeting. The first six members were Joseph Smith, Jr., Oliver Cowdery, Hyrum Smith, Samuel H. Smith, Peter Whitmer, Jr., and David Whitmer. All of these men were baptized, were given the Gift of the Holy Ghost, and were confirmed members of the Church.

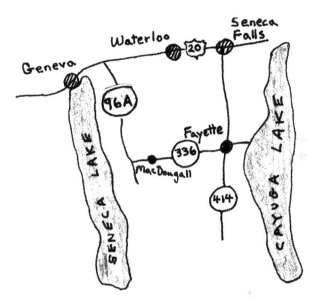

Commenting on the setting up of this kingdom, Joseph Smith said:

> The keys of the kingdom of God are committed unto man on the earth, and from thence shall the gospel roll forth unto the ends of the earth, as the stone which is cut out of the mountain without hands shall roll forth, until it has filled the whole earth. . . .
>
> [B]e prepared for the days to come, in the which the Son of Man shall come down in heaven, clothed in the brightness of his glory, to meet the kingdom of God which is set up on the earth.
>
> Wherefore, may the kingdom of God go forth, that the kingdom of heaven may come. (*Doctrine and Covenants*, 65:2 & 5-6)

B. What Is the Relationship Between This Kingdom and the Existing Christian Churches in the World?

Baptism is the gateway to membership into this kingdom, and so the six original members were each baptized on April 6th, even though they may have already been baptized at an earlier time in their lives (*HC* 1:76; and Joseph Fielding Smith, *Doctrines of Salvation* [Salt Lake City, Utah: Bookcraft, 1955] vol. 2:336). As others desired to unite with the kingdom, some of them desired to do so without rebaptism. But the Lord told Joseph Smith that this was a "new and everlasting covenant," and that even though an individual may have been previously baptized, he must be baptized again at the hands of a Priesthood bearer of this Church in order to enter into God's kingdom. The Lord said:

> Behold, I say unto you that all old covenants have I caused to be done away in this thing; and this is a new and an everlasting covenant, even that which was from the beginning.
>
> Wherefore, although a man should be baptized an hundred times it availeth him nothing, for you cannot enter in at the strait gait by the law of Moses, neither by your dead works.
>
> For it is because of your dead works that I have caused this last covenant and this church to be built up unto me, even as in days of old.
>
> Wherefore, enter ye in at the gate, as I have commanded, and seek not to counsel your God. Amen. (*Doctrine and Covenants*, 22:1-4)

The Church of Jesus Christ of Latter-day Saints is the kingdom of God, the divine organization to which all disciples of Christ should unite. It is the ensign to the nations—to all disciples of Jesus everywhere—inviting them to come and learn God's ways and to walk in his paths. It is the kingdom to which all of God's disciples in the Christian world today will eventually unite in fulfillment of Daniel's prophecy.

The relationship of this kingdom to the many other Christian churches of today is like the relationship between Jesus' followers and the followers of John the Baptist, about which John said: "He must increase, but I must decrease" (John 3:30). In time, all of Jesus' disciples will gladly unite with this kingdom when the Spirit of God bears witness to their souls that it is in very deed the Kingdom of God on earth. Until that time, this kingdom does not seek to destroy anything good, but merely seeks to promote good, to edify, to uplift, to help succor those who stand in need of succor, and to continue to proclaim to all mankind without apology the divinity of this kingdom.

C. Salvation Is an Individual Matter—
So Why Do We Need a Church?

The need for a definite organization to carry on the work of the Lord is something that is questioned by many people today. Often heard is the statement that it doesn't matter what particular church or denomination one belongs to—or even if one belongs to any organized church at all—as long as one believes in Jesus Christ. After all, it is said, it is Christ's atoning sacrifice, not a church, which saves us from sin.

Salvation is and always has been an individual matter—an individual gift from the Lord, Jesus Christ. But Jesus himself established a church (a divine organization) to carry the gospel message to the world, so that all might benefit from His eternal gospel. The purpose of Christ's Church today is identical to what it was in the meridian of time; its purpose is to do the work of the Lord—to preach the gospel and to administer the ordinances of the gospel to those who believe the gospel. Christ's Church exists to help people temporally and spiritually.

Jesus told his apostles that he would "build up [his] church"

(Matthew 16:17). And Jesus himself called twelve apostles (Matthew 10) and "other seventy" (Luke 10:1) as officers in his church. After Jesus' crucifixion, the apostles further built up the church as the Lord directed them by revelation. Pursuant to this authority, they called other officers in Christ's Church, including bishops (or pastors), deacons, teachers, and evangelists. (See, e. g., Acts 6:1-6; 14:23; 20:17 & 28; 1 Corinthians 12:28-29; Ephesians 4:11-16; Philippians 1:1; and Titus 1:5 & 7).

The apostle Paul anciently wrote to the Ephesians:

> And he gave some, apostles; and some, prophets; and some, evangelists; and some, pastors and teachers;
>
> For the perfecting of the saints, for the work of the ministry, for the edifying of the body of Christ:
>
> Till we all come in the unity of the faith and of the knowledge of the Son of God, unto a perfect man, unto the measure of the stature of the fulness of Christ. (Ephesians 4:11-13)

Thus, Paul taught that the purpose of the Church was: (1) To do God's work (the work of the ministry")—including offering the ordinances of the gospel to all the world and tending to the spiritual and temporal needs of all the saints; (2) To teach the saints the gospel, until they come to a "unity of the faith"; and (3) To "edify" and "perfect" the saints until they attain "the measure of the stature of the fulness of Christ."

While anciently, Christ's Church helped the saints to improve, the Church never fully attained its purpose—I don't believe anyone would dispute this; the preaching of the gospel to the world has not been completed; the saints have not come to a unity of the faith; and the professed "saints" have yet to attain perfection. Thus, the needs for which the church was organized still exist. God has not revealed that a church is no longer needed. On the contrary, He has in our day reaffirmed the need for His true Church to accomplish His work in these three areas.

D. There Is Only One True and Living Church of Christ on the Earth Today.

It must be admitted that it is contrary to God's will to teach false doctrines about Him and about what one must do in order to be saved. God does not approve of false teachers and prophets; he condemns them, because they lead people astray. Obedience to the true gospel of Jesus Christ is essential to salvation.

Although some Christians may shy away from a belief in a "one and only true church," such a belief is nevertheless logical and fully supported by scripture. I cannot look at contradicting doctrines about how to become saved and conclude that they are all good; if they contradict, then only one can be correct, although they could all be wrong.

Because of the enormity of the task to search out the one and only true church among all the Christian denominations, many people shy away from the search altogether. But there is a sound approach to this search that is not overwhelming, but rather is inspiring and motivating. We need not frantically worry about seeking out the true Church; God has promised that every ear shall hear the gospel and that every heart shall be penetrated. Jesus has sent and will send his servants to accomplish this task until every soul has had an opportunity to hear and accept the gospel. Jesus has promised to seek us out—it is our responsibility to prepare ourselves so that when his servants do come, we will receive them and accept the Master's message.

And how can we prepare ourselves? We must come to know God. Christians especially have an advantage in this area because we have the word of God in the Bible to aid us.

Jesus taught that we should come to know God the Father and His Son, Jesus Christ (John 17:3). And Jesus also taught that we can accomplish this by obeying his commandments (John 14:21 and 1 John 2:3). When we keep God's commandments we begin to understand what it is like to live a life of absolute integrity and faith—and as we do this we come to understand some of the feelings and desires that God has. Jesus prayed that all of his disciples might be one with him, just as he was one with God the Father (John 17:11). Obedience to the commandments brings this about.

The course that every one of us should pursue is nothing less than purifying our hearts and our desires so that we rejoice in righteousness and virtue, but never in iniquity. We must cultivate a love in our heart for everyone. And we must pray for God's help in this divine task. The apostle John taught that by keeping the commandments the love of God is perfected in us (1 John 2:5). We must study his word and develop a powerful faith in Him—faith that He will bless us and accomplish His work through us if we will be strict in obeying His commandments. We must be courageous in seeking purity and compassion.

If we will live a VIRTUOUS LIFE and have FAITH IN GOD then we will not be numbered among those about which Jesus said: "of whom ye say, that he is your God . . . ye have not known him (John 8:54-55).

Like death, one never knows when God's messenger will come to us. All we can do is prepare for that moment. One who is so prepared will have a full and successful life, whether the opportunity comes to him in his youth or in his old age; whether in this life or in the next. (See John 5:25; 1 Peter 3:18-19 & 4:6; and 1 Corinthians 15:29). But the pure and undefiled gospel of Jesus Christ will be presented to every soul before the great and last day—God has so decreed. And to us is left the responsibility to prepare and receive it when presented.

Through this approach, the prospect of having to seek out the pearl of great price from among all the rubbish is not overwhelming. Of course we will want to search, and we should. But if we truly come to know God, we will be able to obtain his divine guidance in the search, and we will be able to obtain his confirmation when we find the gem for which we have searched.

We previously discussed the belief prevalent among many people today that salvation can be attained without belonging to any particular church. This is so, they say, "because salvation is an individual matter." But there is a serious flaw in this reasoning that we should recognize.

Of course salvation is an individual matter. Paul counseled that each must "work out [his] own salvation with fear and trembling" (Philippians 2:12). It is Christ's atoning sacrifice that saves us from sin—not a church. But *if* the ordinances of salvation (i.e., baptism and bestowal of the Gift of the Holy Ghost) are essential for salvation; and *if* they may be administered only by one having God's actual authority, *then* we must find an authorized minister of Christ to obtain salvation. And *if* God's true servants may be found only in one particular church, *then* we must find that church to obtain salvation. As will be shown in the following discussion, each of these conditions is necessary—Jesus Christ himself established them.

Consider what the scriptures teach about the importance of authority in the ministry. Didn't Jesus give his apostles power and authority? Of course he did; the power He gave them was real (Matthew 10:1). When Jesus "chose" and "ordained" his apostles, he commanded them to "go and bring forth fruit" (John 15:16). He gave them responsibility to do His work and the power to do it; he gave the twelve "power against unclean spirits, and to heal all manner of sickness" (Matthew 10:1). And later, when Jesus gave his apostles the power that "whatsoever ye shall bind on earth shall be bound in heaven" (Matthew 18:18), wasn't this authority also real? Of course it was.

When the Jews came to John to be baptized, it was because he had God's authority to baptize. Likewise, Jesus sought out John to be baptized—because John had authority to do it. And when John declared that Jesus had greater authority than he—the power to baptize with fire and the Holy Ghost—wasn't John speaking about a real difference between his authority and the greater authority that Jesus had? Of course he was (Matthew 3:11; Mark 1:7 and Luke 3:16).

When the Bible teaches that baptism and conferral of the Gift of the Holy Ghost must be performed by one holding authority from God, this is not meaningless rhetoric; it is the truth. The gentile Cornelius sought out Peter to be baptized because Peter had authority (Acts 10).

The Lord sent Ananias to Saul to heal him and to baptize him because Ananias had God's authority to do these things (Acts 9). When Philip preached and baptized in Samaria (Acts 8), it was because he had been given authority to do so (Acts 6:1-6). But Philip, like John the Baptist, did not have authority to baptize with fire and the Holy Ghost—so he didn't, just like John the Baptist did not confer the Gift of the Holy Ghost. Both of these men knew the limits of their authority, and they would not presume to take upon themselves an authority they did not possess. They knew, as Paul taught the Hebrews, that "no man taketh this honour unto himself, but he that is called of God" (Hebrews 5:4). So how were the saints in Samaria given the opportunity to receive the Gift of the Holy Ghost? The apostles sent Peter and John to Samaria, because they did have the authority to bestow the Gift of the Holy Ghost. Then Peter and John "laid their hands on them, and they received the Holy Ghost" (Acts 8:17).

While Peter and John were in Samaria, Simon the sorcerer recognized the great power that Peter and John possessed, and he offered them money so that he, too, could have this power. But the power of God cannot be bought for money, nor can it be obtained merely because one desires it. Peter rebuked Simon because, he said, "thy heart is not right in the sight of God." "Thy money perish with thee." "Repent therefore of this thy wickedness" (Acts 8:21, 20 & 22).

No man taketh this authority upon himself—one must be "called of God, as was Aaron" (Hebrews 5:4 and John 15:16). And how was Aaron called? God revealed to Moses that authority should be given to Aaron and his sons (Exodus 28:1-3), and that Moses should "anoint them, and consecrate them, and sanctify them, that they may minister unto me [God] in the priest's office" (Exodus 28:41).

The practice of bestowing the priesthood (God's authority) by the laying on of hands was followed both in Old Testament and New Testament times. Like Aaron, so was Joshua called to the priesthood by revelation from God, and the priesthood was bestowed on him when Moses laid his hands on him (Numbers 27:18-23). And so did this same procedure govern the bestowal of priesthood authority in the days of the apostles; that is how Philip and Stephen received their authority (Acts 6:5-6; see also Acts 13:1-3).

Actual priesthood authority was required in New Testament times to perform a valid baptism. That is why Paul re-baptized some saints in Corinth; when he found that certain saints had not received a proper baptism, he re-baptized them (Acts 19:1-5). Neither will a baptism be valid in the eyes of God today, unless it is performed by one having God's authority; the principles of the gospel of Jesus Christ are the same today as they were in the days of the Apostle Paul.

God's authority was real in the past. Ordaining men to the priesthood was not a meaningless act in the days of the apostles. Neither is it a meaningless doctrine today. Finding an authorized servant of Christ from whom to obtain a baptism for the remission of sins was essential for salvation in the days of Jesus and the apostles. And it is essential today. The authorized servants will be found in the true church of Jesus Christ. Thus, the search for individual salvation includes the search for Christ's true church.

Today the priesthood bearers in The Church of Jesus Christ of Latter-day Saints are the only ones on earth possessing this authority. Though this may be a hard doctrine for some to believe, it is nevertheless both plausible and in harmony with the teachings of the Bible. God would not have sent John the Baptist and the apostles Peter, James and John to restore this authority, if it still remained on the earth. As presumptuous as this may appear to some, it is nevertheless the truth; the Spirit of God so bears witness. And we dare not shrink from fulfilling our divine commission to declare these glad tidings to all the world. It is a matter of eternal importance for all.

To some, it is considered prudish or ignorant to declare one's personal religion or denomination to be the *only* one that has a fullness of the truth. Some are offended at such an exclusive belief because it implies that no other denomination possesses God's authority. But there is no need for the disciples of Christ to take offense at this.

In November of 1830, a preacher in Ohio named Sidney Rigdon and over a hundred members of his congregation were baptized into The Church of Jesus Christ of Latter-day Saints by Parley P. Pratt (who had previously been associated with Rigdon). After two weeks of earnest investigation, Rigdon become convinced that this was the true church of Christ restored to the earth. Rigdon had been looking for the true New Testament church that practiced the laying on of hands for the gift of the Holy Ghost and healing of the sick. Rigdon had been a Campbellite minister, but his search led him to part ways with the Campbellites. Immediately following his baptism, Rigdon travelled to New York to meet the Prophet Joseph Smith. After meeting with Joseph Smith, the Lord revealed the following to Rigdon about his previous ministry and about the future work that the Lord had in store for him:

> I say unto my servant Sidney, I have looked upon thee and thy works. I have heard thy prayers, and prepared thee for a greater work.
>
> Thou are blessed, for thou shalt do great things. Behold thou wast sent forth, even as John, to prepare the way before me, and before Elijah which should come, and thou knewest it not.
>
> Thou didst baptize by water unto repentance, but they received not the Holy Ghost;
>
> But now I give unto thee a commandment, that thou shalt baptize by water, and they shall receive the Holy Ghost by the laying on of the hands, even as the apostles of old. (*Doctrine and Covenants* 35:3-6)

As I have reviewed this revelation it has occurred to me that the Lord looks upon the hearts of men; and he knew that the heart of Sidney Rigdon was right—that he desired to further the work of the Lord; and the Lord did not condemn Sidney because he had not previously known the gospel of Jesus Christ in its fullness. Rather the Lord commended Sidney for the work he had done, and called him to an even greater work. Yes, this would mean cutting off his ties with his former church. Yes, this would mean publicly admitting to the world that his former religion did not have the gospel of Jesus Christ in its fullness. Yes, this meant that Sidney Rigdon would hereafter declare to the world that The Church of Jesus Christ of Latter-day Saints was in very deed the kingdom of God on earth. But, again, the Lord did not dwell upon the inadequacies and errors in Sidney's prior beliefs. The restoration of the gospel did not come forth to tear down that which was good, but came forth to increase faith in Christ and to build upon the truths that they already had.

In 1828, the Lord revealed to Joseph Smith that although he would shortly establish again on the earth his divine church organization, it was not his intent to condemn the work of his valiant disciples in the existing corrupted churches. In fact, in the broad sense, Jesus taught Joseph that all of his faithful disciples already constituted his church. Joseph's prophetic mission was not to tear down, but to build up Christ's church. The Lord revealed this to Joseph:

> Behold, I do not bring it to destroy that which they have received, but to build it up.
>
> And for this cause have I said: If this generation harden not their hearts, I will establish my church among them.
>
> Now I do not say this to destroy my church, but I say this to build up my church;
>
> Therefore, whosoever belongeth to my church need not fear, for such shall inherit the kingdom of heaven.
>
> But it is they who do not fear me, neither keep my commandments but build up churches unto themselves to get gain, yea, and all those that do wickedly and build up the kingdom of the devil—yea, verily, verily, I say unto you, that it is they that I will disturb . . . .
>
> Behold, this is my doctrine—whosoever repenteth and cometh unto me, the same is my church. (*Doctrine and Covenants* 10:52-56 & 67)

But the Lord also revealed to Joseph Smith that the divinely restored "church" was His kingdom on earth and that it was established for all of his disciples to unite with, participate in, contribute to, and benefit from. In a revelation to Joseph Knight, Sen., the Lord revealed: "[I]t is your duty to unite with the true Church" (*Doctrine and Covenants* 23:7). In the sense that "church" refers to the organized kingdom of God on earth, there is only one "true and living church upon the face of the whole earth" (*Doctrine and Covenants* 1:30). And that is the organization that the prophet Joseph Smith set up under the inspiration and direction of Almighty God—The Church of Jesus Christ of Latter-day Saints.

And so today, the message from the Lord Jesus Christ is one that invites all to come to Him, to recognize Him and His church and His living prophet. Yes, believing and accepting this message would require one to demonstrate one's belief in this divine work by being baptized into The Church of Jesus Christ of Latter-day Saints at the hands of the Priesthood bearers in the Church as a witness to God and to all the world that he believes this to be true and that he covenants to keep all of God's commandments.

Just as some of the early reformers looked forward to the day when Christ would again manifest himself to set things right in preparation for the Second Coming, so in the early 1800s there were many who were looking for it and who, like Sidney Rigdon, recognized and embraced the message of the restoration when they heard it. Two other individuals who were anxiously looking for the restoration of the kingdom of God to the earth were Wilford Woodruff and Willard Richards.

Wilford Woodruff grew up in Connecticut in the early 1800s and was influenced by Robert Mason, who was known as "old Prophet Mason." Mason taught that "no man had authority to administer in the things of God without revelation from God; that the modern religious societies were without that authority;" and "that the time would come when the true Church would be established" (HC 3:337). Woodruff believed this and prayed for the coming of a divine messenger to do it. In 1830 he was impressed that God was about to set up his kingdom.

Then, in 1833, at the age of 26, when he and his brother heard the gospel taught, he and his brother both immediately read *The Book of Mormon*, believed the message, and were baptized two days later (*Id.*).

In 1835, at the age of 31, Willard Richards was practicing medicine near Boston. From his youth he had been intensely interested in religion. He became convinced that all existing Christian sects were wrong, but he believed that God would soon set up a church on earth that would teach the whole truth. In the summer of 1835 a copy of *The Book of Mormon* came into his hands. He read it twice, then sought out the Elders of the Church to make a more thorough investigation of this work. Thereafter, he concluded that this was the work of God for which he had been looking, and he was then baptized by the Elders (*Id.*, 2:470).

Just as ancient Israel fell away from the truth and from the true and living God, so did early Christianity fall away from the truth. And just as God called prophets anciently to set things right, so did He in our day call the prophet Joseph Smith to be an instrument in His hands through whom He restored His Gospel and His authority to the earth.

CHAPTER 13

God Sends His Messengers to All the World

I n April, 1830, another stone was laid in the foundation of the great latter-day restoration. The Priesthood of God had been restored to the earth in 1829; the translation of *The Book of Mormon* was completed in 1829, and in 1830, 5,000 copies of the book came off the press; and then on April 6, 1830, the Lord directed Joseph Smith to formally organize the Church of Jesus Christ again upon the earth. At this point the restoration of all things had not yet occurred, but the small "stone" had been "cut out of the mountain" and was ready to roll forth to fill the whole earth.

The next step in the Lord's work was to roll the stone forward; and for this the Lord called many messengers to announce to the world the occurrence of these great events and to begin to gather the elect from the four quarters of the earth.

A. God Promised to Send Many Messengers in the Last Days.

The participation of *many* messengers was foretold in numerous ancient prophecies. Isaiah foretold that God would send "messengers" in the last days to gather scattered Israel "one by one" (Isaiah 27:12; see also Isaiah 18:2-8 & 66:19). And Jeremiah prophesied that God would set up new "pastors" after his own heart to lead Israel in the last days (Jeremiah 3:15), and that God would send "many fishers" and "many hunters" to gather Israel in the last days (Jeremiah 16:16).

B.   God Chooses and Authorizes His Messengers.

So, who became God's many messengers? Those whom God called and ordained. Not just anyone could be a messenger; first and foremost, God's messengers had to be selected and authorized by God. Just as Jesus told his original apostles: "Ye have not chosen me, but I have chosen you, and ordained you" (John 15:16). And, as Paul wrote to the Hebrews: "And no man taketh this honour unto himself, but he that is called of God, as was Aaron" (Hebrews 5:4). A person's desires to be a messenger is not enough to qualify him to be such—God must appoint the messenger if he is really to be God's messenger.

The same controls have continued to be practiced by the Lord in the last days. The Lord told Joseph Smith: "[I]t shall not be given to any one to go forth to preach my gospel, or to build up my church, except he be ordained by some one who has authority" (*Doctrine and Covenants* 42:11). Joseph Smith taught that the principles that governed the transfer of God's priesthood in the Bible continued in effect: "A man must be called of God by prophecy and by the laying on of hands by those who are in authority to preach the gospel and administer in the ordinances thereof" (*Pearl of Great Price*, Fifth Article of Faith, p. 60).

The need for such restrictions in the transfer of God's authority should be self-evident. If the messengers are to be God's messengers, then God must do the appointing. No one can appoint himself to be the agent for another, and certainly not for God.

Despite these restrictions and controls, God nevertheless did call hundreds of messengers to proclaim his messages to the world. And he gave these messengers his priesthood—the authority to speak and act in his name. And the Lord instructed them that part of their message was to declare their authority to the world. There was to be no mistake about who His messengers claimed to be. The Lord's servants were to work in an open and straightforward manner—not by trickery nor cleverness nor by the sophistry of men—but in perfect plainness. God's messengers were to plainly announce their authority, and the Holy Ghost would witness to the souls of the hearers that it was true. During Jesus' ministry, he told the disbelieving Jews: "And ye have not his word abiding in you: for whom he hath sent, him ye believe not" (John 5:38). The Lord has never changed this pattern for declaring his messages. In modern times, like in Jesus' day: "He that receiveth whomsoever [Christ] send[s] receiveth [Christ]" (John 13:20). And he that rejects Christ's messengers, of whom the Holy Ghost bears witness, rejects Christ.

C. God Introduces His Modern Messengers and Sends an Invitation and a Warning to the World.

In 1830 and 1831, the Lord sent out dozens of messengers to proclaim his word to the world. And the Lord continued to reveal new and explanatory truths to Joseph Smith and the other disciples. In 1831, the Lord commanded Joseph Smith to compile many of these revelations into a separate book, which he did, and which is known today as *The Doctrine and Covenants*. In November, 1831, in Hiram, Ohio, the Lord revealed to Joseph Smith a preface to this book. This revelation includes an invitation to all the world to come unto Christ, and it is a statement of the authority of God's latter-day servants:

> And the voice of warning shall be unto all people, by the mouths of my disciples, whom I have chosen in these last days.
>
> And they shall go forth and none shall stay them for I the Lord have commanded them.
>
> Behold, this is mine authority, and the authority of my servants . . . .

Wherefore the voice of the Lord is unto the ends of the earth, that all that will hear may hear. . . .

And the arm of the Lord shall be revealed; and the day cometh that they who will not hear the voice of the Lord, neither the voice of his servants, neither give heed to the words of the prophets and apostles, shall be cut off from among the people. (*Doctrine and Covenants* 1:4-6, 11 & 14)

D. Fulfillment of Moses' Prophecy that God Would Raise Up a Prophet Like Him.

This modern revelation gives additional meaning to a prophecy of Moses about a latter-day messenger; this is a prophecy that we alluded to at pages 31-36, but we have not yet fully discussed it; yet it is a prophecy that we need to understand because of the warning that it has for us. Here is the text of Moses' prophecy:

I will raise them up a Prophet from among their brethren, like unto thee, and will put my words in his mouth; and he shall speak unto them all that I shall command him.

And it shall come to pass, that whosoever will not hearken unto my words which he shall speak in my name, I will require it of him. (Deuteronomy 18:18-19)

The identity of this future prophet was a puzzle for the Israelites. They understood that the prophet would be an Israelite, since he would be raised up "from among their brethren." And they knew he would be great, because he would be "like unto [Moses]." And they also knew that this prophet's message would be extremely important to heed, because those who would not hearken would be punished. When Peter quoted this prophecy in Acts 3:22-23, he used stronger words for the warning part of that prophecy; he said that "every soul, which will not hear that prophet, shall be *destroyed* from among the people" (Acts 3:23 [emphasis added]).

In the days of Jesus and John the Baptist, the Jews were curious to know whether Jesus or John might be "that prophet." John told the Jews that he was not "that prophet" (John 1:21). But Christ was that prophet, as Peter taught in the third chapter of Acts.

1. Peter Identifies "That Prophet" to Be Christ.

Speaking to the "men of Israel," shortly after the Day of Pentecost, Peter made reference to this prophecy of Moses to warn them that they should repent before it gets too late. Peter said:

> Repent ye therefore, and be converted, that your sins may be blotted out, when the times of refreshing shall come from the presence of the Lord;
>
> And he shall send Jesus Christ, which before was preached unto you:
>
> Whom the heaven must receive until the times of restitution of all things, which God hath spoken by the mouth of all his holy prophets since the world began.
>
> For Moses truly said unto the fathers, A prophet shall the Lord your God raise up unto you of your brethren, like unto me; him shall ye hear in all things whatsoever he shall say unto you.
>
> And it shall come to pass, that every soul, which will not hear that prophet, shall be destroyed from among the people. (Acts 3:19-23)

By implication, Peter identifies Christ to be "that prophet," because it was the words of Christ that he was speaking to them; Jesus was the prophet that was "raise[d] up," both in the sense of growing up and in the sense of being raised up on the cross; it was the gospel of Christ that Peter was preaching; and Peter made it clear that if they did not hearken to the words of Jesus delivered to them by him that they would be "destroyed from among the people."

Thus, while Peter was not "that prophet," he nevertheless was delivering the words of that prophet. And the message of Peter was that those who were hearing him would be destroyed at the last day if they did not hearken to the words of Christ that he was communicating to them.

2. Peter Gives a Broad Meaning to Moses' Prophecy—Peter's Words Must Also Be Heeded!

The agency of Peter and the other apostles is unmistakably established in the New Testament. To the Twelve apostles Jesus said:

> He that receiveth whomsoever I send receiveth me; and he that receiveth me receiveth him that sent me. (John 13:20)

> [I]f they have kept my saying, they will keep yours also. (John 15:20)
> He that receiveth you receiveth me, and he that receiveth me receiveth him that sent me.
> And whosoever shall not receive you, nor hear your words, when ye depart out of that house or city, shake off the dust of your feet.
> Verily I say unto you, It shall be more tolerable for the land of Sodom and Gomorrha in the day of judgment, than for that city. (Matthew 10:40 & 14-15)

Peter understood that those who rejected his words, would actually be rejecting the words of Jesus. And Peter understood that the penalty for rejecting his words as one of Jesus' apostles was the same as for rejecting the words of Jesus himself. Peter knew that he had Jesus' actual authority.

An understanding of the authority of God's agents is every bit as important for us as it is for Peter and all those who are God's agents—because we will be held accountable for accepting or rejecting the words of God's messengers. And, for us, the value of any prophet's words lies in the divine source of those words; that is, the words of the prophets are the words of God. Thus, disobedience to the words of a prophet is disobedience to God, both of which will someday bring God's retribution to the disobedient.

From the historical hindsight that we now have, we know that the fulfillment of Moses' prophecy has not occurred—because those who have rejected the words of Jesus have not all been destroyed.

3. Moroni and Christ Comment on Moses' Prophecy.

If the interpretation of Moses' prophecy was not made abundantly clear by the words of Peter, it has been by the words of divine messengers in our day. When the angel Moroni appeared to Joseph Smith on September 21, 1823, he quoted Acts 3:22-23 to Joseph and explained: "that prophet was Christ; but the day had not yet come when 'they who would not hear his voice should be cut off from among the people,' but soon would come" (*Pearl of Great Price*, Joseph Smith—History 1:40). Later, when Joseph Smith translated the gold plates, he learned that Jesus had taught the same thing to the Israelites in ancient America; Jesus told them: "I am he of whom Moses spake, saying: A prophet shall the Lord your God raise up unto you . . . . And . . . every soul who will not hear that prophet shall be cut off" (*Book of Mormon*, 3 Nephi 20:23).

4. Christ Prophesied that Moses' Prophecy Will Also Be Fulfilled Through the Coming of a Prophet Other than Himself.

Jesus then explained to the ancient Americans that in the last days He would send his "servant" to do a great and marvelous work (*Book of Mormon*, 3 Nephi 21:9-11). Jesus said:

But behold, the life of my servant shall be in my hand . . . .

Therefore it shall come to pass that whosoever will not believe in my words, who am Jesus Christ, which the Father shall cause *him* to bring forth unto the Gentiles, and shall give unto *him* power that *he* shall bring them forth unto the Gentiles, (it shall be done even as Moses said) they shall be cut off from among my people who are of the covenant. (*Book of Mormon*, 3 Nephi 21:10–11)

Thus, Jesus applied this prophecy of Moses to a future divine messenger, as well as to himself. (See also, *Book of Mormon*, 2 Nephi 3:6-15.) This is completely consistent with the way that Peter used Moses' prophecy, for Peter told the men of Israel that the day would come that they would be destroyed if they rejected the words of Jesus that he was delivering to them.

5. The Destruction Predicted by Moses for Rejecting "That Prophet" Is in Large Part the Destruction of the Wicked to Occur at the Last Day.

Jesus taught that the destruction prophesied by Moses will be fulfilled in large part in the same day when the burning prophesied by Malachi will be fulfilled (Matthew 24:51-56; see also D&C 133:63-64). The burning will be a part of that destruction. The Lord says that the destruction will occur because: "[Y]e obeyed not my voice when I called to you out of the heavens; ye believed not my servants, and when they were sent unto you ye received them not" (*Doctrine and Covenants* 133:71).

Further commenting on this day of judgment, Jesus told the ancient Americans that the fulfillment of this prophecy would bring a complete overhaul of society, with all doers of iniquity being uprooted and "cut off" (*Book of Mormon*, 3 Nephi 21:13-19). Jesus said that "all lyings, and deceivings, and envyings and strifes, and priestcrafts, and whoredoms, shall be done away (*Id.*, v. 19).

When all "lyings" and "deceivings" are eliminated, a great host of society will be eliminated with them. When all "whoredoms" are "done away" together with all their participants, another great host of society will be eliminated. Then, in the event there remain any practitioners of "priestcraft" who were not eliminated as liars, deceivers and whoremongers, they will then be eliminated for their counterfeit preaching.

Nephi made this commentary about the day in which Moses' prophecy would be fulfilled:

> For the time speedily shall come that all churches which are built up to get gain, and all those who are built up to get power over the flesh, and those who are built up to become popular in the eyes of the world, and those who seek the lusts of the flesh and the things of the world, and to do all manner of iniquity; yea, in fine, all those who belong to the kingdom of the devil are they who need fear, and tremble and quake; they are those who must be brought low in the dust; they are those who must be consumed as stubble; and this is according to the words of the prophet. (*Book of Mormon*, 1 Nephi 22:23)

6. The Importance of Moses' Warning Today—We Must Heed the Words of God's Messengers Today.

The broadened meaning of Moses' prophecy that Peter and Jesus gave to it has great import for us; when we think of its warning in conjunction with the prophecies of divine messengers to come to earth in the last days, it is clear that we must look for and hearken to the words of God delivered by messengers who will come in the last days.

While the day of destruction spoken of by Moses has not yet come, it will come shortly. And in our day the Savior has called and authorized new apostles and disciples to declare His messages to the world. To these servants and to us, the rest of the world, Jesus has declared their authority and the consequences for failing to heed them:

> And the voice of warning shall be unto all people, by the mouths of my disciples, whom I have chosen in these last days.
>
> And they shall go forth and none shall stay them, for I the Lord have commanded them.
>
> Wherefore, fear and tremble, O ye people, for what I the Lord have decreed in them shall be fulfilled.
>
> And verily I say unto you, that they who go forth, bearing these tidings unto the inhabitants of the earth, to them is power given to seal both on earth and in heaven. . . .
>
> [A]nd the day cometh that they who will not hear the voice of the Lord, neither the voice of his servants, neither give heed to the words of the prophets and apostles, shall be cut off from among the people. . . .
>
> What I the Lord have spoken, I have spoken, . . . whether by mine own voice or the voice of my servants, it is the same. (*Doctrine and Covenants* 1:4-8, 14 & 38)

These words are clear and unmistakable. Let there be no question that the Priesthood leaders in The Church of Jesus Christ of Latter-day Saints do boldly state their authority. We do not aim to offend; but we must give the loud and clear message for which Christ's disciples are seeking—that God has sent new apostles and prophets to the earth again; that he has restored the fullness of his gospel in its purity and beauty.

As one of God's messengers to the world, with all my heart I seek to declare the message with the clarity and dignity it deserves, so that the Holy Ghost can be shed forth in bearing witness to the truthfulness of the message. We do not wish to be overbearing nor to offend; but neither do we dare to allow timidity or fear to divert us from sharing the message with all who will hear us. And so, we attempt to share this message—and some believe it; and others reject it without even finding out what the message is. Some are even anxious to point out the errors of our message without knowing what the message is.

During his mortal ministry, Jesus told the Jews: "He that is of God heareth God's words: ye therefore hear them not, because ye are not of God" (John 8:47). Imagine how offensive this must have been to those who heard him. But Jesus could not alter the truth to make it palatable to those who were steeped in traditions full of falsehoods.

And so today, neither Jesus nor his servants will water down the truth in order to avoid offending. We don't aim to offend; but we cannot say that our message and our divine mandate is anything less than what it is. We strive to declare it in solemnity of heart and in the spirit of meekness; but we will not apologize for or compromise what God has commanded us to declare.

The fundamental question that our message requires one to answer is: Is this message the word of God? Is it divine? By the power of the Holy Ghost, God will confirm the divinity of this message to those who *know* Him and who inquire of Him.

Jesus declared to the Jews that if they knew God the Father, then they would also recognize that he was in very deed their savior. But, he told them, "ye have not known him" (John 8:19 & 54-55). On another occasion Jesus told the Jews that they searched the scriptures because they thought that in them they would obtain eternal life; but, he said, "they are they which testify of me" (John 5:39). Jesus told them that they did not even believe in Moses, who wrote of him. Then Jesus said: "But if ye believe not his writings, how shall ye believe my words?" (John 5:47). Again, Jesus made the point that we have the responsibility to believe the word of God coming from his prophets just as much as if it comes directly from his own mouth. And why is this so? Because the Holy Ghost bears testimony to men of the truthfulness of the word of God from God's own voice as well as from the voice of his servants.

And so we testify that our message is divine. I know that those who are in harmony with the Spirit of God will acknowledge this to be true when it is presented to them in the spirit of love and humility and unshakable firmness.

CHAPTER 14

The Vision of Heaven and Hell—Three Degrees of Glory

While the Bible teaches of "heaven" and "hell," it leaves unanswered many questions about them. Today the different Christian denominations have a variety of different beliefs about them.

On February 16, 1832, in Hiram, Ohio, as Joseph Smith and Sidney Rigdon were studying and pondering the biblical teachings about heaven, they were contemplating the words of Jesus recorded in John 5:29, pertaining to the resurrection. While pondering these things, they saw in vision God the Father and His Son Jesus Christ, after which another glorious vision was unfolded to them. The Prophet Joseph gave the following account of a vision that was unfolded to him and to Sidney Rigdon:

> [T]he Lord touched the eyes of our understandings and they were opened, and the glory of the Lord shone round about.
>
> And we beheld the glory of the Son, on the right hand of the Father . . . .

>And now, after the many testimonies which have
>been given of him, this is the testimony, last of all,
>which we give of him: That he lives!
>
>For we saw him, even on the right hand of God;
>and we heard the voice bearing record that he is the
>Only Begotten of the Father—
>
>That by him, and through him, and of him, the
>worlds[47] are and were created, and the inhabitants
>thereof are begotten sons and daughters unto God.
>(Doctrine and Covenants 76:19-20 & 22-24)

After this vision was closed, another vision was unfolded to Joseph and Sidney in which they saw heaven, and they saw that there were three general levels or glories of heaven. They saw that the righteous and valiant disciples of Christ are received into a **celestial kingdom**; that those who were good and honorable people, but who were deceived by the craftiness of men and who were not valiant in their testimonies of Jesus are received into a **terrestrial kingdom** (of lesser glory); and that those who were evil—who received not the gospel of Jesus Christ and who were liars, adulterers, whoremongers, sorcerers, etc.—they are ultimately received into a **telestial kingdom** (of still lesser glory), after the resurrection and after first having suffered the wrath of God in hell. (See *Doctrine and Covenants*, Section 76.) The above description is a summary—there is a lot more depth and detail described in the written account. Of particular interest to me was the description of the glory of those in the highest kingdom. About them Joseph wrote: "They are they into whose hands the Father has given all things—They are they who are priests and kings, who have received of his fulness, and his glory; . . . Wherefore, as it is written, they are gods,[48] even the sons of God" (*Doctrine and Covenants* 76:55-56 & 58). "These are they whose bodies are celestial, whose glory is that of the sun, even the glory of God, the highest of all" (*Id.*, v. 70). In

---

[47] See also Hebrews 1:2.
[48] See also John 10:30-35 and Psalm 82:6. See also discussion that is to follow and the discussion in chapter 8, section J.

summary, the information that the Lord revealed in this vision can expand and enlighten our understanding of heaven and hell.

A. Hell.

There are in Christianity today a multitude of diverse beliefs about hell, each based on a different way of interpreting the same scriptures. Joseph and Sidney's vision clarifies the truth about hell. This vision teaches that hell is a place of punishment for unrepentant sinners from the time of their death until the time of their resurrection (*Doctrine and Covenants* 76:84 & 104-106). At the time of resurrection, hell will end (verses 104-106), except for the sons of perdition, for whom hell, or the second death (verse 37) will continue.[49] Biblical support for this interpretation can also be found in Psalm 16:10; Matthew 25:41 & 26:24; 2 Peter 2:4; and Revelation 20:13).

Hell, then, is not the final, eternal resting place for the wicked, except for the sons of perdition. Except for those few, all will receive a glorious heavenly reward in the resurrection, differing in magnitude and brilliance according to the difference in the quality of their characters.

---

[49] Satan and a host of angels that followed him in rebellion against God were cast out of heaven and down to earth for a time (Revelation 12:7-15). Their ultimate destiny is to be cast into hell for ever and ever (Isaiah 14:12-15 and Revelation 20:10). Jude describes those who joined Satan in rebellion as "angels which kept not their first estate" (Jude 1:6). The rest of the host of heaven who did not rebel against God in this pre-earth life war have been blessed to come to earth and experience mortality as human beings. And of those, only the sons of perdition will be relegated to never-ending torment in hell. For all the other humans who, after death, are punished in hell (including some very wicked people), their punishment will have an end, and they will be resurrected to receive a reward from God for what good they have done.

In 1829, the Lord revealed to Joseph Smith that "eternal" punishment was synonymous with "God's" punishment—referring to the quality of punishment in hell, rather than to the duration of "eternal" punishment (*Doctrine and Covenants* 19:6-12). Thus, eternal punishment and eternal torment in hell will terminate (Revelation 20:13)—except for Satan, his angels and the sons of perdition (Revelation 20:10 & 14) when the demands of the broken laws have been met and the individual comes forth in the resurrection of the unjust.

B.   Heaven.

The second important teaching that was clarified and developed in this vision was that of the varying levels of heavenly rewards to be bestowed at the Judgment Day according to men's and women's works. While the Bible teaches that men will be judged according to their works (see, e. g., John 5:29; 1 Peter 1:17 and Revelation 22:12), it gives little additional information about the different rewards available or about the qualifications for them. Paul briefly alluded to different degrees of glory in the resurrection when he wrote to the Corinthians:

> There are also celestial bodies, and bodies terrestrial: but the glory of the celestial is one, and the glory of the terrestrial is another.
> There is one glory of the sun, and another glory of the moon, and another glory of the stars: for one star differeth from another star in glory.
> So also is the resurrection of the dead. . . .
> (1 Corinthians 15:40-42)[50]

In his second epistle to the Corinthians, Paul also taught of there being different levels of glory in heaven when he wrote of a man in Christ being "caught up to the third heaven" (2 Corinthians 12:2). The implication from this verse is that there are at least three different heavens or stations within heaven.

Joseph and Sidney's vision taught that even wicked people would ultimately receive heavenly rewards in a glorious "telestial" kingdom for the good that they did. A more glorious heavenly blessing in the "terrestrial" kingdom is to be bestowed on all good and honorable

---

[50] Paul's main theme in this passage has to do with the difference between our corruptible, mortal bodies and the future, incorruptible bodies that we will have in the resurrection. Nevertheless, as Paul said, in the resurrection we will receive bodies of different degrees of glory, just as the sun, the moon and the stars differ in glory.

men and women. And the most prized and the most glorious of all eternal rewards—an inheritance in the "celestial" kingdom—will be bestowed upon all those who were not only good and honest, but who also believed in Christ, who were valiant in their testimonies of Him, who were baptized in His name for the remission of their sins, and who obeyed his commandments. To these valiant disciples of Christ, God promises the greatest of his blessings—to give them "all things" and to bestow on them a "fulness" of His "glory" (verses 55-56 & 59).

Hours could be spent discussing the meaning of the truths revealed through this vision. That will not be undertaken here, since it is the intent of this book only to introduce the major messages that God has revealed in the latter days. However, there is one teaching introduced in this vision about which I will include additional discussion here and in the next chapter—that is the promised blessing that the highest "celestial" blessing is for people to become "gods" (verse 58).

C. The Crowning Heavenly Blessing—A Man and A Wife Can Become Gods.

The Church of Jesus Christ of Latter-day Saints boldly proclaims the divine potential of man, amplifying truths that are taught in the Bible. (See, e .g., Deuteronomy 10:17; Psalm 82:6; John 10:33-36; Romans 8:17; 1 Peter 3:7 and Hebrews 1:14.) Consider some modern-day messages from God that have given further details about the exalted crown in store for the faithful.

At the close of the prophet's account of his and Sidney's vision, he wrote that they were shown other "great and marvelous" mysteries about God's kingdom that they were commanded not to write (verses 114-115). But he wrote that these things would be revealed on an individual basis by the Holy Ghost to his disciples who seek them in faith and purity. One of these truths, I submit, was what Joseph Smith later did write down under the Lord's direction on May 16, 1843:

> In the celestial glory there are three heavens or degrees;

And in order to obtain the highest, a man must
enter into this order of the priesthood [meaning the
new and everlasting covenant of marriage];
And if he does not, he cannot obtain it.
He may enter into the other, but that is the end
of his kingdom; he cannot have an increase. (*Doctrine
and Covenants* 131:1-4)

These verses elucidate two important principles. First, there
are varying degrees of glory and reward even within the celestial
glory, just as there are in the telestial and terrestrial glories.
Second, the most glorious blessing available to mankind in the
hereafter is the opportunity to live with one's spouse eternally
and to continue to enjoy the privilege of having "increase" (i. e.,
exercising procreative powers). Few explanatory details about
this have been revealed, so there remains a multitude of questions
about the specifics of this exalted state. But still, the Spirit of God
witnesses to the divinity of this doctrine. And on an individual
basis, God can reveal more information to those who seek it in
faith and purity (verse 116).

God's promise that we can be "heirs of God, and joint-heirs with
Christ" (Romans 8:17) has more than symbolic meaning; it is literally
true. In the resurrection, not only will we be like him in our immortal
bodies, but we have the potential to be like him in spirit and glory, as
well. (See, e. g., 1 John 3:2-3 and Matthew 5:48; see also Galatians 3:29
& 4:7; Titus 3:7; Hebrews 1:2 & 14; and James 2:5.) This condition of
supreme resurrected glory is referred to as "exaltation."

God has promised to bless his faithful servants with the same
quality of life that He enjoys (Revelation 21:7 and *Doctrine and Covenants*
84:33-38), which is the most sublime expression of Godly love. We
cannot fully comprehend it at this time. And God has revealed that
these crowning blessings of eternal exaltation are made available
only to husbands and wives who are joined together in the true
and everlasting covenant of marriage and who are valiant in their

testimonies of Jesus (*Doctrine and Covenants* 131:1-4 and 132:19-20).[51] The next chapter will continue the discussion of the ordinance and covenant of eternal marriage.

---

[51] The Lord revealed to Joseph Smith that Abraham, Isaac and Jacob have already been resurrected and received inheritance in the highest of God's kingdoms, such that they now are "gods" (*Doctrine and Covenants* 132:37). That there are many "gods" in this sense is consistent with biblical scriptures. (See e. g., Psalm 82:1 & 6; and John 10:30-36.) Undoubtedly, Adam and Eve have also received their crowns of exaltation. However, the fact that Adam and Abraham are now "gods" in one sense does not raise them to the level of "God" as far as man's worship is concerned. Some Mormon critics, who have been overly anxious to criticize the Mormon belief in man's divine potential, have mistakenly claimed that Mormons worship or used to worship Adam. (See appendix C, below.) But this accusation is false; God the Eternal Father and His Only Begotten Son, Jesus Christ, and the Holy Ghost are the only proper objects of man's worship. And, even with regard to those three, the sole ultimate object of all worship is God the Eternal Father, who is the Supreme Being.

CHAPTER 15

The Return of Elijah the Prophet

In December of 1832, the Lord told Joseph Smith that the saints should build a holy temple in the city of Kirtland, Ohio. That temple was built; it was dedicated on March 27, 1836.

On April 3, 1836, following the dedication of the Kirtland Temple, four glorious visions were given to Joseph Smith and Oliver Cowdery in the temple, which include the following:

> The veil was taken from our minds, and the eyes of our understanding were opened.
>
> We saw the Lord[52] standing upon the breastwork of the pulpit, before us; and under his feet was a paved work of pure gold, in color like amber.

---

[52] This was the fourth major appearance of the Savior to Joseph Smith, each of which revealed significant doctrinal truths to Joseph Smith. Joseph's first vision (1820) was to call him to be a prophet, to teach him the true nature of God, to explain that existing Christian denominations had been corrupted, and to announce the forthcoming restoration of the pure gospel of Jesus Christ. When the Savior appeared to Joseph Smith and Sidney Rigdon in Hiram, Ohio on February 16, 1832, the Savior revealed to them that people will attain different degrees of glory in heaven according to the quality of the character that they develop in this life and according to how valiant they were in the testimony of Jesus. (See chapter 14, above and *Doctrine and Covenants* Section 76.) On January 21, 1836, the Lord appeared to Joseph in the Kirtland Temple and told him: "All

His eyes were as a flame of fire; the hair of his head was white like the pure snow; his countenance shone above the brightness of the sun; and his voice was as the sound of the rushing of great waters, even the voice of Jehovah, saying:

I am the first and the last; I am he who liveth, I am he who was slain; I am your advocate with the Father. . . .

For behold, I have accepted this house, and my name shall be here; and I will manifest myself to my people in mercy in this house. . . .

After this vision closed, the heavens were again opened unto us; and Moses appeared before us, and committed unto us the keys of the gathering of Israel from the four parts of the earth, and the leading of the ten tribes from the land of the north.[53]

After this, Elias appeared, and committed the dispensation of the gospel of Abraham, saying that in us and our seed all generations after us should be blessed.

After this vision had closed, another great and glorious vision burst upon us; for Elijah the prophet,

---

who have died without a knowledge of this gospel, who would have received it if they had been permitted to tarry, shall be heirs of the celestial kingdom of God (*Doctrine and Covenants* 137:7). This next appearance of the Savior, on April 3, 1826 (as will be explained in this chapter), was in connection with the restoration of special authority held by several ancient prophets.

None of these above-mentioned appearances is the Second Coming in the clouds of heaven (1 Thessalonians 4:16-17) that "all flesh" shall see "together" (Isaiah 40:5 & 52:10; and Matthew 24:30)—but all were preparatory to it. This appearance in the Kirtland Temple in 1836 was in fulfillment of Malachi's prophecy that "the Lord, whom ye seek, shall suddenly come to his temple" (Malachi 3:2), an event to occur before the Second Coming.

[53] The keys to the gathering of Israel encompasses the authority to preach the gospel of Jesus Christ to all the earth. This dispensation from heaven inaugurated the gathering of Israel from the four quarters of the earth.

who was taken to heaven without tasting death, stood before us, and said:

Behold, the time has fully come, which was spoken of by the mouth of Malachi—testifying that he [Elijah] should be sent, before the great and dreadful day of the Lord come—

To turn the hearts of the fathers to the children, and the children to the fathers, lest the whole earth be smitten with a curse—

Therefore, the keys of this dispensation are committed into your hands; and by this ye may know that the great and dreadful day of the Lord is near, even at the doors. (*Doctrine and Covenants* 110:1-16)

These heavenly manifestations in the Kirtland Temple were the fulfillment of two specific prophecies of Malachi about messengers coming to the earth in the last days. Malachi had said that the Lord would send "Elijah, the prophet, before the coming of the great and dreadful day of the LORD" (Malachi 4:5). And Malachi had also prophesied that the Lord himself "would suddenly come to his temple, even the messenger of the covenant" (Malachi 3:1). Let's examine these appearances and these messages a little more closely.

A. The Temple of God—A Place Where God Can Manifest Himself to His People.

Anciently, the children of Israel built a portable temple, called a tabernacle, that they carried with them as they journeyed in the wilderness for 40 years (Exodus 25-27). And after Israel settled in the land of Canaan, the Lord commanded them to build a more permanent structure for a temple (2 Samuel 7:5 and 1 Kings 6). This became known as Solomon's Temple.

The Lord called the temple his "house," and the Israelites called it "the house of the Lord." (See e. g., 2 Samuel 7:5 and 1 Kings 7:51.) Both the tabernacle and Solomon's Temple were sanctuaries where the Lord could and would come (Deuteronomy 31:15; Exodus 29:43; 2 Samuel 7:5 and 1 Kings 9:3).

Like the temples of ancient Israel, the building of the Kirtland Temple was also done by the Lord's commandment and according to His directions. And once completed, it too, was the Lord's "house"; it too was a holy sanctuary where God could come and dwell. Thus, God commanded that it be kept holy. In the event that unholy or wicked people should manage to get in it, they would neither see the Lord nor be with Him because their presence would defile the temple and make it unhallowed, so that God would not dwell there.

B. The Temple of God—A Place for Sacred Ordinances.

Anciently, the temple was a place for the performance of sacred ordinances and ceremonies. (See, e. g., Luke 1:8-9 and 2:24.) And John the Revelator prophesied of the day when the saints would serve God "day and night in his temple" (Revelation 7:15). In our day, after the completion and dedication of the Kirtland Temple, on April 3, 1836, the Lord restored to the earth special authority and special instructions by which important ordinances can be performed in modern day temples.

C. The Crowning Ordinances of the Gospel Are Administered in the Temple.

Baptism into The Church of Jesus Christ of Latter-day Saints is the gateway to the kingdom of God. It is the gate to the path that leads to Eternal Life. But while baptism is the first ordinance of the gospel, it is not the only ordinance of the gospel. The crowning ordinances of the gospel are performed only in God's holy temples. These ordinances include the ordinance and covenant of eternal marriage (through which couples are sealed together for time and all eternity) and the ordinance of sealing children to parents.

The predominant practice of virtually all Christian denominations today is to unite a man and woman in marriage "until death do you part." Do you realize that this termination clause is not found anywhere in the Bible? Jesus said this regarding marriage: "What therefore God hath joined together, let not man put assunder" (Mark 10:9). But I know of only one Christian religion today that performs marriages to endure for time and eternity—that is The Church of Jesus Christ of Latter-day Saints, whose leaders perform this ordinance by virtue of the power restored by Elias and Elijah on April 3, 1836.

D. A Husband and Wife Can Be "Heirs Together" of Eternal Life

Peter wrote that the divine potential of a husband and wife was to be "heirs together of the grace of life" (1 Peter 3:7). The saints of God are the heirs of eternal life; and faithful husbands and wives will be "heirs" of eternal life "together." By teaching this, Peter taught that the marriage union was meant to endure eternally. Paul also taught this when he wrote, "neither is the man without the woman, neither the woman without the man, in the Lord" (1 Corinthians 11:11). But no passage of the Bible says that a couple joined together in an eternal marriage by God would have to be separated in the resurrection.

E. "In the Resurrection They Neither Marry nor Are Given in Marriage."

One scripture that has been sometimes misapplied to discredit the belief in eternal marriage is Jesus' statement: "For in the resurrection they neither marry nor are given in marriage" (Matthew 22:30). Does this statement contradict what Peter and Paul taught? No. Jesus did not say that marriages would not endure past death and into the resurrection; rather he said that they would not "marry" nor be "given in marriage" in the resurrection. Jesus did not say that no marriages would continue in the resurrection. A close look at this passage supports this interpretation.

To understand Jesus' statement, you must keep in mind the context of the dialogue in which it occurs. Jesus made his statement in response to a trick question that the Sadducees put to him; the Sadducees, who did not believe in the resurrection, posed a question to Jesus that was geared to make both the doctrine of the resurrection and the doctrine of eternal marriage look ridiculous; they presented Jesus with the unlikely, but possible hypothetical of a woman who was in turn married to seven brothers, not having children by any of them. In such a case, they asked, to which of the seven would she be married in the resurrection? The Sadducees were not only trying to ridicule the resurrection, but also the doctrine of marriage that would continue after death. The Sadducees, however, premised their question on the assumption that the eternal companionship question had not been resolved before the woman and the brothers died.

The trick behind this question was that it sought to elicit an answer from Jesus that would require him to repudiate either the doctrine of the resurrection or the doctrine of eternal marriage. They thought they had Jesus trapped: If Jesus affirmed the reality of the resurrection, then the Sadducees reasoned that it would result in an absurdity—for the woman to either be married to seven men or she would have to choose to which of the brothers she would be married in the resurrection. On the other hand, if Jesus were to avoid this absurdity by denying the resurrection, then the Sadducees would still have Jesus beat because a denial of the resurrection was an implicit denial of eternal marriage. They thought they had Jesus in checkmate.

But the Sadducees were so lacking in understanding that their supposed trap only ensnared themselves. Armed with the truth, Jesus turned the tables; He first responded: "Ye do err, not knowing the scriptures, nor the power of God" (Matthew 22:29). Not only did the Sadducees err in denying the resurrection, but they also erred in failing to understand the purposes and procedures behind God's commandment that if a deceased man was childless that his brother should raise up seed in the deceased's name with his widow (Deuteronomy 25:5-10). Any subsequent, earthly marriage was not intended to endure eternally—it was only a temporary, earthly marriage to raise up seed for the deceased brother; those children would eternally belong to the wife and the first husband.

Such a marriage was limited in purpose and differed from an eternal marriage for time and eternity.

One of the errors in the Sadducees' hypothetical was that they did not understand that the commandment for brothers to raise up seed to a deceased brother was originally premised on the existence of an eternal marriage between the wife and their brother, the first husband. Since the Sadducees' hypothetical omitted this, it demonstrated their ignorance of the scriptures.

From the point of view of the other brothers who each subsequently married the first brother's wife, this arrangement was not unfair because such a temporary marriage did not preclude them from making an eternal marriage with another woman, by whom they could raise up seed for themselves. (Historically, polygamy was an acceptable practice among Israelites. Abraham, Jacob, Moses, Gideon, David and Solomon all had multiple wives. See also, Deuteronomy 21:15-17 and 17:17.)

So, returning again to Jesus' dialogue with the Sadducees, their hypothetical presumed that none of the seven marriages was sealed eternally—that they were all "until death do you part." If that were the case, then, as Jesus taught, they would neither "marry" nor be "given in marriage" in the resurrection. After the resurrection, it would be too late.

F. The Restoration of the Doctrine and Ordinance of Eternal Marriage.

The Lord made known to the prophet Joseph Smith that eternal marriages are made only when performed by a servant of God possessing the sealing power and only when the couple enters into and abides by a special covenant, called the "Abrahamic covenant," in which they promise to love and serve God with all their heart. Elias restored this covenant on April 3, 1836.

1. Elias Restored the Covenant of Abraham.

The man Elias who appeared to Joseph and Oliver is not to be confused with Elijah, who also appeared later on this same day. This Elias was a prophet who lived in Abraham's era. Elias restored the dispensation of the gospel of Abraham—the ordinances and covenants by which Abraham received the promise from the Lord that he would be a father of many nations with a posterity as numerous as the sands of the sea shore (Genesis 17:4-7 & 22:17).[54] The dispensation

---

[54] The Abrahamic covenant includes the divine authorization for a righteous man to be married to more than one wife when authorized and performed by one holding the keys to this covenant. After Joseph Smith received the priesthood keys to do this, and after the Lord commanded the Church to practice it (*Doctrine and Covenants*, Section 132), plural marriages were performed in the Church until the 1880s. Under the leadership of Brigham Young, Joseph Smith's successor, this practice drew national attention and widespread criticism. In 1878, the U. S. Supreme Court, in *Reynolds v. United States*, 98 U.S. 145, upheld the constitutionality of anti-bigamy laws and rejected the Mormons' argument that the "free exercise" clause of the First Amendment guaranteed them the right to practice plural marriages (polygamy). The Supreme Court differentiated the protection of religious beliefs and religious practices; it said that the First Amendment does not preclude Congress from prohibiting conduct that it believes to be bad, just because a person claims that conduct to be a religious belief and practice. After this decision, additional anti-bigamy laws with harsher penalties were enacted. In 1885, the Idaho Legislature passed a law disenfranchising all people who taught polygamy, whether or not they practiced it. The U. S. Supreme Court upheld the constitutionality of this law in February, 1890. In 1887, Congress passed the "Edmunds-Tucker Law," which disincorporated the Church and authorized the federal government to confiscate the Church's property. Thereafter, the federal government did seize the Church property. After having exhausted all avenues of appeal, the Church squarely faced the dilemma of either obeying God or obeying the Constitutional law of the land that the Lord had commanded them to obey (*Doctrine and Covenants* 58:21-22; 98:5-6; and 101:80). Then, in 1890, in response to President Wilford Woodruff's appeal to the Lord for assistance, the Lord revealed to him that the practice of plural marriage should be suspended. President Woodruff then issued a declaration called the "Manifesto," which was sustained by the Church at its October Conference in 1890, and which did suspend the practice of plural marriage. (See, William E. Berrett, *The Restored Church* (Salt Lake City: Deseret Book Co., 1965) pp. 316-320. This suspension does not alter the Mormon doctrine that plural, eternal marriages will exist in the eternities; it

of the gospel of Abraham, restored by Elias, includes the ordinance and divine covenant with God by which a husband and wife are sealed together for time and eternity, and the ordinance and covenant by which family relationships can also continue eternally. (Bruce R. McConkie, Conference Address, April 2, 1983; *Ensign*, May 1983, p. 22; and McConkie, *A New Witness for the Articles of Faith* (Salt Lake City: Deseret Book Co., 1985) pp. 322 & 508.)

2. Elijah Restored the Sealing Power of the Priesthood.

After the vision of Elias closed, Elijah the prophet appeared and committed to Joseph and Oliver the keys of the sealing power of God, whereby *all* ordinances performed on earth, including baptism and conferral of the Holy Ghost, and including the marriage and sealing ordinances restored by Elias, will have efficacy in heaven as well as on earth (*Id.*).

Included in the authority restored by Elijah was the priesthood power by which all ordinances of salvation can be performed for the living and the dead.

G. The Hearts of the Fathers and the Children Shall Be Turned.

You will recall from our previous discussion of Malachi's prophecy (in chapter 2) that Elijah would come again before the Second Coming of the Lord. He prophesied that Elijah would come and "turn the heart of the fathers to the children and the heart of the children to their fathers, lest I come and smite the earth with a curse" (Malachi

---

suspended the practice of a religious belief, but it did not change any doctrine. One application of plural marriage that was not affected by the laws and court decisions in the United States is the provision that if a man's wife dies, he may have another wife also sealed to him for eternity. This, of course, is not a violation of earthly anti-bigamy laws, but it is an ongoing practice of eternal, plural marriage. Except for this one application, plural marriage is not practiced in the Church today anywhere in the world.

4:6). Part of the meaning of this prophecy is that children's hearts are turned to their fathers when they go to the temple of God and there act as proxies in receiving all the ordinances of salvation (including baptism and eternal marriage) in behalf of their ancestors who did not have the opportunity to receive them while they lived. The Lord revealed to Joseph Smith that the fulfillment of Malachi's prophecy was inaugurated with Elijah's restoring the keys of this sealing power to the earth.

With regard to the Priesthood power conferred by Elijah, Joseph Smith explained:

> [T]he earth will be smitten with a curse unless there is a welding link of some kind or other between the fathers and the children, upon some subject or other—and behold what is that subject? It is the baptism of the dead. . . . [F]or it is necessary in the ushering in of the dispensation of the fulness of times, which dispensation is now beginning to usher in, that a whole and complete and perfect union, and welding together of dispensations, and keys, and powers, and glories should take place, and be revealed from the days of Adam even to the present time. (*Doctrine and Covenants* 128:18)

H. The Gospel Will Be Preached to the Living and to the Dead.

We know that God is just and will give all of his children the opportunity to hear the gospel at some time before the resurrection. Jesus and Peter both taught this. John records that Jesus said: "the hour is coming, and now is, when the dead shall hear the voice of the

Son of God" (John 5:25).[55] And lest one might fail to grasp the literal meaning of this prophecy, Jesus went on to say:

> Marvel not at this: for the hour is coming, in the which all that are in the graves shall hear his voice,
>
> And shall come forth; they that have done good unto the resurrection of life; and they that have done evil, unto the resurrection of damnation. (John 5:28-29)

Peter taught that this prophecy had been fulfilled, at least in part, when he wrote:

> For Christ also hath once suffered for sins . . . being put to death in the flesh, but quickened by the Spirit:
>
> By which also he went and preached unto the spirits in prison;
>
> Which sometime were disobedient, when once the longsuffering of God waited in the days of Noah, while the ark was a preparing, wherein few, that is, eight souls were saved by water. (1 Peter 3:18-20)

Peter alluded to this truth again, later in the same epistle, when he wrote: "[F]or this cause was the gospel preached also to them that are dead, that they might be judged according to men in the flesh, but live according to God in the spirit" (1 Peter 4:6).

---

[55] The truth of this principle was confirmed on January 21, 1836, when the Lord revealed to Joseph Smith: "All who have died without a knowledge of the gospel, who would have received it if they had been permitted to tarry, shall be heirs of the celestial kingdom of God; Also all that shall die henceforth without a knowledge of it, who would have received it with all their hearts, shall be heirs of that kingdom; For I, the Lord, will judge all men according to their works, according to the desire of their hearts. And . . . all little children who die before they arrive at the years of accountability are saved in the celestial kingdom of heaven" (*Doctrine and Covenants* 137:7-10).

I.   Baptisms and Other Ordinances for the Dead.

We see that the scriptures make it clear that the gospel will eventually be taught to all mankind—if not on earth during their lives, then later in the world of the spirits awaiting the resurrection. But what about Jesus' commandment that one must be baptized in order to enter the kingdom of heaven—Does it apply to those who have died without having the opportunity to hear the gospel message and accept it through baptism? Yes! God is just and will make this and all ordinances of the gospel available to all of the children either during their mortal lives or in the spirit world through vicarious ordinances that the living perform for their dead ancestors. This was what the apostle Paul was referring to when he wrote to the Corinthians: "Else what shall they do which are baptized for the dead, if the dead rise not at all? Why are they then baptized for the dead?" (1 Corinthians 15:29).[56]

Of course, a vicarious baptism does not guarantee salvation for the dead any more than a living person's baptism guarantees his salvation. Nevertheless, it is an essential ordinance of salvation for all mankind, and it is through the priesthood authority restored by Elijah that we can do this vicarious work today. Since the performance of these ordinances is just as important for our dead ancestors as our own baptisms are for us, we can understand why Malachi said that Elijah

---

[56] The Smith and Goodspeed translation of the Bible renders this verse as follows: "Otherwise what do people mean by having themselves baptized on behalf of the dead? If the dead do not rise at all, why do they have themselves baptized on their behalf?" (From John A. Widtsoe, *Evidences and Reconciliations* [Salt Lake City, Utah: Bookcraft, 1943] p. 100.)

An interesting historical note with regard to this teaching is that Marcion and his Christian followers practiced vicarious baptisms for the dead in the second century. T. Edgar Lyon, *Apostasy to Restoration* (Salt Lake City: Deseret Book Co., 1960), pp. 97-102. The Council off Carthage (397 A.D.) denounced any further administration of vicarious baptisms for the dead. Le Grand Richards, *A Marvelous Work and A Wonder* (Salt Lake City: Deseret Book Co., 1950, 1976) pp. 180.

would have to restore this authority to the earth "lest I [the Lord] come and smite the earth with a curse" (Malachi 4:6).

You may recall that Abraham secured great spiritual blessings by virtue of his making a covenant with God and by his keeping his part of that agreement. (See, e. g., Hebrews 11:8-9.) All of the ordinances of the gospel—including the ordinance of baptism—are given to us with an accompanying covenant. The ordinances are symbolic of the eternal blessings that will be ours if we are true and faithful to our part of the covenant. (See also chapter 17 for further discussion of the ordinance of baptism.)

From 1836 until today, and from today until the end of the millennium, faithful couples have and will have the opportunity to enter into the covenant of eternal marriage. They have the opportunity to be married together for all eternity and to have all of their children sealed to be with them eternally, in an eternal, extended family relationship. All may receive this great blessing if they will covenant with the Lord to obey all of his commandments. And for those who receive these exalting ordinances and who are thereafter true and faithful to the Lord, the Lord will fulfill his part of the covenant and grant us eternal life with our spouses and children.

Some Christians who are not Latter-day Saints believe that they will be together with their spouses in the resurrection, even though their churches' doctrines deny this. The Church of Jesus Christ of Latter-day Saints is the only Christian denomination I know of whose doctrine endorses this belief and preaches and practices the way to attain this eternal blessing. The Spirit of God bears witness to all devout followers of Christ that the marriage union is intended by God to endure eternally. How can any couple who believes that their marriage can continue after death be content belonging to a denomination that denies the very possibility of its happening? To those who will hearken unto the Spirit of God, "he will guide you into all truth" (John 16:13), including the true doctrines and ordinances pertaining to eternal marriage.

From 1836 until today, one of the major responsibilities of the saints in the Church of Jesus Christ has been to receive for themselves these sacred temple ordinances, but also to return again and again to the temples to perform these ordinances vicariously for and in behalf of their deceased ancestors. In order to accomplish this, Latter-day Saints diligently seek out genealogical data about their ancestors.

To some, this doctrine of gospel ordinances for the dead seems incredible. But it demonstrates that God means what he says, and that he says what he means. This is the way whereby God gives everyone the opportunity to be baptized into the kingdom of God. If no one can enter into the kingdom of God except he be born of the water and the Spirit (John 3:5), then a just and loving God must provide a way for all of his children to be born again. Vicarious ordinances for the dead are a part of God's plan for giving all of the human race the opportunity to partake of the eternal blessings of the gospel of Jesus Christ.

Some are critical of this doctrine because it is so broad in scope—to endeavor to perform baptisms for every soul in the world's existence who has reached the age of accountability and who has not had an opportunity to be baptized is a vast undertaking, involving many billions of people. We recognize all of this. But the worth of every individual soul is great. God's love extends to every living soul the opportunity to receive the blessing of baptism. The enormity of the task is of no consequence; in God's eternal plan he provides this opportunity for every living soul. Just as many people will not have the opportunity to hear the gospel until they get to the spirit world, neither will they have the opportunity for baptism until then. Therefore, God has provided for vicarious baptisms for the dead to bless those who accept the gospel in the spirit world. These spirit world converts will need others who are living on earth to be baptized for them, much like we all needed the Savior to pay the price for our sins in Gethsemane and on the cross.

For those of us here on earth who serve as proxies to perform these baptisms, it is a great spiritual blessing for us to be privileged to go to the House of the Lord and enjoy the presence of His Spirit as we do this holy work. Personally, this service reminds me of my own covenants with God and of the blessings that I have been promised; and my spirit is uplifted and my determination to serve God is strengthened as I review the promises that I have made to Him to serve Him with all my heart.

Perhaps God could say some magic words and accomplish His work in some other way. But His doctrine was never controlled by considerations of expediency and convenience. On the contrary, His gospel recognizes and teaches the value of *every* human soul. It is God's plan to give every soul the opportunity to covenant to serve Him, and in return to obtain God's greatest blessings. Each and every soul will have the opportunity to secure God's covenant blessings—to return back to His presence, if we will. Every single soul is precious in the sight of God.

Individuals are important to Him. He knows each of us by name, and the baptismal covenant of every single person is a great event for God and for that person. A mass baptism would be a convenient way to get it over with, but it would also diminish the beauty and the importance of the covenant for each individual. It would demean rather than honor the souls for whom the ordinances are being performed.

However long it takes to complete this ordinance work for the dead, it will eventually be completed—all will be given the opportunity to accept or reject the gospel of Jesus Christ; and all will be given the opportunity to demonstrate their faith in Christ and their willingness to obey him by entering into the waters of baptism.

In the meantime, the ordinance work continues. Some souls, who accepted the gospel when it was preached to them in the spirit world, rejoice and are blessed by the ordinances that we perform for them here, now. Other souls are still waiting for us to perform this work for them. And in a small way, but in a most important way, I have been able to bring the blessings of baptism to many individuals. The Spirit of God bears witness to my soul that this is true; and His Spirit fills my soul with peace and love as I do my best to help.

The Apostle Paul wrote:

> Eye hath not seen, nor ear heard, neither have entered into the heart of man, the things which God hath prepared for them that love him.
>
> But God hath revealed them unto us by his Spirit: for the Spirit searcheth all things, yea, the deep things of God. (1 Corinthians 2:9-10)

Some of these great and marvelous "things" are available to mankind today, and are revealed to the pure in heart by the Spirit of God as they engage in God's holy work in His temples.

Isaiah prophesied of the day when the earth would be defiled because its inhabitants will have "transgressed the laws, changed the ordinance, and broken the everlasting covenant" (Isaiah 24:5). Today, those who teach that man can be saved merely by believing in Christ, without receiving the ordinance of baptism and without covenanting with God through baptism to obey His commandments—those people have changed the ordinance of baptism, and they espouse a false doctrine which has indeed "changed the covenant."

But the covenant and ordinance of baptism has now been restored, so that we can once again have this ordinance performed in a manner pleasing to our Father in Heaven. And with the return to the earth of the ancient prophets Elias and Elijah, God has also restored to the earth additional ordinances and covenants for the blessing of mankind—both for the living and for the dead. These crowning covenants are for the further growth and blessing of the disciples of Christ in this life and in the world to come.

The Fulfillment

PART IV

MESSAGES FROM CHRIST TODAY

CHAPTER 16

Believe in Christ

From 1820 until today there have been many messages from God to man. There will be many more as the Lord chooses to make His will manifest. However, the most fundamental message—and the one that bears repeating again and again—is that there is a God; that He is the Father of our spirits; that Jesus Christ is His Only Begotten Son; that Jesus Christ is our Redeemer; and that we can return to dwell with God the Father and Jesus Christ if we will (1) believe in Christ; (2) repent of our sins; (3) be baptized for a remission of sins; (4) receive the Gift of the Holy Ghost; and (5) continue to obey the commandments of God.

This chapter and the next four chapters discuss some of the things that we must do to obtain eternal life. These chapters discuss important messages from God for all the world today. First, we will focus on God's commandment that we should believe in Christ.

A.   Conditions of Salvation.

It is believed by some that Christ offers salvation *unconditionally*. Some assume that God loves everyone "unconditionally" and that he offers salvation to everyone "unconditionally." As superficially appealing as a concept of "unconditional salvation" may be, it is not taught in the Bible. Just the opposite is taught—one must believe in Christ to be saved—and that is a *condition*; salvation is conditioned upon faith in Christ. Those who deny that this is a condition of salvation are only fooling themselves.

Paul taught that God sends preachers to teach the conditions of salvation. He wrote:

> For whosoever shall call upon the name of the Lord shall be saved.
>
> How then shall they call on him in whom they have not believed? And how shall they believe in him of whom they have not heard? And how shall they hear without a preacher? (Romans 10:13-14)

If Christ offered salvation without conditions there would be no need to preach the gospel. But there are conditions, and preachers are sent to declare what those conditions are.

When Paul said that "whosoever shall call upon the name of the Lord shall be saved," did he mean that even the man who takes the name of the Lord in vain would be saved by his profanity? Of course not! Any grade school child can understand that the "call upon the name of the Lord" must be done with sincerity. And Paul went on to state that one must first "believe" in Christ before he can "call upon" Christ for salvation. It's not enough just to say some magic words. Word and acts must be accompanied by earnest and faithful intent.

Although some ministers may shy away from talking about "conditions of salvation," they must nevertheless confess that "conditions" are an integral part of their work. If salvation were given without people's compliance with conditions, then there would be no need for either ministers or religion. But there are conditions of salvation, and God sends his messengers to make those conditions known to us.

B.   Salvation is a Conditional Gift.

Some people are uncomfortable with the concept of "conditional" salvation because they think that it implies that salvation can be earned. Salvation cannot be earned. But, the fact that salvation is conditioned upon obedience to the gospel of Christ does not imply that it is earned. No amount of works can "earn" salvation, for it is a gift. (See, e. g., Ephesians 2:8-9.) But God commands us to "work out [our] own salvation" (Philippians 2:12). And we are commanded to be good and to obey God in order to be saved. (See, e. g., John 5:29; Matthew 7:21; Hebrews 5:9 and Revelation 2:23.) The Bible teaches that God's gift of salvation is a conditional gift—conditioned upon obedience to God.

It is contended by some that a "conditional gift" is a contradiction in terms. But this is simply not true. Conditional gifts are a common reality in our society. For example, wealthy people sometimes make donations to charitable institutions with conditions attached, such that the institution must meet the condition in order to obtain and/ or retain the gift. The institution can comply with the condition and obtain the gift, or it can reject the gift. For another example, real property can be conveyed subject to conditions and with a reversion clause. Then, if the conditions are violated the recipient of the gift can lose the property, which can revert back to the giver of the gift. In the law, the existence of conditions does not negate the fact that a gift was given; neither is the gift ever earned by the efforts of the recipient to satisfy the conditions. The condition merely insures that the giver's purposes are served by the gift.

Similarly, the gift of salvation does not cease to be a gift just because God conditions its bestowal upon obedience to His gospel. Salvation remains a gift because no amount of works could ever save a single soul without Christ's atoning sacrifice. There is nothing illogical or contradictory about the gift of salvation being offered conditionally. We should thank God that he has revealed his commandments to us, so that by obedience to them we can satisfy the conditions of salvation and qualify to receive that priceless gem.

Let's now discuss what the Bible teaches about the conditions of salvation.

C.   Belief in Christ—Key to Eternal Life.

Jesus taught that belief in him was the key to eternal life. (See, e .g., John 6:40 &47; and 8:24.) The apostle John echoed this theme in this beautiful and often quoted passage: "For God so loved the world, that he gave his only begotten Son that whosoever believeth in him should not perish, but have everlasting life" (John 3:16). To believe in Christ—to have faith in Him—is the key to eternal life. The belief that John spoke of was not a shallow, uncommitted belief. John remembered well the Lord's condemnation of hypocrites (Matthew 23). John was familiar with what Jesus taught the multitude in the Sermon on the Mount: "Not every one that saith unto me, Lord, Lord, shall enter into the kingdom of heaven; but he that doeth the will of my Father which is in heaven" (Matthew 7:21).

An individual's mere mental acceptance of Jesus as the Redeemer does not guarantee eternal life for him. Neither does lip worship of Jesus secure eternal life for an individual. While we must believe with our hearts and witness to the world with our words that Jesus is the Savior, these acts are not sufficient. The ancient saints knew and the apostles taught that an individual must demonstrate both faith and works of righteousness in order to obtain salvation. Jesus said: "If ye continue in my work, then are ye my disciples indeed" (John 8:31). And to those who may have wanted to believe that faith without the works of faith was sufficient to save, James wrote: "But be ye doers of the word, and not hearers only, deceiving your own selves" (James 1:22). John echoed this when he wrote: "[L]et us not love in word, neither in tongue; but in deed and in truth" (1 John 3:18). John the Baptist, also taught the necessity of living God's commandments when he denounced the unrepentant Pharisees and Sadducees who had come to him; to them he said: "O generation of vipers, . . . Bring forth therefore fruits meet for repentance" (Matthew 3:7-8).

But while mere mental acceptance of the Savior is not sufficient to save, it is nevertheless the indispensable starting point and continuing element of saving faith.[57]

D. Saving Faith—Essential to Salvation.

The "belief" that John said would cause one to obtain "everlasting life" (John 3:16) was that kind of belief and faith that motivates works of righteousness. Of this faith James wrote: "I will shew thee my faith by my works" (James 2:18). There can be no question that saving faith is that faith which is the moving force for good in a person's life—it is the force that makes a saint say: "Regardless of the consequences, I will do what is right. Though I may suffer ridicule, persecution or harm for doing what's right, I will do what's right anyway. I will do the will of God, and let the chips fall where they may." There can be no question that Jesus had this attitude in mind when he spoke of the hypocrites who would be denied entrance into the kingdom of God. Again, I repeat Jesus' warning: "Not every one that saith unto me, Lord, Lord, shall enter into the kingdom of heaven; but he that doeth the will of my Father which is in heaven. . . . And then I will profess unto them, I never knew you: depart from me, ye that work iniquity" (Matthew 7:21 & 23).

The Book of Mormon prophets Amulek, Samuel and Benjamin confirmed what James taught about works of repentance and obedience being a part of faith in Christ. Amulek said that we must "exercise[] faith unto repentance" to be saved (Alma 34:16). Samuel explained that: "if ye believe on his name ye will repent of all of

---

[57] A one-time belief in Christ is not sufficient to save a person. An individual must exercise an enduring faith in Christ. In the parable of the sower, Jesus taught that the seeds that first sprouted on the rock, but later wilted and died under the heat of the day, represent those that "have no root, which *for a while believe*, and in the time of temptation fall away" (Luke 8:13 [emphasis added]). Thus, Jesus taught that it is not enough to just believe "for a while." One must live a life of belief.

your sins, that thereby ye may have a remission of them through his [Christ's] merits" (*Book of Mormon*, Helaman 14:13). And Benjamin summarized it this way:

> Believe in God; believe that he is, and that he created all things, both in heaven and in earth; believe that he has all wisdom, and all power, both in heaven and in earth; believe that man doth not comprehend all the things which the Lord can comprehend.
>
> And again, believe that ye must repent of your sins and forsake them, and humble yourselves before God; and ask in sincerity of heart that he would forgive you; and now, if you believe all these things see that ye do them. (*Book of Mormon*, Mosiah 4:9-10)

Clearly, the saving faith—the saving belief—is that which motivates one to obey the commandments of God and the ordinances of His gospel.

E.   Salvation Comes Through the Grace of Christ.

Through the grace of Christ, God offers to everyone the most choice and desirable of all blessings—eternal salvation and in this life an endowment of God's power (particularly through the Gift of the Holy Ghost). God has sent messengers to the world to declare these glad tidings—to declare that they are available to all, equally and freely, on the conditions of faith, repentance, baptism and receiving the Gift of the Holy Ghost. When we do our best to obey God with all our heart, then God can fill us with divine love and with increased capabilities, by which we can produce works of righteousness. We cannot produce such fruits of righteousness without the grace of God—but neither will God bring them to pass in us without our best effort.

The apostle Paul wrote that "by grace are ye saved through faith; and that not of yourselves: it is the gift of God: Not of works, lest any man should boast" (Ephesians 2:8-9). Some have interpreted this to mean that salvation is not conditioned upon one's repenting of sins and obeying the commandments of God. But Jesus taught that we must obey his commandments in order to obtain salvation and to enter into the kingdom of God. The predominant theme of Jesus' preaching was that we must repent and be good. (See, e. g., Matthew 4:17; 5:5-10, 16, 19-20, 22, 28, 48; 6:14 & 33; 7:1-5, 21-27: 11:20; 12:50; 18:4 & 21-35; 19:16-30; 21:28-32; 22:35-40; 23:1-39; 25:31-46; 28:19-20; Mark 7:20-23; Luke 5:32; 6:27-49; 10:25-37; 11:42-46; 12:5, 16-21 & 41-48; 13:1-5 & 23-24; 24:46-48; John 8:1-11 & 31; 13:34-35; 14:15 & 21; 15:10, 14 & 17; & 21:14-17.)

Jesus taught that God would "reward every man according to his works" (Matthew 16:27). Jesus taught that there will be a judgment, and that "they that have done good" would come forth unto "the resurrection of life," while "they that have done evil" would come forth unto "the resurrection of damnation" (John 5:29; see also Romans 2:6-7 & 13; Galatians 6:7-9; and Revelation 20:12-13, where the apostles Paul and John repeat this teaching). Faith *and* works are conditions to meet to qualify for the gift of salvation. As James wrote: "[B]y works a man is justified, and not by faith only. . . . For as the body without the spirit is dead, so faith without works is dead also" (James 2:24 & 26).

Jesus and his apostles repeatedly preached the *need* to repent and do good. Their teachings leave no room to doubt that faith *and* works of righteousness are conditions of salvation. Nevertheless, neither a person's faith nor his works of righteousness save him. Without Jesus' atoning sacrifice, all faith and works would be for naught. Faith and works are merely two conditions that God has set for us to meet before he bestows the gift of salvation upon us. The fact that conditions are imposed, does not make salvation any less of a gift.

No man can save himself. Works can never earn salvation. It is by the grace of Christ that we are saved, after we do all that we have been commanded to do. (See, e. g., *Book of Mormon*, 2 Nephi 25:23.) Salvation by the grace of Christ through faith is the free gift of God to us (Ephesians 2:8-9). And it is offered on the conditions of our believing in God and obeying his commandments, including the commandment to be born of the water and of the spirit (John 3:5 and Mark 16:16).

The doctrines of repentance, obedience and righteousness are predicated on the agency and accountability of the individual for his own actions. The fairness of the judgment at the last days is also based upon the individual's responsibility for both his successes and for his mistakes. The grace of Christ does not supersede and replace the accountability of the individual. The grace of Christ demonstrates God's faith in us—acknowledging that we can change and become better. The grace of Christ permits the repentant individual to change and overcome sin and return into God's presence, whereas without Christ's grace an individual's sins would be eternal and immovable barriers to one's returning to God's presence.

The Book of Mormon prophet Lehi explained that we must have a repentant heart to partake fully of Christ's grace. He taught:

> Wherefore, redemption cometh in and through the Holy Messiah; for he is full of grace and truth.
>
> Behold he offereth himself a sacrifice for sin, to answer the ends of the law, unto all those who have a broken heart and a contrite spirit; and unto none else can the ends of the law be answered.
>
> Wherefore, how great the importance to make these things known unto the inhabitants of the earth, that they may know that there is no flesh that can dwell in the presence of God, save it be through the merits, and mercy, and grace of the Holy Messiah. (*Book of Mormon*, 2 Nephi 2:6-8)

The notion that God's grace saves a person regardless of that person's actions is a false and pernicious doctrine. Salvation does not come by merely professing with the mouth that Jesus is the Christ, without having to obey any other commandments of God. Those who teach this, teach plain, old hypocrisy—the same hypocrisy that was repeatedly condemned by Jesus and the apostles. Two verses in

Romans, chapter 10, which have sometimes been taken out of context to attempt to establish this false doctrine are verses 9 and 13, which state: "[I]f thou shalt confess with thy mouth the Lord Jesus, and shalt believe in thine heart that God hath raised him from the dead, thou shalt be saved. . . . For whosoever shall call upon the name of the Lord shall be saved" (Romans 10:9 & 13). If these were the only verses in the Bible that talked about how to obtain salvation, perhaps one would be justified in believing that no other requirements for salvation existed. But other verses describe additional requirements for salvation. These other requirements cannot be ignored, just because some verses don't mention them.

The grace of Christ does not eliminate the need to obey God; rather the grace of Christ can most fully bless our lives when we learn to walk in obedience to God. Thus, Peter admonished the saints to "grow in grace" (2 Peter 3:18).

Through Christ's grace, all will one day be resurrected from the dead. Through Christ's grace all may be forgiven of their sins through faith in Him, through repentance, through baptism and through reception of the Gift of the Holy Ghost. Through the grace of Christ, when we do these things God sanctifies us and fills us with the love of God (through the Holy Ghost). And thereby we are enabled to lay hold on eternal life.

Only through Christ's grace are we saved—we cannot be saved without it. But Christ's grace does not do for us what God has commanded us to do for ourselves. The grace of Christ does not sanctify and give eternal life to the unrepentant hypocrite.

F.   Learn the Truth about God.

When Jesus said, "This is life eternal that they might know thee, the only true God, and Jesus Christ" (John 17:3), he introduced a profound and powerful approach to religion. If one compares knowing God with knowing a friend, one realizes that true friends have similar interests and desires; they communicate with one another; they will do things for one another. Don't the same principles apply to our friendship with God and to our knowledge of God? Of course they do.

When Peter admonished the saints to "grow in grace, *and in the knowledge of our Lord and Saviour Jesus Christ*" (2 Peter 3:18 [emphasis added]), he taught that even after being born again we can and should continue to get to know God better. John confirmed this; he taught that the purpose of this life was for us to engage in the continuing process of perfection; he taught the saints that our eternal potential was to "be like him [Christ]," and that "every man that hath this hope in him purifieth himself, even as he is pure" (1 John 3:2-3). This purifying process is one and the same as learning to obey all of God's commandments; and engaging in this purifying process is the way to come to know God. John explained this when he wrote:

> [E]very one that loveth is born of God, and knoweth God.
>
> He that loveth not knoweth not God; for God is love. . . .
>
> And hereby we do know that we know him, if we keep his commandments.
>
> He that saith, I know him, and keepeth not his commandments, is a liar, and the truth is not in him.
> (1 John 4:7-8 & 2:3-4)

Actually, there is nothing more important to know than to know God and to know the truth about God—to learn that he exists; to learn what he is like; to learn what our relationship is to him; to learn how we can come to know him in this life and how we can be with him in the hereafter. In fact, that is what the gospel of Jesus Christ is all about. And that is one reason why baptism is so important. Jesus told Joseph Smith that baptism and the other ordinances of the gospel exist to help us come to know God; the Lord has revealed that "without the ordinances [of the gospel], and the authority of the priesthood, the power of godliness is not manifest unto men in the flesh" (*Doctrine and Covenants* 84:21).

G. Believe the Truth About God.

It should go without saying that belief in Christ encompasses belief in the true nature of Christ. Belief in falsehood has no real value. God exists with a particular nature and with particular attributes. Regardless of whether or not man knows what God is like—God is what he is.

Can man learn what God is like? YES! The scriptures we have mentioned above teach that we can learn what God is like—in fact, that is the very purpose of life. The quest to know God and to know what he is like is not an impossible dream or an incomprehensible mystery; rather, God has commanded us to obtain such knowledge—as Peter and John taught, we should grow in the knowledge of God by obeying God's commandments.

Part of the belief in Christ and in God the Father that we should develop includes coming to understand their nature and attributes. Chapter 7 discussed some of these. Later, chapter 17 will discuss in further detail "how" we can come to know God. But here, let's discuss Jesus Christ, the "only begotten Son" of God, and why it is that we should believe in Him.

H. The Testament of the Divine Sonship of Jesus.

I think the most beautiful story ever told is that of the conception and birth of Jesus:

> [T]he angel Gabriel was sent from God unto a city of Galilee, named Nazareth,
>
> To a virgin espoused to a man whose name was Joseph, of the house of David; and the virgin's name was Mary.
>
> And the angel came in unto her, and said, hail, thou that are highly favoured, the Lord is with thee: blessed art thou among women.

And when she saw him, she was troubled at his saying, and cast in her mind what manner of salutation this should be.

And the angel said unto her, Fear not, Mary: for thou hast found favour with God.

And, behold, thou shalt conceive in thy womb, and bring forth a son, and shalt call his name JESUS.

He shall be great, and shall be called the Son of the Highest: and the Lord God shall give unto him the throne of his father David:

And he shall reign over the house of Jacob for ever; and of his kingdom there shall be no end.

Then said Mary unto the angel, How shall this be, seeing I know not a man?

And the angel answered and said unto her, The Holy Ghost shall come upon thee, and the power of the Highest shall overshadow thee: therefore also that holy thing which shall be born of thee shall be called the Son of God. . . .

And Mary said, Behold the handmaid of the Lord; be it unto me according to thy word.

. . .

And so it was, that, while they were there, the days were accomplished that she should be delivered.

And she brought forth her firstborn son, and wrapped him in swaddling clothes, and laid him in a manger; because there was no room for them in the inn. (Luke 1:26-35 & 38; and 2:6-7)

The importance of Mary's testimony about the conception of Jesus is unsurpassed in scripture. Mary's testimony of Jesus' divine heritage explains how he possessed the power to make an atoning sacrifice for all mankind. Indeed, except for the powers that Jesus inherited from his immortal Father, he could not have redeemed the world.

As these verses in Luke teach, Jesus is in very fact the son of God.

The scriptures teach this. They teach that Jesus is the "only begotten Son of God." The literal interpretation of this teaching is glorious; it does not diminish the glory and majesty of God. But it does raise man to a godly level; it affirms that man is superior to the animals; the world was made for man, and man is lord over the animals and over all the earth. The literal meaning of Mary's testimony gives added depth to the statement of Paul: "Know ye not that ye are the temple of God, and that the Spirit of God dwelleth in you?" (1 Corinthians 3:16). All of us are indeed the spirit children of God. (See, e. g., Acts 17:28-29; Romans 8:16-17 and Hebrews 12:9.) When we address God in prayer as "our Father which art in heaven" (Matthew 6:9), the title "Father" is not a meaningless appellation—the title describes an eternal truth. As sons and daughters of God, we are indeed "heirs of God, and joint-heirs with Christ" (Romans 8:17). It is literally and verily true that Jesus is the only begotten son of God in the flesh. (See also appendix D.)

I. Jesus Brought About the Resurrection of the Dead.

Because of his divine sonship, Jesus is the only soul to ever live who had the power within himself to prevent his own suffering, to prevent his death, and to possess the power to live again if he should die. Jesus specifically taught this on at least two occasions, as the apostle John records:

> For as the Father hath life in himself; so hath he given to the Son to have life in himself. (John 5:26)

> Therefore doth my Father love me, because I lay down my lie, that I might take it again.
> No man taketh it from me, but I lay it down of myself. I have power to lay it down, and I have power to take it again. (John 10:17-18)

Because of Jesus' divine sonship, he was able to resurrect himself.

So, at the age of 33, after Jesus allowed his enemies to crucify him and kill him, he let his body remain lifeless in the tomb until the third day, at which time he put his spirit back into his body and resurrected himself. His body and spirit were then eternally reunited—never to be separated again. Jesus was the first man to be resurrected, and he was the only man having the power to resurrect himself—a power he inherited from his immortal Father.

Following the resurrection of Jesus, many of the saints were likewise resurrected (Matthew 27:52-53). By virtue of his divine sonship, Jesus was able to accomplish this. How it is done, I do not know. But it is done. And the Spirit of God testifies of this eternal truth. A person can know this truth, just like Job did when he said: "I know that my redeemer liveth . . . . And though after my skin worms destroy this body, yet in my flesh shall I see God" (Job 19:25-26).

Certainly, there is no more wonderful miracle than that of the resurrection that will happen to all of us one day. It is the free gift to all mankind: "For as in Adam all die, even so in Christ shall all be made alive" (1 Corinthians 15:22). For this great gift I thank the Savior and I thank God the Eternal Father, whose plan provided such a blessing.

J.   Jesus Suffered the Penalty for the Sins of Mankind.

Our dependence upon Jesus for the gift of resurrection is too obvious to require any discussion; the effect of death leaves an obvious need for a redeemer. But we are also dependent upon Jesus for freeing us from eternal punishment for our sins. Our need to be redeemed from the consequences of our sins is just as real as the need for resurrection. Sometimes the effects of sin are not readily apparent to the mortal eye—but they separate our spirits from God. Sins kill faith, hope, happiness and love.

When we disobey even one commandment of God, this disobedience separates us from Him. This effect on us is real, although it is not a tangible effect that can be detected by the five senses. But there is a spiritual effect that is just as real as are our emotions. No unclean thing can dwell in God's presence, and our sins separate us from God—they alienate us from God. Once separated from God by sin, we become unholy and tainted with sin. Though we could refrain from ever sinning again, God's presence has nevertheless been withheld from us; we would be ever banished from His presence unless a reconciliation could be made—unless someone else can satisfy the demands of justice, forgive our sins, and allow us to return to God's presence. Jesus is the one who does this service for us. He paid the price for all our sins, and He gives us reconciliation with God if we keep God's commandments, including entering into the covenant of baptism, witnessing to God that we will do His will. Jesus freely forgives our sins and makes possible this marvelous reconciliation on the condition of our believing Him and obeying His words. Jesus' atoning sacrifice was and is fully effective to remit the sins of those who lived before his time as well as those who lived after.

K.   We Must Obtain and Retain a Remission of Our Sins.

Because of the forgiveness of sins that God has given me, I know of the power of Jesus' atoning sacrifice. It is real! There is not a greater blessing that anyone can have in this life. It causes the soul to rejoice. But, as the prophet Benjamin taught, it is not enough to obtain it—one must retain a remission of his sins by continuing to do the things that brought the forgiveness in the first place:

> [A]s ye have come to the knowledge of the glory of God, or if ye have known of his goodness and have tasted of his love, and have received a remission of your sins, which causeth such exceedingly great joy in your souls, even so I would that ye should remember, and always retain in remembrance, the greatness of God, and your own nothingness, and his goodness and long-suffering towards you, unworthy creatures, and humble yourselves even in the depths of humility,

calling on the name of the Lord daily, and standing
steadfastly in the faith . . . . [I]f ye do this ye shall
always rejoice, and be filled with the love of God, and
always retain a remission of your sins. (*Book of Mormon*,
Mosiah 4:11-12)

The atonement of Christ provides a means for us to re-enter God's
presence. Upon the condition of our faith and repentance, Jesus took
upon himself the punishment for our sins. Since Jesus was sinless, he
could approach God the Father in our behalf. This he did; he made
intercession for all those who repent of their sins and obey his gospel.
In our behalf he agreed to and did suffer the punishment for our sins
to satisfy the eternal law of justice—which requires a punishment for
every sin. Thus, the atonement of Christ was able to provide us mercy
without violating the law of justice.

L.   The Miracle of Forgiveness.

The miracle of forgiveness of sins is the most powerful miracle
that a person can experience. The effects of sin are real; and so is
the effect of Christ's atonement. Because of the grace of Christ our
sins can be blotted out and we can rejoice in joy and love. I thank my
Father in Heaven for this blessing in my life. I am grateful to the Lord
Jesus Christ for what he has done for me and for all mankind. With
all my heart I want to retain a remission of my sins so that my life can
be blessed with the companionship of the Holy Ghost and so that I
may inherit eternal life.

Let's now turn to a discussion of some additional commandments
that we must obey to obtain salvation—commandments that we will
obey if we have the saving faith in Christ.

CHAPTER 17

Be Baptized for the Remission of Sins and Receive the Gift of the Holy Ghost

A. God's People Covenant to Obey Him and to Keep His commandments.

Abraham, Isaac and Jacob (Israel) covenanted with God and were promised great blessings for them and their posterity. Thereafter the prophets often referred to the "peculiar" or "chosen" status of the Israelites. (See, e. g., Exodus 6:4; & 19:5; Deuteronomy 5:2; & 7:6.) A covenant is more than a mere promise; it is an agreement; it is a two-way promise. A covenant is made when one party does or promises to do something for another party, and when that other party does or promises to do something for the first party in return.

In Old Testament times, the Lord promised Abraham that he would have a great posterity, that he would be the father of many nations, and that the land of Canaan would be an everlasting possession for him (Genesis 17). In return, Abraham promised to obey all of God's commandments. One of the specific commandments that Abraham was given was that he and all of his male descendants were to be circumcised.[58] The LORD told Abraham that this act was to "be a token of the covenant betwixt me and you" (Genesis 17:11). The Bible then records that "the selfsame day" that God gave him this commandment, Abraham circumcised all the males in his household and that he himself, at the age of 99, was also circumcised (Genesis 17:23-24).

The versions of the Old Testament that we have today do not mention the covenant and ordinance of baptism. This "plain and precious" truth was wrongfully omitted from the Old Testament (*Book of Mormon*, 1 Nephi 13:29). But the Lord revealed to Joseph Smith 189 years ago that God introduced the ordinance of baptism to Adam, and that God's people have practiced this ordinance throughout history— Enoch and Noah both preached baptism for the remission of sins (*Pearl of Great Price*, Moses 6:59-66; and 8:23-24). Bible scholars will recognize that Jesus did not introduce the ordinance of baptism, for John was baptizing before Jesus' ministry began. And it should be noted that John was not criticized by the Jewish leaders for introducing any new doctrine when he taught baptism for a remission of sins. Scholars in ancient history recognize that ablutions, or washings for the cleansing of sin were performed by Israelites and Jews prior to the time of Jesus.[59] Baptism was not new with John the Baptist. And, now, the discovery of the Dead Sea Scrolls and other ancient scriptural texts (e. g., "The Apocalypse of Adam"—one of the Nag Hammadi texts) confirm that the covenant and ordinance of baptism was first practiced during the days of Adam.[60]

---

[58] With the resurrection of Jesus, the law of circumcision was ended. (See, e. g., Acts 21:21; 1 Corinthians 7:19; and Galatians 5:6 & 6:15.)

[59] "Baptism," *American People's Encyclopedia*, 1956 ed., 3:056; Nibley, pp. 72 & 144; Potter, p. 49; and Letter from Dr. S. Kent Brown, Director, Egyptian Microfilming Project, Brigham Young University, June 3, 1987.

[60] Lucetta Mowry, *The Dead Sea Scrolls and the Early Church* (Indiana: Univ. of Notre Dame Press, 1966), 237, quoted in Vernon W. Mattson, Jr., *The Dead Sea Scrolls and Other Important Discoveries* (Salt Lake City: Buried Records Productions, 1979), 102.

B.   Through Baptism We Covenant to Obey God.

Baptism is an act of submission to a servant of God (signifying the person's submitting to the will of God) and of God's promise to cleanse him from sin. Baptism is an ordinance—an outward act, symbolic of this covenant between God and man. The ordinance of baptism is the act that makes the covenant binding. Just as one's signature is often required to make a binding written contract today, so the performance of the act of baptism makes a binding contract between God and an individual.

An ordinance is an outward act, prescribed by God, by which an individual enters into a covenant with God, promising to do certain things in exchange for receiving promised blessings from God. The outward acts of the ordinance are symbolic of at least some parts of the spiritual reality of the accompanying covenant.

The covenant of baptism is very simple: God promises to give eternal life to all those who repent of their sins and serve God with all their hearts and keep all of his commandments (John 3:5; Mark 16:16; and Acts 2:37-38). This covenant between God and man is made binding by the ordinance of baptism—when the person is baptized by an authorized servant of God.

The symbolism of baptism is plain and precious. When God's servant immerses the candidate in the water, this is symbolic of God's washing away his sins. Just as only Christ can wash away our sins, so only one who holds God's priesthood can authoritatively perform the ordinance of baptism. When the candidate is lowered completely into the water, this immersion is symbolic of the death and burial of one's former life of sin and disobedience. When God's servant raises the person out of the water, this is symbolic of rebirth to a new life in Christ; it is also symbolic of our future resurrection from the dead.

The symbolism of baptism serves to teach and remind us of the real meaning of the covenant that this ordinance accompanies. Because baptism is an outward, physical act, it is more easily remembered by us. Because it requires us to go to some inconvenience to be baptized, it will not be lightly entered into. By participating in this ordinance, we witness to all the world and to God that we do promise to obey His commandments. And by submitting ourselves to be immersed in the water by God's servants, it is a demonstration of our submissiveness to God and to God's authorized servants.

If a person does not promise with real intent to obey God, and if that person does not earnestly attempt to obey all of God's commandments, he would only be fooling himself if he were to think that his having been baptized would bring him eternal life with God. Baptism, like a signature, creates a binding covenant or agreement, but it does not guarantee that we will perform our part of that agreement.

C.   Repentance Must Accompany Baptism.

If one covenants to obey God through the ordinance of baptism, it is only logical that the candidate for baptism should demonstrate his sincerity by repenting of his sins prior to baptism. John the Baptist taught this to the hypocritical Sadducees and Pharisees who came to him when he was baptizing in the Jordan River. Matthew records:

> Then went out to him Jerusalem, and all Judaea, and all the region round about Jordan,
>
> And were baptized of him in Jordan, confessing their sins.
>
> But when he saw many of the Pharisees and Sadducees come to his baptism, he said unto them, O generation of vipers, who hath warned you to flee from the wrath to come?
>
> Bring forth therefore fruits meet for repentance: ...
>
> [E]very tree which bringeth not forth good fruit is hewn down, and cast into the fire.
>
> I ... baptize you with water unto repentance ....
> (Matthew 3:5-8 & 10-11)

Jesus likewise instructed his apostles to teach that repentance was to accompany baptism. Luke records that Jesus told them that "repentance and remission of sins should be preached in his name among the people" (Luke 24:47). And, after the ascension of Jesus, Peter continued to preach that repentance must accompany baptism; on the Day of Pentecost he instructed those who believed to "[r]epent and be baptized" (Acts 2:38).[61]

Those who teach a doctrine of salvation that denies the requirement of repentance, teach a false doctrine. By what authority do they change the gospel that Jesus taught? Clearly, they have no such authority. Repentance continues to be a requirement for salvation in the kingdom of God for those capable of committing sin.

There are some who teach that repentance consists of merely changing from a state of non-belief in Christ to belief in Christ—that repentance is nothing more than accepting Christ as one's Savior and believing that salvation comes through this belief. Others believe that repentance is merely an attitude of willingness to submit to God's will. Both of these beliefs about repentance are incomplete. The full meaning of repentance encompasses stopping from disobeying and starting to obey God's commandments. This was one of the predominant

---

[61] With regard to the practice of baptizing infants, the Lord revealed to the prophet Mormon that such a practice was an abomination. The Lord said: "Behold, I came into the world not to call the righteous but sinners to repentance; the whole need no physician, but they that are sick; wherefore, little children are whole, for they are not capable of committing sin" (*Book of Mormon*, Moroni 8:8). Commenting on the erroneous practice of baptizing infants, Mormon wrote:

> [I]t is a solemn mockery before God, that ye should baptize little children. Behold I say unto you that this thing shall ye teach—repentance and baptism unto those who are accountable and capable of committing sin; yea, teach parents that they must repent and be baptized, and humble themselves as their little children, and they shall all be saved with their little children. . . .
> But little children are alive in Christ, even from the foundation of the world; if not so, God is a partial God, and also a changeable God, and a respecter of persons; for how many little children have died without baptism! . . .
> For awful is the wickedness to suppose that God saveth one child because of baptism, and the other must perish because he hath no baptism. (*Book of Mormon*, Moroni 8:9-10, 12 & 15)

themes of Christ's teaching, as we pointed out previously. (See chapter 16, section E, and the scriptures cited there.) True repentance also includes having "godly sorrow" for sin (2 Corinthians 7:10) and, to the extent possible, making restitution for injury caused by one's sins. (See, e. g., Exodus 22—the general principle of restitution, like the Ten Commandments, was not repealed by Christ.)

Nevertheless, repentance does not "earn" either forgiveness or salvation; it is a condition God has set to be met in order to obtain forgiveness for sins.

D.   One Must Be Baptized to Be Saved.

A person who denies that baptism is necessary in order to obtain salvation is mistaken. Who is he who thinks he can counsel God or dictate to God what his terms of salvation should be? It is not the sinner's prerogative to decide whether or not he will comply with the terms and conditions that God has set for obtaining salvation. Jesus' divine decree that a man must be born of the water and of the spirit in order to enter the kingdom of God (John 3:5) has not been rescinded. In fact, before Christ ascended to heaven, he reemphasized that this was the message his apostles were to carry to all the world: "He that believeth and is baptized shall be saved; but he that believeth not shall be damned" (Mark 16:16). And thereafter, the acts and epistles of the apostles bear out that they continued to preach and practice the ordinance of baptism for the remission of sins and for salvation. (See, e. g., Acts 2:37-38; 3:19; 8:12-13 & 36-38; 9:17-18; 10:47-48; 11:16-18; 16:15; 18:8; 19:1-6; 22:16; Romans 6; 1 Corinthians 1:14-16; and 1 Peter 3:21.)

E.   Baptism Must Be Performed by an Authorized Servant of God.

One aspect of the baptism ordinance that is sometimes ignored is the need for baptism to be performed by one who actually holds God's authority. Such was anciently an indispensible requirement. Jesus would not have ordained the apostles and given them his authority if it was not necessary (John 15:16; Matthew 10; and Mark 16:15-16). The apostles anciently found it necessary to re-baptize those who had been baptized by unauthorized persons (Acts 19:1-6). And the Apostle Paul clearly taught that no man taketh the priesthood of God upon himself unless he "is called of God, as was Aaron" (Hebrews 5:4)—that is by prophecy and by the laying on of hands by one already having God's authority (Exodus 28:1-3 & 28; see also Numbers 27:18-23). Just as God has not rescinded the commandment that all mankind must be baptized in order to be saved, neither has He rescinded the requirement that baptisms must be performed only by his authorized servants.

Some may dispute this requirement, but I cannot help but see the wisdom for it. The symbolic meaning of baptism is altered if one dispenses with the requirement of an authorized administrator. And even more importantly, no imposter has authority to bind God to a contract to bless someone. If someone enters into a covenant with an imposter to obtain blessings from God, then there would be no legal, binding or actual covenant made with God. Any good that would result would be because of the person's efforts to obey God, not because the baptism was adequate or valid—the baptism would not have any binding effect on God. God is the one who established that actual authority to baptize is required; He must have his reasons for this.

Obviously, God is aware of the many invalid baptisms that have been performed—either invalid because of lack of authority, improper procedure, having the wrong covenant, or a combination of these errors. And while God is certainly displeased with false priests and pastors who create and/or perpetrate false doctrines, I don't believe God condemns anyone for sincere efforts to obey God's commandments according to the light and knowledge that one has. One who has not been baptized by an authorized servant of God, but who desires to keep all of God's commandments, will happily be baptized by one holding God's actual authority when the opportunity is given.

F.   One Must Receive the Gift of the
Holy Ghost to Be Saved.

When John baptized in the Jordan River, he taught that there would come one after him, who was greater than he, who would baptize with fire and the Holy Ghost (Matthew 3:11). John apparently did not have the authority to bestow the Gift of the Holy Ghost. But John taught his disciples to look for and receive this baptism of fire. Jesus taught that being born of the water (baptism) and being born of the spirit (the Gift of the Holy Ghost) were both essential for salvation (John 3:5). Jesus taught his disciples that after his departure He would send the Holy Ghost to them (John 14:16-19 & 26; 15:26 & 16:7 & 13-14). The scriptures teach that Jesus bestowed the Gift of the Holy Ghost on his apostles when he "breathed" on them and said, "Receive ye the Holy Ghost" (John 20:22). Jesus instructed his apostles to wait at Jerusalem until the Holy Ghost would come (Acts 1:4-5 & 8), then they could commence their apostolic missions. On the Day of Pentecost, the Holy Ghost did fall upon them and manifested himself to a multitude of people in a wondrous and powerful way (Acts 2).

As the apostles carried the gospel to the world, they clearly taught a two-part ordinance for salvation. Baptism was the first part, and the laying on of hands for the Gift of the Holy Ghost was the second. One illustration of this is found in Acts, chapter 8, when the gospel was brought to Samaria. Philip, who had been called and ordained to the ministry by the apostles (Acts 6:1-6), preached to the Samaritans and baptized those who believed. But he did not bestow the Gift of the Holy Ghost on them (Acts 8:12). He did not have such authority. Later, when the apostles heard that the Samaritans had received the gospel, they sent Peter and John to Samaria, so that those disciples might receive the baptism of Spirit as well as the baptism of water (Acts 8:14-17). Philip, like John the Baptist, had authority to baptize, but not authority to confer the Gift of the Holy Ghost. The apostles, having greater authority, could both baptize and confer the Gift of the Holy Ghost.

G. The Gift of the Holy Ghost Is Bestowed by the Laying on of Hands by an Authorized Servant of God.

While the Holy Ghost can and does manifest himself to devout seekers of God without the laying on of hands (see, e. g., Acts 2:37 and Acts 10:44-48), the apostles nevertheless clearly taught that baptism and the laying on of hands for the Gift of the Holy Ghost was essential for salvation. Thus, when on the Day of Pentecost, the Holy Ghost pricked the hearts of Peter's audience, he nevertheless commanded them to be baptized and to receive the Gift of the Holy Ghost (Acts 2:37-38). The apostles bestowed the Gift of the Holy Ghost by the laying on of hands (Acts 8:17-20; 19:6 and Hebrews 6:2).

H. The Gift of the Holy Ghost— Companionship of the Holy Ghost—Is Conditioned upon Obedience to God.

Peter taught that the continuing companionship of the Holy Ghost comes through obedience to God's commandments. This blessing, Peter said, "God hath given to them that obey him" (Acts 5:32). The Gift of the Holy Ghost is the right to the constant companionship of the Holy Ghost; it is the right to and the blessing of enjoying an increased portion of the Spirit of God. Thus, Peter taught that after receiving a witness from the Holy Ghost that the gospel of Jesus Christ was true, one still had need to repent, to be baptized and to receive the Gift of the holy Ghost in order to be saved (Acts 2:37-38).

I. When the Authority of the Apostles Disappeared from the Earth, the Power to Baptize and to Bestow the Gift of the Holy Ghost Was Lost.

Paul taught the Ephesians that apostles and prophets were the foundation of Christ's church (Ephesians 2:19-20). He also taught that they were essential officers in the church until the saints were unified and perfected (Ephesians 4:11-14). We have previously discussed the apostasy of the early Christian church after the death of the apostles. (See chapter 8.) Once the authority to baptize and to bestow the Gift of the Holy Ghost was lost, the Gifts of the Spirit soon disappeared, also. Reformer John Wesley commented on the absence of these gifts after the second or third centuries. (See chapter 9, section B.) The reappearance of the spiritual gifts of tongues, prophecies, revelations, visions and healings would not be expected without the Lord's first restoring the authority to baptize and to bestow the Gift of the Holy Ghost.

J.   God Foretold of False Doctrines, Changed Ordinances and Broken Covenants.

While it is disconcerting to entertain the idea that false doctrines of salvation abound in and among Christian churches today, it was nevertheless prophesied by Jesus and other prophets that this would happen in the last days. (See chapter 9, above.) Jesus said that before his second coming, "there shall arise false Christs, and false prophets, and shall shew great signs and wonders; insomuch that, if it were possible, they shall deceive the very elect" (Matthew 24:24). And Isaiah wrote of our day when he said:

> The earth also is defiled under the inhabitants thereof; because they have transgressed the laws, changed the *ordinance*, broken the everlasting *covenant*. . . .[T]his people draw near me with their mouth, and with their lips do honour me, but have removed their heart far from me. (Isaiah 24:5 & 28:13 [emphasis added])

In our day, Isaiah's prophecy about the transgressed laws, changed ordinance and broken covenant has unquestionably been fulfilled. But, as God's prophets have predicted, in these latter days, God has restored his pure covenants and ordinances to the earth again. One of these restored covenants and ordinances is baptism of water and of the Spirit.

K.   The Authority to Baptize Has Been Restored.

The authority to act in the name of God has been restored to the earth. Chapter 10 related the account of the restoration of that authority when the resurrected John the Baptist conferred the authority to baptize upon Joseph Smith and Oliver Cowdery. With the restoration of this authority (called the Aaronic Priesthood) comes the great opportunity for all mankind to obtain great spiritual blessings in covenanting with God, through baptism, to serve Him and keep His commandments.

God has a great and marvelous mission for every one of his covenant children to fulfill in this life. He has kept many of his noblest spirits in reserve to be born in these latter days to accomplish a great work for Him. But the starting place for learning and doing that important calling is to humbly submit to baptism at the hands of God's chosen servants.

In 1830, shortly after the Lord commanded Joseph Smith to organize the Church of Jesus Christ, some raised the question of whether they needed to be baptized into this church if they had already been baptized in some other denomination. The Lord revealed the following answer to this inquiry:

> Behold, I say unto you that all old covenants have I caused to be done away in this thing; and this is a new and an everlasting covenant, even that which was from the beginning.
>
> Wherefore, although a man should be baptized an hundred times it availeth him nothing, for you cannot enter in at the strait gate by the law of Moses, neither by your dead works.

For it is because of your dead works that I have caused this last covenant and this church to be built up unto me, even as in days of old.

Wherefore, enter ye in at the gate, as I have commanded, and seek not to counsel your God. Amen. (*Doctrine and Covenants* 22:1-4)

L.   The Authority to Bestow the Gift of the Holy Ghost Has Been Restored.

When John the Baptist bestowed the Aaronic Priesthood upon Joseph Smith and Oliver Cowdery in May, 1829, he told them that he was acting under the authority of Peter, James and John. He said that these three apostles would soon visit them and give them the authority that they possessed—the Melchizedek Priesthood—which greater authority would empower them to confer the Gift of the Holy Ghost on those who are baptized. A short time later, Peter, James and John did appear to Joseph and Oliver at Harmony, Pennsylvania, and conferred their higher authority upon them. The authority of the apostles, which had been taken from the earth with the departure of the apostles, was now restored. And with this restoration, once again mankind has the opportunity to receive the Gift of the Holy Ghost. With this Gift, once again we can expect those recipients to experience the gifts of visions, tongues, prophecy, healings, revelations and miracles in their lives as they seek to do the work of God.

M. Summary.

Can one be saved without being baptized and receiving the Gift of the Holy Ghost? No. It is not enough to just believe in God. "The devils also believe, and tremble" (James 2:19). When John wrote that "whosoever believeth in him [Christ] should not perish, but have everlasting life" (John 3:16), he did not mean that a person who believes need not be baptized. Rather he meant that a person who believes in Christ will do what Christ commands, including being baptized. "Then said Jesus to those Jews who believed on him, If ye continue in my word, then are ye my disciples in deed" (John 8:31). Those who believe in Jesus, obey Jesus. When Peter preached on the Day of Pentecost, those who believed his words asked the apostles:

> Men and brethren, what shall we do?
>
> Then Peter said unto them, Repent, and be baptized every one of you in the name of Jesus Christ for the remission of sins, and ye shall receive the gift of the Holy Ghost.
>
> For the promise is unto you, and to your children, and to all that are afar off, even as many as the Lord our God shall call. (Acts 2:37-39)

Now that God has restored his Priesthood authority to the earth, the marvelous blessings of salvation are once again available to all the world.

CHAPTER 18

Unite with The Church of Jesus Christ of Latter-day Saints

We have previously quoted from Paul's epistle to the Ephesians to highlight the truth that the church of Christ exists to bring about a unity of the faith (Ephesians 4:13). From the moment of its inception, The Church of Jesus Christ of Latter-day Saints has proclaimed that this will be accomplished by uniting with it. God has declared that it is "the only true and living church upon the face of the whole earth" (*Doctrine and Covenants* 1:30). The Church continues to reaffirm this—that it is the very kingdom of God on earth spoken of by Daniel (Daniel 2:44 and *Doctrine and Covenants* 65:2); and that it is God's will that all should join it, through receiving the ordinance of baptism as discussed in the preceding chapter.

I have now shown that the "Mormon" message of restoration is plausible; once a person comes to understand the "Mormon" point of view, the logic and soundness of that message becomes apparent. Mormonism is not a reckless and hasty concoction of nonsense; on the contrary, it is fundamentally sound and profound, and it is in harmony with the teachings of the Bible.

But the ultimate questions remain: Is the message of Mormonism divine? And, Is The Church of Jesus Christ of Latter-day Saints really the work of God? The answers to these questions can come only from Him. I give my witness that the Spirit of God testifies to me that the message of Mormonism is divine—that it is the work of God.

To those who are sincerely wrestling with the question of the truthfulness of these claims, I would like to share some thoughts I have had about the valiant disciples of Christ who do not belong to The Church of Jesus Christ of Latter-day Saints.

A. The Disciples of Christ Will Come to a Unity of the Faith.

The multiple variations of doctrines taught in the many Christian denominations today witness the widespread dissatisfaction that the disciples of Christ have had with Christian churches and their doctrines throughout the centuries. Every protestant must confess that his church sprang from an effort to correct problems and errors that crept into Christianity. It is also obvious to even the most casual observer of Christianity today that Christians have not come to a unity of the faith; significant doctrinal differences exist and persist among the many Christian denominations. While efforts are currently being made to unite Christianity in some ways, the ecumenical movement alone will never bring Christianity to "a unity of the faith."

When the saints come to a "unity of the faith" it will not be the result of debate and negotiation about what the gospel of Jesus Christ should be. It will be accomplished by God himself setting things straight and revealing the truth and setting up an ensign to which all Christians and all the world will come.

B. A Conversation about Conflicting Doctrines of Salvation.

A few years ago, I attended a luncheon meeting of the Full Gospel Businessmen's Fellowship International in Washington, D. C. The group in attendance was comprised of Christians from many different denominations. After lunch, the program included a speech by an Episcopalian judge and three or four other men who briefly shared their testimonies of Jesus Christ. I felt the presence of the Spirit at this meeting. One gentleman in particular spoke a few words that touched me deeply. In a humble, but sure manner, he said that he had seen the Lord. He shared his witness that Jesus was the Christ and of the importance of being pure and good.

On the way home from the luncheon I was talking with two ministers who had also been in attendance; one was the pastor of a Southern Baptist congregation; the other pastored an Assembly of God congregation. In the course of our conversation we discussed the fact that the men in attendance had varying doctrinal beliefs about the gospel of Jesus Christ, but they were united in their belief that only through Him could one be saved. Specifically, the Southern Baptist minister and the Assembly of God pastor each explained their respective doctrines about how to obtain salvation: According to one, once you are "born again" your salvation is eternally secured, and the rest of your life you go about in a saved condition. On the other hand, the other pastor believed that you can be "born again" and know the Lord, and thereafter lose your salvation through sin.

The seeker for truth must candidly acknowledge that these two ministers teach different doctrines of salvation.

C. When Christ Comes He Will Set Things Right.

As we continued our conversation, both of the ministers acknowledged that there were conflicting doctrines taught in the various Christian denominations. But they both agreed that when Christ comes he would set things right, and that they would then correct any of their wrong beliefs and unitedly follow Him.

These ministers recognized that God would eventually correct false doctrines so that Christ's church would be unified around the truth. This is good because a desire for unity should not take precedence over the love of truth. These brethren were willing to overlook doctrinal differences they have with at least some other religions.

Later in the conversation, when I explained that I belonged to The Church of Jesus Christ of Latter-day Saints, the Southern Baptist pastor was quick to point out some errors that he perceived in my church's doctrine; baptism for the dead was one in particular that he criticized. Rather than finding an attitude of interest in the message of the restoration, I found instead, in the one minister, an attitude of determined and aggressive criticism of Mormonism. For some reason he could tolerate error in some denominations, but he could not tolerate what he perceived to be error in Mormonism. The pastor said he believed that Christ would set things right, but he was determined that Mormonism was not accomplishing that.

Though many Christians, including their paid ministers, may be loath to admit it—God has spoken from Heaven to set things right in his church; He has sent messengers to the earth to unify his disciples around the truth. But too many Christians are not looking for heavenly messengers to bring Christianity to a unity of the faith. Nevertheless, God has spoken to set things right—it is happening right before their eyes, and they are blind to it.

If Christians today will sincerely distinguish between what they know and what they don't know about the gospel of Jesus Christ, then they will look forward to and embrace the messages that the Lord promised to send to the world by messengers before His Second Coming.

D. The Parable of the Ten Virgins Is a Prophecy That Will Be Fulfilled.

I am optimistic that many Christians will embrace the truths brought by God's messengers. But I also know that many will not. In the parable of the ten virgins (Matthew 25:1-13), Jesus foretold that half of the virgins, who were looking forward to the coming of the bridegroom, were not wise and were not prepared when he did come.

I believe this means that many who expect the Lord to shortly come again will nevertheless not be found ready when he does come.

Part of the preparation that is required if we are to be found among the five virgins who were prepared is that we must look for, listen to and heed the divine messengers that God will send in the last days. These messengers will not hide the fact that they are divinely commissioned, but they will boldly declare their authority in meekness and solemnity of heart.

This message of restoration is not one of condemnation of Jesus' disciples who love God with all their hearts and souls. But it is a message of condemnation to hypocrites who profess to be of God, but whose hearts are set on riches or glory or other vain things of the world. But to those who seek to obey God and "live . . . by every word that proceedeth out of the mouth of God" (Matthew 4:4), this message of restoration will edify and uplift. Those who embrace it will find their own spiritual abilities magnified as the Lord opens to their understanding many great and important gospel truths that had hitherto been hidden from them.

There are thousands upon thousands of courageous and loving disciples of Christ in the many different Christian denominations— people who have a firm conviction that Jesus Christ is the Savior of the world. When these people take the time to prayerfully and thoroughly consider the message of The Church of Jesus Christ of Latter-day Saints, they will come to know of its truthfulness, and they will embrace it with conviction and enthusiasm.

Nevertheless, it is a fact that unless someone listens for and hearkens to this message, he or she will not receive the witness from God of its truthfulness. A man or woman who is so busy in his professional life that he does not have time to study and consider the word of God denies himself great spiritual blessings which otherwise could be his. So, too, the individual who is set in his own ways and his own habits and practices, and who will not prayerfully consider the messages of God delivered by Joseph Smith and God's living messengers today—that individual will likewise deny himself great and marvelous blessings that he might otherwise have.

But I do say, as the Spirit of God bears witness, that the day will soon come when millions of devout Christians around the world, who are not now members of The Church of Jesus Christ of Latter-day Saints, will come to hear and recognize and embrace the message of the restored gospel, when it is taught to them by the servants of the Lord in this Church. The missionary messengers of the Lord will continue to raise their voices around the globe as this marvelous work and a wonder rolls forth to fill the earth.

And how will you respond when the "Mormon" missionaries appear at your door? Some valiant Christians may know the Bible better than the young servants of the Lord called to declare his heavenly message to them. Please remember that the measuring stick of a disciple of Christ is not how high he would score on a chapter-and-verse scripture test. The mark of a true messenger from Christ is whether he has the love of God in his heart, and whether he has faith in Christ, and whether he is actually commissioned by God to do His work.

I know that some Christians feel that the members and missionaries of The Church of Jesus Christ of Latter-day Saints need to be converted, rather than the other way around. As a member of this Church, I have come to understand some gospel principles from great men and women of other denominations. But the truthfulness of the restored gospel is not based upon the premise that a member or missionary of this Church must know more about every principle of the gospel of Jesus Christ than everyone to whom he proclaims his message. The fact that you may understand some points of doctrine better than the messenger that God sends to you does not mean that his message cannot be true. The fact that one person hears and accepts God's message before another person does not make that person better or smarter than another. So, while you may have some wise counsel to give to the Lord's messenger, do not let your pride prevent you from hearing and recognizing and accepting the divine message that will be delivered to you by one who may be less wise than you. The Spirit of God bears witness to the truthfulness of the message of the restored gospel. Hearken to it. Don't dismiss the message just because you may feel you understand more about life and the gospel than he who brings you the message of the restoration.

E. Truth Will Prevail—Falsehoods Will Be Exposed.

You will recall that in the opening pages of the book we discussed the widespread propaganda in the world, aimed at destroying and hampering the work of The Church of Jesus Christ of Latter-day Saints. All of these efforts will eventually fade as they are exposed to the light of day. But God will bless his disciples, and He will ultimately prosper the work of His servants; their work will shine more and more brilliantly as the day wears on. The Lord will bring the blessings of the gospel to his disciples throughout all of Christendom and to all the world—to those who love Him with all their heart and who desire to keep his commandments.

F. "I Have . . . Prepared Thee for a Greater Work."

I am thankful for the opportunity God has given me to do His work—to share His word with my brothers and sisters. There is no greater joy that I have experienced than sharing the messages of God with my friends. I know that many of my brothers and sisters in Christ who are not in this Church share with me that love and joy that comes in discussing the word of God and in sharing our witnesses of Him with others. My testimony is that the great and marvelous works prophesied to precede the Second Coming of our Lord are unfolding before your eyes, and you may not have recognized it as such. The work of God is moving forward. God's work is being done by His servants in The Church of Jesus Christ of Latter-day Saints. Russell M. Nelson is now (2019) God's prophet to the whole world. He is bringing about God's holy purposes under the inspiration and direction of the Lord God Almighty, with the assistance of hundreds of thousands of fellow servants holding the Priesthood of God.

All disciples of Jesus can best serve the Lord if they will accept the truth that The Church of Jesus Christ of Latter-day Saints is the very

Kingdom of God on earth. Disciples of Christ who reject this truth make a serious mistake, which, if not corrected, will alienate them from Him whose disciples they want to be. Disciples of Christ will accept this truth because they will be in tune with the Spirit of God who bears witness of it. It is the gospel of Jesus Christ. *There is no truth that is not a part of The Church of Jesus Christ of Latter-day Saints.*

There are many men and women of deep and profound faith in the power of God who do not yet believe The Church of Jesus Christ of Latter-day Saints to be the Kingdom of God on earth. But once these men and women embrace this message from God they will be magnified in their powers and abilities to carry the gospel to the ends of the earth.

Already there are thousands of Christians preaching the gospel of Jesus Christ to the extent of their understanding throughout the world. And when these men and women come to recognize that this Church is indeed the Kingdom of God on earth, and after they obey the ordinances of the gospel, the Lord will endow them with power to do an even mightier work for God. The Lord's message to them will be similar to His message to Sidney Rigdon: "Behold, verily, verily, I say unto my servant Sidney, I have looked upon thee and thy works. I have heard they prayers, and prepared thee for a greater work" (*Doctrine and Covenants* 35:4).

When these spiritual giants embrace the restored gospel of Christ, the world will witness a marvelous work and a wonder wrought by the power of God.

I fully believe that the Lord has blessed the efforts of Christians from many denominations, just as He blessed Sidney Rigdon before the message of the restored gospel was presented to him. But the day will come when all true disciples of Jesus will unite around the true gospel principles; they will unite with The Church of Jesus Christ of Latter-day Saints. That day will come, and the vision of its unfolding is exciting.

Because of the great scriptural knowledge that some of these men and women already have, and because of the successes that they have already enjoyed, they may be tempted to rest on their laurels and believe that they have all there is to have. I think it will be difficult for many of them to accept that the Lord would deliver his divine message to them via an 18- or 19-year-old missionary. But that is exactly what is happening to thousands of people each day. God has indeed "chosen the foolish things of the world to confound the wise," and "the weak things of the world to confound the things which are mighty" (1 Corinthians 1:27). In the eyes of a sophisticated world, the Lord's young servants may appear foolish and weak. But in eternal reality, the pure young servants of God are armed with His power, enabling them to go forward with the strength and wisdom of the Lord.

So, if these great men and women will hold fast to the fundamentals of the gospel—if they will stay close to God and be submissive to His will, in due time they will come to confess that The Church of Jesus Christ of Latter-day Saints is God's kingdom on earth. And when these men and women then humbly offer their services to the servants of the Lord, to help the kingdom of God grow in whatever capacity God's servants may call them to labor—when these great men and women come to that point and are willing to humble themselves and obey the counsel of God's living prophet, then God will magnify them and make them greater in His work than they ever were previously.

God has set up His kingdom on earth as he promised. He has restored the authority of the Priesthood as the prophets foretold. He has restored the gospel in its purity and in its power and in its fullness to the earth. He has set up an ensign for the nations. It is now up to his disciples to look for it, recognize it, and come to it.

Will all of Jesus' disciples unite with The Church of Jesus Christ of Latter-day Saints when God's message is properly presented to them? Yes! Those who come unto the Father and who know the voice of the good shepherd will accept the invitation of the servants of the Lord to be baptized by an authorized administrator for the remission of sins and for entrance into the kingdom of God on earth. Like Saul of old, who kicked against the pricks and resisted the spirit of the Lord for a time, there will be many disciples who will not recognize and embrace God's message at first—but in time, all of the Lord's disciples will unite in this divine work.

The key to the realization of this miracle is the fulfillment of Peter's admonition that all disciples of Christ should "grow in grace and in the knowledge of our Lord" (2 Peter 3:18). The next two chapters will discuss this admonition and challenge.

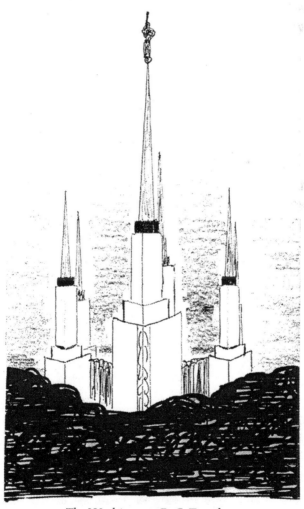

The Washington, D. C. Temple,
on I-495, in Kensington, Maryland

CHAPTER 19

Come to Know God

B efore Jesus retired to the garden of Gethsemane to commence his suffering for the sins of mankind, Jesus prayed that his disciples "might know thee the only true God, and Jesus Christ, whom thou hast sent" (John 17:3). Jesus said that "this is life eternal, that they might know" God (*Id.*) In other words, Jesus was saying that to come to know God is to achieve "eternal life." Thus, the basic purpose of life is to come to know God. The apostle John the Beloved made this one of the central themes of the fourth gospel. In chapter 14, John quotes Jesus as saying: "He that hath my commandments and keepeth them, he it is that loveth me: and he that loveth me shall be loved of my Father, and I will love him, and will manifest myself to him" (John 14:21).

A. What Does It Mean "to Know God"?

One of the most lofty and uplifting thoughts to contemplate is that God wants to reveal himself to us. I remember contemplating this thought as an eighteen-year-old freshman at college. And as I considered it, my heart yearned to talk to my Father in Heaven. I believed the words of the prophets that God would make himself known to me if I would obey His words and put Him first in my life.

I fasted and prayed earnestly that I might know Him. I repented of my sins, so that I might know Him. I had previously been baptized and had received the laying on of hands for the Gift of the Holy Ghost. But, now, ten years later, I had a great desire to actually receive the companionship of the Holy Ghost—to actually experience a real spiritual rebirth. As a result, there came a time when He accepted my sacrifice of a broken heart and a contrite spirit, and He poured out His Spirit upon me. I had felt His Spirit before, on many occasions, but on this particular occasion, I was immersed in the love of God; every particle of my being felt aglow with the love and knowledge of God. By the power of the Spirit, I knew God lived; I knew Jesus was my Savior; and I was filled with compassion and concern for my family and friends and all mankind in a way I had never before experienced. I had previously been baptized by water, and I had received the laying on of hands for the Gift of the Holy Ghost, but on this occasion I was literally baptized by the Spirit; I felt purified and cleansed before God.

This experience is part of what it means to know God. Unless we come to know the Holy Ghost from personal experience, we don't really know God. We may understand the words and phrases that describe God; but unless we get to know Him personally, by receiving the Holy Ghost, we can't know Him in the most important way.

Throughout history, there have been those who have actually seen God, and to whom God has spoken. But it is the power and influence of God that accompanies such an appearance or vision that has the greatest effect on the soul of man. God is a God of Glory. Satan can produce some counterfeit apparitions, but he cannot replicate God's glorious power and love. This is one of the keys by which we can discern Godly manifestations from the manifestations of false spirits.

God has not taught that we need to see him to know him. But He taught that we should receive the Holy Ghost to know Him. Jesus taught that it is the mission of the Holy Ghost to testify of Him. "[T]he Comforter . . ., which proceedeth from the Father, he shall testify of me" (John 15:26).

To feel the unseen power of the Holy Ghost, and to have his

companionship and guidance, is an important part of what it means to know God.

I do not believe it is God's purpose for us in this life to be constantly guided by the Spirit of God to the extent that He makes all decisions for us and removes all trials, tribulations and stumbling blocks from us. If this were God's plan, then once we came to know Him, there would be no more growth for us—we would become mere puppets. God's plan for us does not relegate us to such a helpless condition. We are his children; each of us possesses a spark of divinity—our spirit; and God has clothed that spirit with a mortal body and a mind, both of which he wants us to learn to develop and to control. Once one is born again the growth process does not stop; God's plan is to help it continue. He has not constantly endowed me with marvelous outpourings of His Spirit. But the experiences I have had have been transformational. I believe this is what Peter was referring to when he admonished the saints to "grow in grace and in the knowledge of our Lord and Saviour Jesus Christ" (2 Peter 3:18). As we grow in grace and in the knowledge of God, and as we develop our divine potential, the love and light of God's Spirit will glow in us more and more brightly, until, as John said, we become like Him (1 John 3:2). Until then, God wants us to continue to use our intellect and abilities in living—but always subjecting them to His will.

With regard to the guidance and revelation that He will regularly give to us, the Lord's admonition to Oliver Cowdery is counsel that can be broadly applied in decision making to combine our own intelligence with the Spirit of God:

> [Y]ou must study it out in your mind; then you must ask me if it be right, and if it is right I will cause that your bosom shall burn within you; therefore, you shall feel that it is right.
>
> But if it be not right you shall have no such feelings, but you shall have a stupor of thought that shall cause you to forget the thing which is wrong. (*Doctrine and Covenants* 9:8-9)

This passage mentions one particular manifestation of the Spirit of God—a burning in the bosom. One who knows God can expect to experience this. But there are also other ways that God manifests himself to man. He can fill our souls with joy and peace and love and conviction. He can give us premonitions and warnings. He can reveal truths to us—both past, present and future. He can fill our souls with great faith in His power. He can give us patience. He can fill our souls with Godly desires for righteousness and abhorrence of sin. And He can manifest His power through us in spiritual gifts—the gifts of tongues, prophecy, visions, healings, interpretation of tongues, the power to work great miracles, and the power to convince and influence people.

There are many ways that the Spirit of God can work in our lives. To experience these spiritual gifts is to know God.

But in my experience, God does not bestow these gifts indiscriminately on everyone. These gifts of God are given for the benefit of man, and they are administered by and through God's servants whose hearts are one with him—who love the Lord with all their hearts. Those who are not anxiously engaged in His work don't usually experience these spiritual gifts.

In another important sense "to know God" means to think and feel the way God does. If we don't understand His point of view—if we don't feel the same way about things as He does—then we don't really know God. If we don't obey his commandments, that indicates that we are out of harmony with God. If we felt the same way about things as God does, we would always obey His commandments. John undoubtedly had this in mind when he wrote: "And hereby we do know that we know him, if we keep his commandments. He that saith, I know him, and keepeth not his commandments, is a liar, and the truth is not in him. But whoso keepeth his word, in him verily is the love of God perfected" (1 John 2:3-5).

One of the commandments one must live in order to know God is to love one another. Unless we learn to love others and to be a loving person, we don't really know God. As John also said: "He that loveth not knoweth not God; for God is love" (1 John 4:8). In essence, to know

God is to become like Him, to talk to Him, to receive communication from Him, and to experience the power and influence of His Spirit in our lives.

B.   How to Come to Know God.

The starting point in the quest to know God is to comply with the first principles of the gospel of Jesus Christ so that one may receive the Gift of the Holy Ghost. Reduced to the simplest terms, one comes to know God through receiving the Gift of the Holy Ghost—the baptism of fire and of the Spirit is a spiritual endowment of the knowledge of God.

The apostle John clearly taught that after we receive the Gift of the Holy Ghost we must continue to keep God's commandments in order to know God and in order to have the love of God in us (1 John 2:3-5). When Peter admonished those who had previously been baptized and given the Gift of the Holy Ghost to "grow . . . in the knowledge of [God]" (2 Peter 3:18), he confirmed that the quest to know God does not terminate at one's initial spiritual rebirth. The quest to grow in the knowledge of God continues throughout life. And in a very real sense, the more Godly attributes we develop, the better we know God.

We discussed the first principles of the gospel of Jesus Christ in the previous chapters. The fundamental gospel message is the same today as it was in the days of Jesus and the apostles—one can come to know God through believing in the Atonement of Christ, through repenting of one's sins, and through covenanting with God through baptism to keep God's commandments, and then through receiving the Holy Ghost by the laying on of hands of the servants of God. In making and keeping this covenant, one receives the promised spiritual blessing—one receives the companionship of the Spirit of God and the accompanying knowledge that God the Eternal Father lives and that Jesus Christ is our Redeemer.

C. The Purpose of Christ's Church Is to Bring Us to God—So that We Come to Know Him.

It is the purpose of the Church of Jesus Christ to bring all mankind to Him; it is the purpose of the Church of Jesus Christ to make the ordinance and covenant of baptism available to all who sincerely desire to love God and keep his commandments; and it is the purpose of Jesus' Church to help His disciples to improve and become more God-like.

The Apostle Paul explained that God called apostles, prophets, pastors and teachers in Christ's church to do the following: "For the perfecting of the saints, for the work of the ministry, for the edifying of the body of Christ: Till we all come in the unity of the faith, and of *the knowledge of the Son of God*, unto a perfect man, unto the measure of the stature of the fulness of Christ" (Ephesians 4:12-13 [emphasis added]).

There are today many different Christian churches which teach many different doctrines about God, about what he is like, and about what it means to know him. Much of what is taught is false, and no false doctrine can help one to come to know God. In the quest to come to know God it is absolutely essential that we come to know the whole truth about God. We must lay hold of as many truths about God as we can, and we must also identify and reject the erroneous concepts about God that may be urged upon us. We must discern the genuine from the counterfeit. We must seek the pearl of great price, until it is found; but we don't want to settle for white, plastic, costume jewelry.

I believe that Christians from many denominations can also know God. But those who have come to know God in some degree will want to grow in that knowledge and improve their relationship with Him. It is to you that this book is most particularly addressed. To you I am saying: Consider these messages that I testify are from the Savior. If you will openly consider these messages and embrace them with all your hearts, the Lord will pour out His Spirit upon you in greater abundance than ever before. You will find that acceptance of these messages will cause you to grow in the knowledge of the Lord. But professed Christians who state that The Church of Jesus Christ of Latter-day Saints teaches falsehoods about God and Jesus Christ—these people show that they don't know God very well; in fact, they expose themselves as having a shallow and flawed understanding about the nature of God.

Up until now the Holy Ghost may have come upon you from the time to time; but only through receiving the Gift of the Holy Ghost at the hands of actually authorized servants of God can you obtain the right to the constant companionship of this member of the Godhead. The search to know God and the search for God's messengers of salvation go hand in hand. If you know God you will not seek to belittle the message of this book, but you will learn from God himself that this message is true.

CHAPTER 20

Acquire the Qualities of a Disciple of Christ

Whén all is said and done, if we do not obey God with love in our hearts we will not return to live with Him. Jesus said: "If ye continue in my word, then are ye my disciples in deed" (John 8:32). But if we do not obey God, we are not really his disciples.

Those who profess their devotion to God, but who disobey his commandments are hypocrites and liars. John wrote: "He that saith, I know him, and keepeth not his commandments, is a liar, and the truth is not in him" (1 John 2:4). And James wrote: "Thou believest that there is one God; thou doest well: the devils also believe, and tremble. But wilt thou know, O vain man, that faith without works is dead" (James 2:19-20). The man who professes to be a disciple of Christ, but who disobeys and disregards God's commandments is not really a disciple of Christ.

A.   Live the Ten Commandments.

For beginners, a true Christian will obey the Ten Commandments (Exodus 20:3-17):

1. Thou shalt have no other gods before me.
2. Thou shalt not make unto thee any graven image, or any likeness of any thing that is in the heaven above, or that is in the earth beneath, or that is in the water under the earth; Thou shalt not bow down thyself to them, nor serve them . . . .
3. Thou shalt not take the name of the LORD thy God in vain; for the LORD will not hold him guiltless who taketh his name in vain.
4. Remember the sabbath day, to keep it holy. Six days shalt thou labour, and do all thy work: But the seventh day is the sabbath of the LORD thy God: in it thou shalt not do any work, thou, nor thy son, nor thy daughter, thy manservant, nor thy maidservant, nor thy cattle, nor thy stranger that is within thy gates: For in six days the LORD made heaven and earth, the sea, and all that in them is, and rested the seventh day: wherefore the LORD blessed the sabbath day, and hallowed it.
5. Honour thy father and thy mother: that thy days may be long upon the land which the LORD thy God giveth thee.
6. Thou shalt not kill.
7. Thou shalt not commit adultery.
8. Thou shalt not steal.
9. Thou shalt not bear false witness against thy neighbor.
10. Thou shalt not covet thy neighbour's house, thou shalt not covet thy neighbour's wife, nor his manservant, nor his maidservant, nor his ox, nor his ass, nor any thing that is thy neighbour's.

B.   Live the First and Great Commandment.

The true disciple of Christ will put God first in his life in all things—he will love the Lord with all his heart, might and mind—he will keep the first and great commandment, which is: "Thou shalt love the Lord thy God with all they heart, and with all thy soul, and with all thy mind. This is the first and great commandment" (Matthew 22:37-38).

Those who are not interested in putting God first in their lives are shunning that which is of greatest worth to them.

Those who like to learn about the Lord, but who also like to enjoy some of the evils and vices that are popular today are toying with that which is sacred. Those who live lives that purposefully mix sin with sacredness, mock the sacred; that which is sacred is not compatible with sin. Only by constantly striving to eliminate impurity and sin from our lives do we comply with the first and great commandment—to love God with all our heart. Too many people today try to serve God, while at the same time flirting with mammon. This doublemindedness will ruin them. We must not allow ourselves to be among those who the Lord said "draw near me with their mouth and with lips do honour me, but have removed their heart far from me" (Isaiah 29:13). We must not be deceived—God will not be mocked by such hypocrisy. "Not every one that saith unto me, Lord, Lord, shall enter into the kingdom of heaven; but he that doeth the will of my Father which is in heaven" (Matthew 7:21).

Is the most important goal in your life TO DO GOD's WILL? Or do you allow other desires to creep into your life, like weeds, and take control of your life? Do you want to obey God's commandments, or do you regard them as inconvenient or annoying? Do you try to obey the ten commandments, or do you try not to think about them? Only by facing up to God's commandments, and then happily obeying them can we lay claim to salvation. The words of Jesus echo the warning:

> Not every one that saith . . . Lord, Lord, shall enter into . . . heaven; but he that doeth the will of [God].
>
> Many will say to me in that day, Lord, Lord, have we not prophesied in thy name? and in thy name have cast out devils? and in thy name done many wonderful works?

> And then will I profess unto them, I never knew
> you: depart from me, ye that work iniquity. (Matthew
> 7:21-23)

If we are to LOVE GOD WITH ALL OUR HEART, we must develop Godly desires. We do this by programming our minds with wholesome, inspirational and Godly thoughts. There is no greater admonition for us to follow in this regard than the words of the Savior: "Let virtue garnish thy thoughts unceasingly, then shall thy confidence wax strong in the presence of God, . . . the Holy Ghost shall be thy constant companion" (*Doctrine and Covenants* 121:45-46). If we allow our minds to receive unholy, uninspired thoughts, then this mental input will hinder us from developing Godly desires. We must limit, and as much as is possible, we must eliminate ungodly thoughts, including many messages communicated by internet, social media, radio, CD's, tapes, movies, videos, television, books, magazines, and even conversations and messaging—we must discipline ourselves to control the spiritual level of the messages that are around us and of the thoughts that enter into our minds. Our thoughts are in large measure the product of the messages we permit our minds to entertain. No one can love God with all his heart if he has some desires that are not pure and holy. And without controlling our input, we will not be able to control the desires that our minds put out. The challenge to keep this commandment has never been greater in the history of the world than it is for us today. This is especially true for our young people, who are meeting some temptations earlier than those of preceding generations, but having even less experience behind them from which to draw strength to resist.

One who loves God with all his or her heart will have a pure mind. And God's promise is that if we deny ourselves of all ungodliness and love God with all our might, mind and strength, then we will enjoy the Spirit of God in our lives now as well as obtaining salvation eternally through the grace of Christ (*Book of Mormon*, Moroni 10:32-34).

God's messages for the world are always founded on the "first and great commandment" that Jesus gave the world 2,000 years ago—we must love God with all our hearts. God gave this same commandment to Moses and the children of Israel 3,500 years ago (Deuteronomy 6:5), and this is God's message today. There are also other things we should do, but we must build upon the foundation of putting God first in our lives—of loving Him with all our heart and soul. This is the divine motivation that leads to salvation—it is the one that guided Jesus, whose life's mission was to do the will of his Father in heaven (John 4:34; 5:30; & 6:38). This is the sacred motivation that will guide us through the trials that will confront us in life. This is the attitude of faith that will assure our abiding with Him when He comes and will lead us to salvation and eternal life with Him.

C. Live by Every Word of God.

When Jesus was tempted by Satan to turn stones to bread so that he could have something to eat, Jesus responded by reciting words that Moses had delivered to the children of Israel years before: "Man shall not live by bread alone, but by every word that proceedeth out of the mouth of God" (Matthew 4:4). This means not to just obey the written word of God (i. e., the scriptures), but to obey the broader "word of God"—the will of God as made known by God's living prophets and as made known by the Spirit of God to the individual. We should seek to know and to do the will of God in all that we do, just as Jesus Did.

Do you actively and consciously seek to learn what God would have you do in all aspects of your life? I believe this question gets to the heart of Jesus' injunction to live by every word of God.

The scriptures explain that anciently God talked to Moses face to face and gave him instructions. God revealed his will to Isaiah, to Elijah, to Jeremiah, to Samuel, to Malachi, to all of his prophets. And after the ascension of Jesus, God continued to reveal his will to his apostles and prophets. God directed Peter to bring the gospel to the gentiles. An angel freed Peter from prison. Stephen looked into heaven and saw Jesus on the right hand of God. Jesus appeared to Saul in a vision. God inspired Paul to prophesy and to perform miracles. And

God gave the Apostle John the visions and prophecies contained in the Book of Revelation. But did God intend for the Bible to be the last word of God for the remainder of the earth's existence? No. We have reviewed many prophecies that God would deliver his words to the world through messengers in the last days. When God commanded us to live by every word of God, this meant living in obedience to God's *living* prophets—not just to the words of the dead prophets.

Much of Christianity today is absolutely close-minded to even the possibility that God would give us scripture today in addition to what is recorded in the Bible. But in refusing to even consider such a thing, these people put blinders to their eyes to limit that portion of God's word that they will see. I submit that such an attitude is contrary to Jesus' admonition to LIVE BY EVERY WORD THAT PROCEEDETH FROM THE MOUTH OF GOD (Matthew 4:4).

There is no reasonable basis in either scripture or sound logic for anyone to believe that the Bible is to be the final and last word of God for mankind. The Bible teaches just the opposite; it prophesies of additional messages to come from God in the latter days. Some may take scriptures out of context to support a belief that the Bible is God's last words, but in so doing they wrest the scriptures to their own detriment.

The Bible does teach that the Lord withholds revealing himself to people because of unrighteousness (Isaiah 59:1-2). And the Bible reveals that prior to the gathering of Israel in the latter days there will be a famine in the land—not of bread and water, but of hearing the word of God (Amos 8:11-13). But the Bible teaches that in the latter days the heavens will be opened again, and that God will send messengers to the world to prepare the people for Christ's Second Coming.

God never said: "I have revealed all that I am going to reveal to mankind." But He did say that "Eye hath not seen, nor ear heard, neither have entered into the heart of man, the things which God hath prepared for them that love him" (1 Corinthians 2:9). God will yet reveal to those who love Him many great and marvelous things. This applies to us today, just as in the days of the Apostle Paul. God is the same yesterday, today and forever (Hebrews 13:8). But God will not reveal His will for us *if* we are not prepared to receive it. "For precept must be upon precept . . . ; line upon line . . .; here a little, and there a little" (Isaiah 28:10).

The belief that the Bible is the one and only book containing the word of God for us is the devil's blindfold, preventing people from looking for, listening to and obeying God's commandments today. Those who can't see must take off this blindfold so that they can see—and live by the words that proceed today from the mouth of God's living prophets.

D.   Live the Commandment to Love One Another.

The hallmark of any disciple is his adherence to the principles taught by his master. Perhaps the most distinguishing characteristic of a disciple of Christ is the love he has for others. Jesus taught this:

> A new commandment I give unto you, that ye love one another; as I have loved you, that ye also love one another.
> By this shall all men know that ye are my disciples, if ye have love one to another. (John 13:34-35)

John wrote: "He that saith he is in the light, and hateth his brother, is in darkness" (1 John 2:8). And as John also wrote, "let us not love in word, neither in tongue; but in deed and in truth" (1 John 3:18). For just as faith without works is dead (James 2:17), even so, love without works of kindness and service is dead. And as Paul taught:

> Though I speak with the tongues of men and angels, and have not charity, I am become as sounding brass, or a tinkling cymbal.
> And though I have the gift of prophecy, and understand all mysteries, and all knowledge;

and though I have all faith, so that I could remove mountains, and have not charity, I am nothing.

And though I bestow all my goods to feed the poor, and though I give my body to be burned, and have not charity, it profiteth me nothing.

Charity suffereth long, and is kind; charity envieth not; charity vaunteth not itself, is not puffed up.

Doth not behave itself unseemly, seeketh not her own, is not easily provoked, thinketh no evil;

Rejoiceth not in iniquity, but rejoiceth in the truth;

Beareth all things, believeth all things, hopeth all things, endureth all things.

Charity never faileth: but whether there be tongues, they shall cease; whether there be knowledge, it shall vanish away.

And now abideth faith, hope, charity, these three; but the greatest of these is charity. (1 Corinthians 13:1-8 & 13)

The quest to become a loving person is the greatest quest a man or woman can pursue. That quest does not end when one is baptized and born again. We must continue to refine and purify ourselves so that God's love can continue to dwell in us. Throughout life we mold our character by the principles we live and by the habits we make. The Christ-like person is constantly polishing and refining his character, adding Christ-like traits one by one, as he grows in the grace of Christ and in the knowledge of God (2 Peter 3:18), until he eventually attains "the measure of the stature of the fulness of Christ" (Ephesians 4:13).

Jesus' beloved apostle, John, taught that the way to fulfill this quest is to obey all of God's commandments. John said: "But whoso keepeth his word, in him verily is the love of God perfected" (1 John 2:5). Conversely, Jesus prophesied that in the last days "because iniquity shall abound, the love of many shall wax cold" (Matthew 24:12). The ancient American prophet Mormon taught that the Holy

Ghost fills us with the love of God after we have faith in Christ, repent of our sins, covenant by baptism to serve God, and receive the laying on of hands for the Gift of the holy Ghost. Mormon wrote that through the grace of Christ comes the "remission of sins; and the remission of sins bringeth meekness, and lowliness of heart, and because of meekness and lowliness of heart cometh the visitation of the Holy Ghost, which Comforter filleth with hope and perfect love" (*Book of Mormon*, Moroni 8:26). No one will complete his quest to become loving unless and until he becomes a pure vessel in whom the Spirit of God can dwell. This purity can be obtained only through the combination of our repenting of our impure desires and acts and our exerting faith in the atoning blood of Jesus who remits the sins of the truly penitent.

This is what Jesus said to the ancient inhabitants of the Americas in about 34 A.D.:

> And no unclean thing can enter into his kingdom; therefore nothing entereth into his rest save it be those who have washed their garments in my blood, because of their faith and the repentance of all their sins, and their faithfulness unto the end.
>
> Now this is the commandment: Repent, all ye ends of the earth, and come unto me and be baptized in my name, that ye may be sanctified by the reception of the Holy Ghost, that ye may stand spotless before me at the last day.
>
> Verily, verily, I say unto you, this is my gospel. (*Book of Mormon*, 3 Nephi 27:19-21)

In order to have the love of God in our hearts we must repent of our sins and impurities. The closing words of the prophet Moroni, written to us by him in 421 A.D., exhort us to purify ourselves so that we can be sanctified in Christ by the grace of God:

And again I would exhort you that ye would come unto Christ, and lay hold upon every good gift, and touch not the evil gift, nor the unclean thing. . . .

Yea, come unto Christ, and be perfected in him, and deny yourselves of all ungodliness; and if ye shall deny yourselves of all ungodliness, and love God with all your might, mind and strength, then is his grace sufficient for you, that by his grace ye may be perfect in Christ; and if by the grace of God ye are perfect in Christ, ye can in nowise deny the power of God.

And again, if ye by the grace of God are perfect in Christ, and deny not his power, then are ye sanctified in Christ by the grace of God, though the shedding of the blood of Christ, which is in the covenant of the Father unto the remission of your sins, that ye become holy, without spot. (*Book of Mormon*, Moroni 10:30 & 32-34)

God the Eternal Father has promised to bestow the pure love of Christ on all who are true followers of His Son—those who obey God's commandments. Here is the challenge and promise that the prophet Mormon has given us:

Wherefore, my beloved brethren, pray unto the Father with all the energy of heart, that ye may be filled with this love, which he hath bestowed upon all who are true followers of his Son, Jesus Christ; that ye may become the sons of God; that when he shall appear we shall be like him, for we shall see him as he is; that we may have this hope; that we may be purified even as he is pure. Amen. (*Book of Mormon*, Moroni 7:48)

A perfect love casteth out all fear (1 John 4:18), and a perfect love also empowers one to have the courage and faith to do all things in Christ (Philippians 4:13). Those who have a perfect love will have the

Spirit of God with them so that they will recognize and heed the word of God when it is delivered to them by the messengers God will send. This powerful love is necessary to break down the prejudices and barriers and pride and misinterpretations and deceptions and stigmas that sometimes impair the vision and judgment of good people. Those who can attain a perfect love in Christ will recognize and rejoice at and embrace the divine messages that God has delivered to the world in these last days. Then these same disciples of Christ will have their bodies and minds renewed as they join with the Savior and His messengers in declaring to others the glad tidings of the gospel.

THE FULFILLMENT

PART V

THE LORD HAS SENT
HIS MESSENGER

In the opening pages of the book we referred to Malachi's prophecy that God would send a messenger to prepare the world for the Lord's Second Coming. We reviewed this and other biblical prophecies of messages and messengers who were to come in the latter days. After this, we reviewed Joseph Smith's account of several heavenly messengers who came to him; and we reviewed the messages that they delivered to him.

Joseph Smith's story is a spectacular testimony of the marvelous work and wonder wrought by the power of God in our time. Joseph Smith's story is a testimony of the continuing power of God in the world today. Joseph Smith bore witness that angelic messengers delivered messages to him for the salvation and blessing of all the world. Joseph Smith was visited by the ancient prophets Moses, Elias, Elijah, John the Baptist, Peter, James, John and Moroni. These messengers came to "restore all things," as Jesus foretold. And most importantly, God the Eternal Father and his only begotten Son, Jesus Christ, also came to Joseph Smith and delivered messages to him. They came to him before sending the other heavenly messengers; they called him to be the prophet of the restoration—to be God's earthly servant to whom the other heavenly messengers would come.

Each of these angelic visitors gave Joseph Smith specific authority and/or special instructions pertaining to God's work in preparation for the imminent return of Jesus Christ. Each of these heavenly visitors was a "messenger." But Joseph Smith was also a "messenger," as he communicated to the world the divine messages that were delivered to him. Just as John the Baptist was the messenger who came in the "spirit and power of Elias" before Jesus' first coming, so Joseph Smith is the messenger spoken of by Malachi who came in the "spirit and power of Elias" to prepare the way before Jesus' Second Coming.

And what is the central theme woven though the messages of all of these messengers? It is the invitation to come unto Christ, to love Him with all our hearts, to repent of our sins, and to seek out God's authorized servants and to receive from them the ordinance of baptism for the remission of sins and to receive from them the laying on of hands for the Gift of the Holy Ghost.

Joseph Smith was a special witness for Christ in modern times. He courageously and valiantly declared to the world the divine messages that he received. One of the greatest of these messages is *The Book of Mormon*, the translation of the writings on the gold plates, containing the witness of ancient American prophets that Jesus is the Savior of the whole world, and that he appeared to them shortly after his resurrection. If *The Book of Mormon* is not the word of God, then Joseph Smith's testimony is a fabrication. But if it *is* the word of God, then Joseph Smith is necessarily a prophet of God, and his words are of vital importance for all the world.

No prophet of God has brought forth more of the words of God in the history of the world than Joseph Smith. The 872 pages of scripture that he delivered is almost three times as much as was given to us by Moses; it is seven times as much as was given to us by the apostle Paul. And because the Holy Ghost bears witness of all truth (John 16:13), everyone can test the messages of Joseph Smith to ascertain their truthfulness; by the Spirit we can prove all things (1 Thessalonians 5:19-21).

But the question of whether or not the messages of Joseph Smith are divine is a two-edged sword. While an individual is testing them to determine if they come from God, he is also being tested by them, to see if he will recognize and accept God's messages. In evaluating Mormonism, one must keep in mind Nephi's testimony about this test:

> And if ye shall believe in Christ ye will believe in these words, for they are the words of Christ, and he hath given them unto me; and they teach all men that they should do good.
>
> And if they are not the words of Christ, judge ye— for Christ will show unto you, with power and great glory, that they are his words, at the last day; and you and I shall stand face to face before his bar; and ye shall know that I have been commanded by him to write these things, notwithstanding my weakness. (*Book of Mormon*, 2 Nephi 33:10-11)

We must make sure we do not follow the example of the unbelieving Jews, of whom Jesus said: "And ye have not [God's] word abiding in you: for whom he hath sent, him ye believe not" (John 5:38). Like it or not, we will be held accountable for whether or not we heed the words of Christ delivered to us by Joseph Smith. And like it or not, we will be held accountable for whether or not we heed the words of Christ delivered to us by living prophets and apostles of Christ who succeeded Joseph Smith.

As was pointed out in the opening pages of this book, many people *don't like it.* A lot of people *don't like* Joseph Smith and *don't like* doctrines that he taught. That is their privilege. Some of these same people claim that Joseph Smith was a false prophet, that Mormonism is not Christian, and that Mormonism is actually the evil "antichrist" spoken of by the apostle John. But an honest and thorough study of Mormonism refutes all of these claims. Lies and misrepresentations are the only basis for the claim that Mormonism is not Christian. And the Spirit of God testifies that Mormonism is one and the same as the pure gospel of Jesus Christ.

The great slander of Mormonism that exists in some Christian circles thrives on deception; and there are many who unwittingly contribute to the spread of falsehoods about Mormonism, not realizing what they are doing. But no truth-lover will be content to condemn Mormonism based on false accusations. Nevertheless, the accusation that Mormonism is not Christian puts at issue the most fundamental of all religious questions:

WHAT IS THE TRUE GOSPEL OF JESUS CHRIST?

I welcome the open and robust discussion of this issue. As Mormonism is dissected and analyzed to see what it is, I only insist that an evaluation be based upon the truth—not misrepresentations. It has been my great opportunity in these pages to set the record straight on some of the fundamentals of Mormonism. It is now the reader's privilege to get to the bottom of the Mormonism mystery.

If God has poured out his spirit upon millions of faithful members of The Church of Jesus Christ of Latter-day Saints, then how can another Christian argue that the church is anti-Christian or that it is doing the work of Satan. The Spirit indicates just the opposite.

When the apostles of Jesus first took the gospel to the gentiles, the Jewish Christians were at first astonished that a gentile could receive the Holy Ghost as well as a Jew. But this fact led Peter and the others to acknowledge: "Can any man forbid water, that these should not be baptized, which have received the Holy Ghost as well as we? (Acts 10:47).

Similarly, today, I submit that if a Mormon has the Spirit of God with him, then other Christians must acknowledge that God has signaled his acceptance of that person's faith by bestowal of the divine gift. Today, millions of Mormons manifest by their words, their actions, their attitudes, their countenances, their faith, and their compassion that they have received the Gift of the Holy Ghost. It thus becomes an absurdity to take the position that Mormonism is anti-Christian. Spiritual evidence and the fruits of the Spirit prove just the opposite—they prove that Mormonism brings souls to Christ.

The test of the Spirit is the ultimate test of religious truth. Logic and reason have a place in the pursuit of God. But if they lead to a conclusion that is not in harmony with the Spirit of God, then we know that we must examine our presumed facts and our reason to see where we have erred.

I give my solemn witness that *The Book of Mormon* is the word of God—the Spirit of God so witnesses to my soul. And Joseph Smith is the great "messenger" of the latter days, through whom the Lord God has revealed vital information for the blessing of all mankind in preparation for the coming of our Lord and Savior in power and glory. The Spirit of God witnesses to my soul that this is true. The Church of Jesus Christ of Latter-day Saints, or "Mormonism," as it is called, is in very deed the kingdom of God on earth; it is the stone cut out of the mountain without hands that will roll forth until it fills the whole earth; it is the kingdom to which all of Jesus' disciples will come to receive God's choicest blessings; it is the mountain of the Lord's house to which all nations will gather to be taught God's ways in the last days; it is the kingdom that will be given to our Savior when he comes on earth to reign. I give my solemn witness of the truth of these things in the name of Jesus Christ, whose authorized servant I am.

I challenge my friends, my fellow Christians, my fellow disciples of Jesus, to acknowledge the biblical prophecies that God will send messengers to the earth before the Second Coming. I challenge the reader to prayerfully and courageously and humbly consider the truthfulness of the messages of Joseph Smith and of *The Book of Mormon*. If you do, the Lord will manifest to you by his Holy Spirit that these messages are divine. I hope and pray that you will have the desire and faith to obtain this witness, and that you will have the courage and motivation to do God's will when it is revealed to you.

Appendix A

What Mormon Doctrine Is and What It Isn't

Today, virtually everybody searches the internet to look up information and get answers to questions—including questions about Mormon history and doctrine. Years ago, such inquiries were done by researching books, but today the internet has for the most part replaced researching in actual books with paper pages. The amount of information that is instantly available by the touch of a key is vast—and not all of it is true or reliable. The need to distinguish the reliable from the unreliable is a major issue today. To find correct and authentic answers to questions about Mormon doctrine requires some education and some discipline.

Some Mormon critics regularly use unofficial statements of Mormons to establish what they think official Mormon doctrine is. This mistake demonstrates a misunderstanding of what is and what is not Mormon doctrine.

Official doctrine of The Church of Jesus Christ of Latter-day Saints is that which is taught in the four books that we acknowledge as scripture: *The Bible, The Book of Mormon, The Doctrine and Covenants,* and *The Pearl of Great Price.* In addition, official doctrine can be pronounced by the living Prophet and First Presidency. (The First Presidency is the presiding quorum of the Church, comprised of the Prophet-President and two or more counselors. The First Presidency governs the Church under the direction of Jesus Christ through revelation and inspiration.) Because of the existence of these standards, it is an easy matter to verify and confirm what is and what is not "Mormon" doctrine.

Those four books of scripture are canons of scripture for Mormons, just as the Bible is a canon of scripture for all Christians. Mormons often refer to these four canons of scripture as "standard works" because they are the standards against which all teachings may be measured to assess their truthfulness. The apostle Joseph Fielding Smith, who later became the Tenth Prophet and President of the Church, gave this explanation about official Mormon doctrine:

> [T]he Standard Works of the Church are the measuring rods the Lord has given us by which we are to measure every doctrine, every theory and teaching, and if there is anything that does not conform to that which is given to us in the revelations, we do not have to accept it. (Joseph Fielding Smith, *The Signs of the Times* (Salt Lake City, Utah: Deseret Book Co., 1952, 1970) pp. 21-22.)

> The *Bible, Book of Mormon, Doctrine and Covenants,* and the *Pearl of Great Price,* including the Articles of Faith, have been received by the vote of the Church in general conference assembled as the standard works of the Church.
> . . . It is not to be supposed from this that all that has been written outside of the standard works of the Church is discarded and rejected . . . . The point is this, if in these books mistakes are found, "they are the mistakes of men," and the Church as an organization is not to be held accountable for them. . . . (Joseph Fielding Smith, *Doctrines of Salvation* (Salt Lake City, Utah: Bookcraft, 1954) 1:322.)

> Every man who writes is responsible, not the Church, for what he writes. If Joseph Fielding Smith writes something which is out of harmony with the revelations, then every member of the Church is duty bound to reject it. If he writes that which is in perfect harmony with the revealed word of the Lord, then it should be accepted. (Joseph Fielding Smith, *Doctrines*

of Salvation (Salt Lake City, Utah: Bookcraft, 1956) 3:203-204.)

While there are only a few sources of official Mormon doctrine, there are hundreds of secondary sources that comment on Mormon doctrine. For example, Bruce R. McConkie's book, *Mormon Doctrine* (Salt Lake City, Utah: Bookcraft, 2d ed., 1966) is a commentary and a secondary source—not a primary source for Mormon doctrine. It is a valuable tool in locating scriptural sources for doctrine; and many of his opinions give helpful insight. But despite its name, it is not a source for official Mormon doctrine.

A distinction can also be made among the commentaries. A select few commentaries are authorized and published by the Church itself. These books have the Church's endorsement of reliability, and therefore, next to the standard works themselves, they provide the greatest weight in answering doctrinal questions. Included in these are two treatises by James E. Talmage: *The Articles of Faith* (1889, 1968); and *Jesus the Christ* (1915, 1970). Also include is Joseph F. Smith's *Gospel Doctrine* (1919). Also included in this group is Joseph Smith's seven volume *History of the Church*, edited by B. H. Roberts (1914, 1948). (Note, however, that *History of the Church* is a "history" and thus contains numerous pieces of information of a secular nature, such as newspaper reports and letters of correspondence.) Another excellent and reliable secondary source is the collection of books/manuals published by the Church beginning in the late 1990s: *Teachings of Presidents of the Church*, with separate volumes published for many of the Church presidents from Joseph Smith through Howard W. Hunter. Another wonderful source is the *Encyclopedia of Mormonism*, Daniel H. Ludlow, ed. (New York: Macmillan Publishing Co., 1992) 5 volumes. This book was produced by Brigham Young University and involved the work of hundreds of scholars. Another excellent secondary source would be the Seminary and Institute manuals in the Church. These materials are excellent, reliable, and available on line. Finally, the essays published on the Church's website, "lds.org," are also excellent secondary material.

Many other writings exist by prominent Mormon leaders, but unless they are published and endorsed by the Church, they do not necessarily reflect the official position of the Church. This is true even of the Prophet and President of the Church; not every word he says is necessarily the mind and will of the Lord. Joseph Smith taught that "a prophet was a prophet only when he was acting as such" (HC 5:265).

The scriptures do not answer all questions about God's plan for mankind—all truths have not been revealed on non-essential and secondary matters. Members and leaders of the Church often have their own opinions about these matters. But there is a difference between these opinions and official doctrine. Even if such an opinion is true, it is not official doctrine. No individual has the right to proclaim something to be a doctrine—only the Prophet and the First Presidency of the Church have this authority, and even then, the matter would be subject to the sustaining vote of the Church before it would become official doctrine.

It is the responsibility of all Elders in the Church to proclaim and explain the gospel of Jesus Christ to the best of their ability, both in speaking and in writing. Sometimes, in doing so, an Elder may add a personal opinion of his that is not official doctrine—it may be true or it may be false—but the fact that a church leader said it does not automatically make it official doctrine.

Perhaps the most vital secondary source for instruction comes from the semi-annual General Conference addresses of the living prophet, apostles and other general authorities in April and October of each year. Except when explicitly stated, it is not their purpose to pronounce new doctrine. They do, however, preach doctrine to explain, exhort and inspire. In the course of these addresses, specific directions are frequently given to assist in the work of the ministry. But such particular programs and directions are not normally doctrines; programs and leadership policies are subject to change as times and circumstances warrant it. Conference addresses are printed in the *Ensign*, the Church's official monthly publication, which is also a reliable secondary source for the teaching of doctrine.

In the 1800s before the Church made its own publication of

conference addresses, some members collected transcripts of many addresses of Church leaders over many years, and privately had them published in a 27-volume set, called *Journal of Discourses* (London, 1854-1886). These volumes contain many exceptional speeches and inspiring messages. But they are neither published by nor endorsed by the Church, and the Church does not vouch for their accuracy nor for the truthfulness of all that is reported therein.

Because some Mormon critics fail to discern between real sources of Mormon doctrine and the multitude of unofficial secondary sources, the above explanation is many times necessary to resolve a doctrinal question. The tendency of Mormon critics to equate randomly selected statements of a prominent Mormon with official Mormon doctrine is like picking an excerpt from the *Congressional Record* to establish the meaning of the Constitution. Just as one must consult the Constitution itself and the opinions of the U. S. Supreme Court to learn the official meaning of the Constitution, so one must turn to the four books of Mormon scripture and the official statements of the First Presidency to learn official Mormon doctrine. Secondary sources may be true, or they may not be true; they may be helpful or they may not be helpful; but they are not official statements of Mormon doctrine.

Appendix B

Basic Beliefs of The Church of Jesus Christ of Latter-day Saints

---

1. We believe in God, the Eternal Father, and in His Son, Jesus Christ, and in the Holy Ghost.
2. We believe that men will be punished for their own sins, and not for Adam's transgression.
3. We believe that through the Atonement of Christ, all mankind may be saved, by obedience to the laws and ordinances of the Gospel.
4. We believe that the first principles and ordinances of the Gospel are: first, Faith in the Lord Jesus Christ; second, Repentance; third, Baptism by immersion for the remission of sins; fourth, Laying on of hands for the Gift of the Holy Ghost.
5. We believe that a man must be called of God, by prophecy, and by the laying on of hands, by those who are in authority to preach the Gospel and administer in the ordinances thereof.
6. We believe in the same organization that existed in the Primitive Church, namely apostles, prophets, pastors, teachers, evangelists, and so forth.
7. We believe in the gift of tongues, prophecy, visions, healing, interpretation of tongues, and so forth.
8. We believe the Bible to be the word of God as far as it is translated correctly; we also believe the Book of Mormon to be the word of God.
9. We believe all that God has revealed, all that He does now reveal, and we believe that He will yet reveal many great and important things pertaining to the Kingdom of God.
10. We believe in the literal gathering of Israel and in the restoration of the Ten Tribes; that Zion (the New Jerusalem) will be built upon the American continent; that Christ will

reign personally upon the earth; and, that the earth will be renewed and receive its paradisiacal glory.

11. We claim the privilege of worshiping Almighty God according to the dictates of our own conscience, and allow all men the same privilege, let them worship how, where, or what they may.

12. We believe in being subject to kings, presidents, rulers, and magistrates, in obeying, honoring, and sustaining the law.

13. We believe in being honest, true, chaste, benevolent, virtuous, and in doing good to all men; indeed, we may say that we follow the admonition of Paul—We believe all things, we hope all things, we have endured many things, and hope to be able to endure all things. If there is anything virtuous, lovely, or of good report or praiseworthy, we seek after these things.

"Articles of Faith," *Pearl of Great Price*, 60-61. (For a thorough discussion of each of these, see James E. Talmage, *Articles of Faith* (Salt Lake City: Deseret Book Co., 1889, 1968.)

Appendix C

Mormons Do Not Worship Adam

A popular false statement about Mormon doctrine is that we now teach or that we used to teach that Adam is God and that we worship Adam. This is a false representation of what our doctrine is. In support of this misrepresentation, critics point to a statement contained in the *Journal of Discourses*, vol. 1, page 50, reportedly made by Brigham Young: "Adam is our Father and our God, and the only God with whom we have to do."

Adam is the father of the human race, the Patriarch of all mankind; he is Michael the archangel, and he is referred to in the Bible as "the Ancient of Days." But he is not God. Brigham Young knew this, as his many other statements clearly show. If this particular quote is accurate, it does not accurately state Mormon doctrine.

The *Journal of Discourses* is not and has never been an official communicator of Church doctrine. It is not published by the Church. The Church has never vouched for the accuracy of its reporting. Even when accurate, its words do not become official statements of Church doctrine. (See appendix A, "What Mormon Doctrine Is and What It Isn't.") Additionally, with regard to the quotation about Adam in volume 1, page 50, it was the editor of *Journal of Discourses* and not Brigham Young who capitalized the "G" in "God" and the "F" in "Father."

As discussed in chapter 8, section J and chapter 14, sections B and C, Mormon doctrine embraces the belief that the highest eternal potential of man and wife is for them to become gods. Some of our critics have misconstrued this doctrine to state that Mormons believe Adam is God, and that Mormons worship Adam. Both of these conclusions are false. After his resurrection, Adam will become a "god" (if he is not already) in the sense of his becoming an exalted heavenly being. But Adam is not "God." He is not and will not be in the Godhead; and he is not to be worshipped.

But some critics persist and insist that Mormons used to worship Adam in the 1800s, and that we have changed our doctrine to correct this error. This contention is also false. Mormon doctrine about the nature of God has not changed. Chapters 8, 14, 15 and 16, above, give a thorough discussion of the Mormon belief in God.

There is significant biblical support for the Mormon belief that the ultimate potential of mankind is to become like God—to actually become gods. (See chapters 8, 9, 14 and 15, above.) In this respect, Abraham, Isaac and Jacob have become "gods" (*Doctrine and Covenants* 132:37). But they are not "Gods," and they are not to be worshipped. In this sense, Adam is or will be a "god" also. Furthermore, in Adam's case, because he stands as the presiding patriarch over the human race, and because he will yet return to the earth before the Second Coming to do an important work (Daniel 7:9 & 22), Adam unquestionably plays an important role in the destiny of each of us. But he is not God. And it has never been a part of Mormon theology to worship him.

Two other quotes from the *Journal of Discourses* have also been advanced to attempt to prove that Mormons *used* to worship Adam. But these references do not give even a smidgen of support for this accusation. First, *Journal of Discourses* 4:1 has been quoted to try to prove that the Mormon Church taught that Adam is God the Father. But the words in that reference don't say it, and I don't find such a thought even faintly suggested in that speech. All the reference does is show how desperate some critics are to find fault. The use of this citation to claim that Mormonism teaches that Adam is God the Father, completely destroys the credibility of those critics who use it.

Second, *Journal of Discourses* 5:331 has been cited to support the accusation that Mormons *used* to worship Adam. This reported discourse of Brigham Young gives a helpful explanation of the role played by Adam in God's divine plan for the world. In this excerpt, Brigham Young taught that Adam, or Michael, assisted God the Father and Jesus Christ in the creation of the world, just as all of God's spirit children served God in one capacity or another in the pre-earth existence. But this did not make Adam to be "God," and it did not make him one to be worshipped. Adam is not God the Father, and he has not become God the Father.

Finally, if Brigham Young did say that Adam is "the only [g]od with whom we have to do," it is contradicted by what he repeatedly taught about the true nature of God on many other occasions. And *if* he did say it once, the fact that he never repeated it again is an indication that he recognize that those words confused rather than clarified the thought he was trying to express.

Joseph Smith said that "a prophet was a prophet only when he was acting as such" (HC 5:265). Every word spoken by a man who is the prophet is not necessarily and automatically the word of God. We do not blindly embrace as the word of God every single word that a man speaks just because he is the prophet. I, who revere Brigham Young as a prophet, give him this much latitude. Our critics should do likewise; otherwise they are likely to make mistakes and misrepresentations about Mormon doctrine.

Appendix D

The Virgin Birth vs. The Divine Sonship of Christ

The accusation was once made against me that I was not a Christian because I did not believe in the virgin birth. I am a Christian, and my belief about the parentage and birth of Christ is the true doctrine: Jesus Christ is literally the only begotten son of God, and Mary was a virgin who conceived the Son of God.

The term "virgin birth" is not found in the Bible; neither is any doctrine of "virgin birth" expressly taught in the Bible. I know of only two verses from which it could be implied. One is Luke 1:27, which describes Mary as a "virgin" at the time the angel Gabriel visited her and announced that she would subsequently conceive and bear the child Jesus. The second verse is Isaiah 7:14, which states: "Behold, a virgin shall conceive, and bear a son, and shall call his name Immanuel" (Isaiah 7:14). Matthew wrote that Emmanuel (or Immanuel) means "God with us" (Matthew 1:23).[62]

The passage in Luke merely establishes that Mary was a virgin *before* she conceived the child Jesus. In that respect, she was a virgin when she conceived, fulfilling the prophecy in Isaiah 7:14, whether or not the term "virgin" in that verse may be a mistranslation. Matthew and Luke make it clear that Mary did not "know" Joseph or any other man until after the birth of Christ (Matthew 1:25 and Luke 1:34).

---

[62] "Modern biblical scholars point out that Isaiah used the Hebrew word *almah*, signifying a young woman of marriageable age, instead of the word *bethula*, which connotes a virgin." Dr. Charles F. Potter, *Did Jesus Write This Book?* (New York: Fawcett Crest Books, 1965) p. 94.

"The rendering, in Isaiah 7:14, of a Hebrew word, which normally means only young woman, by the Greek *parthenos* or virgin, played into the hands of Christian apologists, who found in Isaiah a prophecy of the virgin birth of Christ." H. G. G. Herklots (M.A.), *How Our Bible Came to Us* (New York: Oxford University Press, 1954) p. 116.

In these respects, Mary could be considered a virgin after Jesus' conception and continuing until after his birth.

But in any event, if a "virgin birth" doctrine precludes the natural paternity of God the Father as the father of Jesus, such a doctrine must be discarded. The Bible repeatedly teaches that Jesus is the "only begotten son" of God. (See, e. g., John 1:14, 3:16 and Hebrews 1:5-6,)

All mankind, including Jesus, are spirit children of God (Hebrews 12:9 and Acts 17:28-29). We lived as spirit beings before our mortal births. (See, e. g., Jeremiah 1:5; Job 38:7; and John 9:2.) Jesus was God before his birth. He is the "word." He was JEHOVAH, the God of Israel before he came to earth as the Babe of Bethlehem. But Jesus is the only one of all mankind whose earthly father is God the Eternal Father. Being the "only begotten son" of God, Jesus inherited the power to live again—to resurrect himself (John 5:26 and 10:18) and to accomplish the work of the atonement for all mankind.

The biblical accounts of the birth of Christ are some of the most sublime verses in all scripture. Jesus was conceived in the manner prophesied by the angel who came to Mary: "The Holy Ghost shall come upon thee, and the power of the Highest shall overshadow thee: therefore also that holy thing which shall be born of thee shall be called the Son of God" (Luke 1:35).

The scriptures give no details about whether the conception of Jesus was accomplished in the customary way or in some other way. We do not know how much Mary even remembers of this event. Verse 35 in Luke implies that Mary was transfigured by the power of the Holy Ghost at the time of the conception. This was undoubtedly necessary to enable her to withstand the presence of God.

God the Eternal Father is the earthly father of Christ. This doctrine is one of the most fundamental of all Christian doctrines; it at the same time establishes the true nature of God and the individuality of Jesus, being separate and distinct from his father. Man was indeed created in the image of God (Genesis 1:26). Jesus looks exactly like his immortal father (Hebrews 1:3). And just as the resurrected Jesus today has an immortal body of flesh and bones (Luke 24:36-39), so does

God the Eternal Father, by whom Jesus was begotten, also possess an immortal body of flesh and bones.

Those who attempt to give preeminence to the non-biblical "virgin birth" doctrine over the biblical divine sonship of Christ doctrine are out of line with the word of God as taught in the Bible. Mary was a virgin in that she did not know any mortal man before the birth of Christ; in this respect she was a virgin at His birth. But any "virgin birth" doctrine that denies that God is the literal father of Jesus and denies that Jesus is His "begotten son" is a false doctrine that must be discarded.

Appendix E

Is Mormonism a Cult?

The word "cult" is a frequently used pejorative term that some use to classify Mormonism. Mormon critics say that Mormonism is a "cult" in order to disparage Mormonism and discourage people from having any involvement with Mormons. But what is a cult?

The word "cult" is not found in the King James version of the Bible. But a lot of people use the word religiously. There are multiple definitions of "cult," but a cult is always something bad—comething to avoid, and something from which we should protect others. A cult is some kind of radical religious group. A cult is an extremist group to which *others* belong—no one believes that he or she belongs to a cult. For example, if members of all the organizations that have been identified as cults were invited to a national cult convention, it is unlikely that anyone would even show up because no one believes that his or her group is a cult—its only other groups that can be cults.

Cults are also regarded as religious groups that follow Satan, either openly or unwittingly. But there is no one, universally accepted meaning of "cult," except to the extent that the term is used to put a negative label on the one associated with it. The word "cult" is so evasive in meaning that its very use becomes nothing more than name-calling.

Being a Mormon, I have often been accused of belonging to a cult. Inevitably the use of the word is an attempt to short-circuit any rational conversation about Mormonism. Once the label "cult" is affixed, the listener immediately accepts the condemnation, and together the speaker and listener move on to discuss something else. Never mind that neither "cult" nor "Mormonism" were defined and understood; that is not important—all that matters is that the negative label be affixed.

A few years ago, I heard a radio evangelist discussing "cults."

There was a little more depth to his analysis than the customary conversation about cults. After this evangelist warned his audience to beware of cults, he at least offered a definition of what he said a cult is. He said that a cult is characterized by three things: It may have extra-biblical scripture; it may believe in continuing revelation from God; and it may believe that an individual's works are necessary for salvation.

When I heard this definition for a cult, I had to chuckle—that definition fits my religion to a "T." If that definition is right, then Mormonism is a "cult." But the interesting thing about the evangelist's definition is that by his definition, the very religion established by Jesus Christ would be a cult. According to the Bible, the three characteristics condemned by the evangelist were all a part of the original gospel of Jesus Christ. Look at each of these characteristics a little more closely.

1. **Belief in extra-biblical scriptures.** There are over a dozen biblical prophecies of latter-day messages and messengers to be sent by God before the Second Coming of the Savior. For starters, see Isaiah 29:14-18; Ezekiel 37:16-17; Malachi 3:1; Matthew 17:11; Acts 3:19-22; and Revelation 14:6; see also chapters 5 and 6. Nowhere did Jesus or any of the prophets condemn the writing down of God's revelations; on the contrary, God's prophets have always done this. The one scripture that is usually cited to support the premise that the Bible is the last and final written word of God is found in the last four verses in the Bible, Revelation 22:18-19. But those verses do not support such a conclusion. The clear meaning of those verses is that they are a warning that no one should change John's word, either by adding to them or by taking away from them. John did not say that the words of the latter-day angelic messenger (of whom he prophesied in Revelation 14:6) should not be written down, neither did he say that such words should be ignored or labeled as devilish. Such an interpretation would be contradictory. The apostle John affirmed that additional scripture would be revealed in the future. (See also chapters 5 and 6.)

2. **Belief in continuing revelation**. The concept that continuing revelation should be a part of true religion is very compelling and is based upon biblical scripture. The apostle Paul told his converts that their faith should not rest on the wisdom of men, but should be based on the power of God (1 Corinthians 2). The apostles were guided and directed by continuing revelation in their ministries. Nowhere in the Bible does it state that future generations should not have God's revelations to guide them. But the Bible does prophesy that there would be a "falling away" from the truth for a time before the Second Coming of the Savior (2 Thessalonians 2), and many prophecies predict an outpouring of God's Spirit in the last days. (In addition to the scriptures mentioned earlier, see also Joel 2, Ephesians 1:10, and chapter 5 of this book.)

3. **Belief that good works are necessary for salvation**. Finally, the condemnation of a religion that teaches the necessity of good works to obtain salvation is really anomalous. Every good parent teaches his/her children to be good—to be patient, forgiving, helpful, courteous, reverent, etc. The need to teach and develop good qualities and Godly characteristics is almost universally acknowledged by good people. And those interested enough to examine the teachings of Jesus in the four gospels will find that one of the themes he most frequently addressed was to be good, to help others, to love one another, and not to be a hypocrite. In the sermon on the mount Jesus said: "Not everyone that saith unto me Lord, Lord, shall enter into the kingdom of heaven; but he that doeth the will of my Father which is in Heaven" (Matthew 7:21). Those who seek to condemn the Mormon affirmation that individuals are responsible for their actions (including their works), frequently base their criticisms on Ephesians 2:8-9, which states that "by grace are ye saved . . . . Not by works, lest any man should boast." But surely Paul did not mean to correct what the Savior had so clearly taught. Paul's statement does not rescind the need to repent and to be good, rather it condemns the proud, and it affirms that all the good works in the world could not and cannot save someone without his/her acceptance of Jesus Christ as the Lord and Savior. No amount of works can save a person. (See chapter 16.)

No one can be saved without faith in Christ. But, nevertheless, Christ commands us to keep his commandments and to do good works. Keeping His commandments qualifies us to receive the conditional gift of salvation. And those who have faith will have the courage and conviction to be good and to do good. All of this Jesus taught.

Mormonism clearly satisfies the radio evangelist's definition of a cult. But each of the three defining characteristics that he labeled as erroneous and bad is actually truthful and good. Each is a part of the gospel taught and practiced by Jesus and his apostles. If Mormonism is a cult, then so is Christianity itself. As long as the Bible and the Holy Ghost are standards by which one tests the truthfulness of religious doctrine, Mormonism will always pass the test. And as for the labeling of Mormonism as a "cult," that has been and will continue to be merely an exercise in name-calling that will only be effective in influencing the biased, the lazy and the superficial thinkers.

Appendix F

This is the reconstructed cabin where the family of Joseph and Lucy Smith lived in 1820, located about two miles south of Palmyra, New York. In the spring of 1820, in a grove of trees behind the home, the fourteen-year-old young man, Joseph Smith, Jr., was called of God to be a prophet, to direct God's work on earth in preparing for the Lord's Second Coming.

This is a current picture of the grove of trees, just west of the Smith cabin home, where God the Father and His Son Jesus Christ appeared to Joseph Smith in 1820.

This is an artist's depiction of Joseph Smith's first vision in 1820. With his own eyes Joseph saw that God the Father and His Son, Jesus Christ, are separate and distinct beings, with bodies of flesh and bones. This statue currently rests at the LDS Visitors Center in Nauvoo, Illinois. Statue is the work of D. J. Bawden.

"The Hill Cumorah is about 4 miles south of Palmyra, New York. This is where Joseph Smith was directed by an angel of God to find the gold plates, buried in a stone box near the top of the hill. This view looks east at the area where a pageant has been performed each July.

In the background is the reconstructed frame home where Joseph and Emma Smith lived in 1829, in Harmony (now Oakland), Pennsylvania, on the banks of the Susquehanna River. It was here, from April to June, 1829, that by the gift and power of God, Joseph translated a portion of the gold plates into *The Book of Mormon*. Oliver Cowdery served as scribe to Joseph during this period of time; Oliver would write down the words dictated by Joseph.

The bronze statue (at the left) depicts John the Baptist, conferring the Priesthood of Aaron on Joseph Smith and Oliver Cowdery. This occurred on May 15, 1829, in Harmony, Pennsylvania, while Joseph and Oliver were engaged in translating the gold plates. Following the ordination, Joseph and Oliver baptized one another in the Susquehanna River, as directed by John the Baptist. The statue to the right depicts Jesus' ancient apostles Peter, James and John, as they conferred their apostolic authority on Joseph Smith and Oliver Cowdery in early June, 1829, also in Harmony, Pennsylvania. This priesthood gave Joseph and Oliver the authority to bestow the Gift of the Holy Ghost and to later organize and lead the Church of Jesus Christ. Statues are duplicates of the work of Avard T. Fairbanks.

This is the reconstructed farm house of Peter Whitmer, Sr., in Fayette, New York (situated between the upper ends of Cayuga Lake and Seneca Lake). It was here that the translation of the gold plates into *The Book of Mormon* was completed in June of 1829. A short distance from the home is where a heavenly vision was unfolded to Oliver Cowdery, David Whitmer and Martin Harris, in which the angel Moroni showed them the gold plates, and where the voice of God commanded them to bear witness to the world that the translation of the plates was true. Their written testimony is published with each copy of *The Book of Mormon*. It was also in this home, on April 6, 1830, where the Church of Jesus Christ was organized under the laws of New York. This brought about the restoration of the church of Christ upon the earth in the last days, with apostles and prophets as its foundation.

This was the home of Joseph Smith, Sr. and his wife Lucy in 1829 and 1830, when the Book of Mormon was being printed. It was in the woods, close to this home in June of 1829, where eight men held and examined the gold plates from which Joseph Smith translated *The Book of Mormon*. The testimonies of these eight witnesses are published with each copy of the book.

Below is the Egbert Grandin Building, which continues to stand, in downtown Palmyra. It was in this building that the first 5,000 copies of *The Book of Mormon* were printed (1829-1830). Martin Harris mortgaged his farm for $3,000 to pay for the printing. Later his farm was foreclosed upon to pay for the publication.

This is the John Johnson farm house in Hiram, Ohio (about 41 miles southeast of Cleveland). It was in the upstairs (left) of this home on February 16, 1832 where a vision was given to Joseph Smith and Sidney Rigdon, in which they saw God the Father and His Son, Jesus Christ. Joseph and Sidney were then shown a vision of three degrees of glory in heaven. (This is recorded in Section 76 of the *Doctrine and Covenants*.)

This is the temple in Kirtland, Ohio (about 23 miles east of Cleveland), which the saints built at great sacrifice. It was here, on April 3, 1836, that the Lord Jesus Christ appeared to Joseph Smith and Oliver Cowdery, after which in sequence the prophets Moses, Elias and Elijah each appeared to Joseph and Oliver and conferred upon them important priesthood authorities.

This is the "Mansion House" in Nauvoo, Illinois, into which Joseph and Emma moved their family in 1843. After a number of years of persecution and deprivation, Joseph and Emma finally secured a comfortable home for their family in this dwelling—about a mile away from the Nauvoo Temple, which was then under construction.

This is the jail in Carthage, Illinois, where on June 27, 1844, an angry mob stormed the jail and assassinated Joseph and Hyrum Smith, who had been arrested on a trumped up charge of treason, and had been denied bail. Statue is the work of D. J. Bawden.

Construction of the Nauvoo Temple began in 1841, and was completed and dedicated in 1846—a year and a half after the prophet's death. The original edifice was destroyed by fire (1848) and a tornado (1850). The Temple was rebuilt in 2002, with the same exterior dimensions, and with substantially the same interior floor plans, including a basement font in which vicarious baptisms are performed for deceased ancestors.

All photographs are those of the author.

BIBLIOGRAPHY

I. Canons of Scripture

The Holy Bible (King James Version—translated in 1611). Unless otherwise noted, all references are to the King James version of the Bible.

The Book of Mormon—Another Testament of Jesus Christ - (Translated from gold plates by Joseph Smith by the gift and power of God—first published in Palmyra, NY by E. B. Grandin, 1830.) Current edition, divided into chapters, verses and with extensive cross-references to it and to the Bible, the Doctrine and Covenants and the Pearl of Great Price (Salt Lake City, Utah: The Church of Jesus Christ of Latter-day Saints, 1981), 532 pp.

The Doctrine and Covenants - revelations and other inspired writings of Joseph Smith and succeeding prophets, first published in 1835, and supplemented with additional writings since then. Current edition—(Salt Lake City, Utah: The Church of Jesus Christ of Latter-day Saints, 1981) 294 pp.

The Pearl of Great Price - selection of revelations translations and narrations of Joseph Smith written between 1830-1842, first published as a group in 1851; became canonized scripture in 1880. Current edition—(Salt Lake City, Utah: The Church of Jesus Christ of Latter-day Saints, 1981) 61 pp.

II. Other Books and Articles

"Baptism," *American People's Encyclopedia*, 1956, ed.

Berrett, William Edwin, *The Restored Church* (Salt Lake City, Utah: Deseret Book, 1965).

Book of Jasher. Translated from Hebrew (Salt Lake City: Deseret Book Co., 1965).

Brown, Dr. Kent S., letter to author dated June 3, 1987.

"Councils," *Encyclopedia Brittanica* 6:634.

"The Falling Away and Restoration of the Gospel of Jesus Christ Foretold" (Salt Lake City, Utah: The Church of Jesus Christ of Latter-day Saints, 1976).

Garrison, W. E., "Bible," *American People's Encyclopedia*, 1956, ed.

Gaster, Theodor H., ed., *The Dead Sea Scriptures*, 3rd ed. (Garden City, NY: Anchor Press, Doubleday, 1976).

Goodspeed, Edgar J., *The Apocrypha—An American Translation* (New York: Vintage Press, 1959).

_____, "New Testament," *American People's Encyclopedia*, 1956 ed.

Grant, Frederick, G., "Revelation," *World Book Encyclopedia*, 1969 ed.

Herklots, H. G. G., *How Our Bible Came to Us* (New York: Oxford University Press, 1954).

"Indulgence," *American People's Encyclopedia*, 1956 ed.

Jackson, Kent P., "Early Signs of the Apostasy," *Ensign*, Dec. 1984.

Lyon, Edgar T., *Apostasy to Restoration* (Salt Lake City, Utah: Deseret Book Co., 1960).

McConkie, Bruce R., Conference Address, April 2, 1983, *Ensign*, May, 1983.

_____, *A New Witness for the Articles of Faith* (Salt Lake City: Deseret Book Co., 1985).

_____, *Mormon Doctrine*, 2nd ed. (Salt Lake City, Utah: Bookcraft, 1966).

Mattson, Vernon W., Jr., *The Dead Sea Scrolls and other Important Discoveries* (Salt Lake City, Utah: Buried Records Productions, 1979).

Merservy, Keith, "Ezekiel's Sticks," *Ensign*, March, 1987, pp. 4-13.

Nibley, Hugh, *An Approach to the Book of Mormon* (Salt Lake City, Utah: Deseret Book Co., 1976).

_____, *Enoch the Prophet* (Salt Lake City, Utah: Deseret Book Co., 1986).

Peterson, Daniel C. and Ricks, Stephen D., "Comparing LDS Beliefs with First-Century Christianity," *Ensign*, March, 1988.

Potter, Dr. Charles E., *Did Jesus Write This Book?* (Greenwich, CT: Fawcett World Library, 1965).

Pratt, Orson, *Divine Authenticity* (Liverpool, 1850).

Richards, F. D., et al., *Journal of Discourses* (London, 1854-1886).

Richards, LeGrand, *A Marvelous Work and A Wonder* (Salt Lake City: Deseret Book Co., 1950, 1976).

Roberts, B. H., "Introduction," *History of the Church of Jesus Christ of Latter-day Saints*, 2nd ed. (Salt Lake City: Deseret Book Co., 1948).

Robinson, James M., ed., *The Nag Hammadi Library* (New York: Harper & Row, Publishers, Inc., 1981).

Schmadt, Raymond H., "Inquisition," *World Book Encyclopedia*, 1969 ed.

Sheen, Fulton J., "Nicene Councils," *World Book Encyclopedia*, 1969 ed.

Smith, *Smith's Bible Dictionary*.

Smith, Joseph, *History of The Church of Jesus Christ of Latter-day Saints*, 2nd ed. (Salt Lake City: Deseret Book Co., 1948).

Smith, Joseph Fielding, *Doctrines of Salvation*, 3 vols. (Salt Lake City: Bookcraft, 1955).

_____, *The Signs of the Times* (Salt Lake City: Deseret Book Co., 1952, 1970).

Starr, Chester G., "Roman Empire," *World Book Encyclopedia*, 1969 ed.

Talmage, James E., *The Articles of Faith* (Salt Lake City: Deseret Book Co., 1890, 1977).

Widtsoe, John A., *Evidences and Reconciliations* (Salt Lake City: Bookcraft, 1943).

TABLE OF SCRIPTURES

OLD TESTAMENT

NEW TESTAMENT

BOOK OF MORMON

DOCTRINE & COVENANTS

PEARL OF GREAT PRICE

INDEX

-Separate and distinct from God the Father: 100-101, 106-108, 296
-Signs of birth: 155
-"Virgin birth": 229-231, 295-297
Jews: 48, 154
Johnson, John, home: 308
John the Baptist: 31-34, 74, 143-146, 150, 169, 174, 175, 185, 222, 236, 279, 305
John the Revelator: 23, 60, 72, 78, 83, 87, 147, 269
Jordan River: 49
Joseph, Stick of: 40-45, 76
Judgment: 196, 210, 225
Judah, stick of: 40-45, 76
Judah, tribe of: 48, 57
Judas Iscariot: 67
Justice: 234
King James Version of Bible: 83, 106, 114, 119, 228
Kingdom of God: xvii, 57-70, 91, 165-179
Kirtland, Ohio: 180, 200-202, 308
Kirtland Temple: 180, 200-202, 308
Knight, Joseph, Sr.: 177
Know God: 17, 170, 227-231
Lamanites: 141
Laying on of hands: 243, 259
Lehi: 139
Lost tribes of Israel: 48
Love: 198, 228, 258, 261, 266-275
Lucifer: see Satan
Luther, Martin: 3, 4, 83, 130, 131
Malachi: 23
Man, his divine potential: 126-127, 197-199, 203-208
Manasseh: 49
Manifesto: 207

Marcion practiced vicarious baptisms for the dead: 211
Marriage, eternal: 197-199, 203-208
Mason, Robert: 178
Mary: 229-231, 295-297
Matthias: 67, 69
Medes: 60-62
Medo-Persian Empire: 60-62
Melchizedek Priesthood: 146, 246, 305
Messenger(s): 19, 24, 26-40, 53, 71-77, 87, 143-147, 150, 153-154, 181-192, 202, 251-252, 275, 279
Messenger of the Covenant is Jesus Christ: 28
Messiah: 3
Methodist Church: 98, 127, 131, 132
Michael: see Adam
Ministers: 10, 107, 251
Missionaries, Mormon: xviii, xx, 11, 253-257
Missionary work: 53-56
Montgomery County, MD: 5
Mormon: throughout
Mormon, ancient American prophet: 140, 152, 272
Mormonism: 298-301
  -Alleged to be satanic: 7
  -Alleged to be not Christian: 9
Mormon doctrine: xviii, 12, 285-289
Moroni: xvii, 138-141, 152, 156-157, 279
Moses: 19, 150, 184-187, 201, 279, 308
Mountains: 30, 49, 50, 62-64, 150, 165, 181
Nag Hammadi: 86, 236
Napoleon: 61
Nauvoo, IL: 309-310
Nauvoo Temple: 309-310
Nebuchadnezzar: 57-62

ABOUT THE AUTHOR

C. Paul Smith has operated a general law practice in Maryland since 1978, after receiving a law degree from Brigham Young University. He is also an author who has written extensively on constitutional, political, historical and religious issues. His publications include: *The State of the Constitution* (2002); *The State of the Constitution—2017; The Fetal Right to Life Argument* (1977); and *The Prophet Joseph Smith—Restoration Issues* (2019).

Paul and his wife, Terry, are parents of twelve children, and grandparents of 35. All nine of their sons are Eagle Scouts, and Paul has been an adult Boy Scout leader for many years, receiving the Silver

Beaver Award in 2013. Eight of Paul and Terry's children have served missions for The Church of Jesus Christ of Latter-day Saints. Paul and Terry recently served a full-time mission in Texas, and Paul served a mission in France (1970-72). He has served in many local church callings including bishop, high councilor and stake Young Men's president. Paul has coached and refereed numerous youth basketball, baseball and softball games. He has also been a local elected official in Maryland, including Alderman of Frederick City and Vice President of the Frederick County Board of Commissioners.